THE BERLIN ENIGMA

MEMORIES - FROM BOY TO SPY

D. F. HARRINGTON

 FriesenPress

Suite 300 - 990 Fort St
Victoria, BC, v8v 3K2
Canada

www.friesenpress.com

Copyright © 2017 by D. F. Harrington
First Edition — 2017

ISBN
978-1-5255-1008-3 (Hardcover)
978-1-5255-1009-0 (Paperback)
978-1-5255-1010-6 (eBook)

1. BIOGRAPHY & AUTOBIOGRAPHY, MILITARY

Distributed to the trade by The Ingram Book Company

To
Olive Emily Meadows
With Love Forever

✻
✻✻

The heart that friendship warms,
That marches on with double shield
To guard it through the warring storms,
On struggling life's great battlefields.

– H. Boyton

Chapter 1

AUSTRALIA 1900 – 1905

Johnny's first impression of life was that of being in a cradle, which was actually the shell of a giant tortoise, lined with the fleeciest of lambskins. Looking down on him with the gravest of concerns imaginable, was Cluba, a middle-aged aborigine who had cared for him since the day he was born. The golden glow of her lovable round face was accented by her thick black hair, which was tied back tightly in a fantastic weave that fell down her back with elegance. Johnny, who was barely four years old, had been burning up with a fever for many days and was now very weak. They were afraid it was the Bubonic plague.

The plague had arrived by ship one day, at their busy little Port town of Fremantle, Australia, and suddenly emerged in the population leaving death and destruction in its path. Within a few months, by the spring of 1900, it had already killed 78 people. Everyone in town who wasn't afraid to leave their home was bustling around, making every effort to contain it. The plague's progress was traced vigilantly, and all of the clothing and bed sheets were burned, leaving telltale plumes of black smoke billowing daily. Many of the public buildings were closed down and sprayed with lime and disinfectant, while the men formed groups to hunt down every rat they could find.

In the nursery where Johnny lay, the sour smell of carbolic acid used to sanitize the room had saturated the air like an unwelcome blanket. A big round tear rolled down Cluba's cheek and fell on the almost lifeless Johnny as she reached down to comfort him, gently rubbing his shoulders.

His eyes opened instantly at her touch, and he quickly smiled and uttered her name, "Cluba," when he saw her familiar face. She jumped back with a little squeal of surprise, and then quickly leaned back in towards him in disbelief. Cluba was breathless and beaming her precious smile, right back at his little charismatic grin. Her relief was so intense when she looked at the thick, deep brown curls on Johnny's brow, which moments before had been lifeless and covered in sweat, but were now lifting off his face and leaping to life, making him look as adorably curious as always, a trait which matched his personality. Little Johnny had survived the first of his many narrow escapes.

Cluba, who had been his only real mom, was now gushing tears of happiness, and when Johnny sat up, she scooped him right up into her arms. Twirling around while holding on to him tightly with one hand, she was speechless but began waving her free fingers in the air in an attempt to get the attention of her oldest son, who had been quietly sitting under the window reading. "Schnozza" she finally blurted out, and Billy quickly jumped up, dropping his book, and fetched her a clean handkerchief from the hutch.

*
**

The two families all lived together in the same house at 22 Carnac Street, in Fremantle. It was typical of a large Australian house at the time, big and flat and made mostly of brick because of the extremely hot climate. There were ten rooms, each of which was open to the air. On the outside was a huge veranda that went all around the house where many people sat in the evening.

Cluba had two sons, Billy, short for Bilyana, the aborigine name for a wedge-tailed eagle and Algernon who got his name just because she liked it, but everyone called him Algi. The three boys, Johnny, Algi and Billy, used to love chasing each other around the veranda, having great fun until they were told to stop, usually by Johnny's mother or by a man named Jocelyn Carr who maintained the house.

It was a busy house with grown ups working at one thing or another and people coming and going all the time. Every man in Fremantle who had a parcel of land would have a vegetable garden. It was Johnny's favourite part of the yard. He really loved vegetables and the vegetable garden, and it got him into a lot of trouble. There was also a lot of fruit around, fabulous peach trees surrounding the house and loads of giant gooseberries and raspberries. The neighbours were only a few hundred yards away with their own garden and chicken coops, another staple then.

The boys used to keep a few ducks as pets and there was a little enclosure for them near the garden, inside of which was a little shed for their shelter. They were white ducks of the English type, as opposed to the native ducks that were black. Quite often the boys would play with the ducks, bringing them out of their cages into the yard, which would bring an angry Mr. Carr running across the open yard and boisterously yelling, "Who let thase bloody ducks out?"

Even as a very young lad, Johnny's first instincts were to hide quickly behind the little wooden shed, which soon resulted in his nickname "Duck." Billy and Algi however, were not quite as nippy in their getaway and quite often could be seen lifted in the air by Jocelyn Carr, who would have one boy in each hand. But Johnny would always emerge to take the tongue lashing along with them. Shuffling uncomfortably in between Billy and Algi, who were trying so hard to look innocent, Johnny would find an inner strength standing with his two best friends, and would always confess with his head tilted down and his big eyes looking up in apology. "It was me, I opened the cage."

Billy was many years older than Johnny and had a nurturing way, always taking the two younger boys with him wherever he went and trying to teach them the aboriginal ways. Algi was a little younger than Johnny, thin and small for his age, and that always made Johnny feel extra comfortable being between them in age and size-wise.

The three of them loved swimming and did so at every opportunity. Johnny's nickname of "Duck" stuck with him as he grew. Whenever he was in trouble near the water, which was often, Johnny would head straight for the river or sea and dive in.

The ocean itself was just a short walk from home, and within a mile from the house was the huge new jetty used for the mooring of the largest ships. It was surrounded by the other wharves and piers stretched along the shoreline, where the most fantastic of sailing ships from foreign parts were moored. Fremantle was the port for Perth, the nearest large town, and Perth was known as the "Gateway to the West" for the Northern Territory. Fremantle was a very busy harbour town.

The three boys spent most of their young lives carefree, playing in the water or getting into mischief on the piers. They were forever sitting on the crates, casually watching and listening to the people around them as their ships would come and go, or playing chase around the cargo if they were bored.

*
**

Johnny's mother probably loved him, but she never went out of her way for him. He could walk outside with nothing on, and she wouldn't even notice. She was a hefty, yet beautiful woman who was getting on in age, which showed in her striking brunette hair that was now lightly streaked with grey. She seemed quite lazy, never worked and was not worried about money because she had a wealthy father who was living in Sydney. His family name was Chappon, of German background. The Chappon family were well-known piano makers in Berlin. In those days German pianos were the best. No one else made pianos like the Germans did, people would say.

The relationship between Johnny and his mother was strained and confusing as neither of them really cared too much for the other. When she was mad, she would yell at him in German, but occasionally in the evenings she would ask him to come and sit down beside her on the chaise lounge and she would sing him a German lullaby.

Mostly though, for what Johnny saw of her, he thought she was fond of only two things in her life. She was partial to liquor, not unusual in this country, and had a liking for the opposite sex, also not unusual. Not that he blamed his mother for that, as she did not see much of his father who was away in Sydney and often travelling for long periods.

There were many times when Johnny's mother sent him to the off-licence, better known as the beer store, with an empty jug for some stout or beer. Liquor laws were really liberal, as he was only five or six years old by then. It was just a little wooden hut about a mile down the road, and there was a very tiny window that you knocked on and if you were lucky, a man would slide it open. Johnny was too small to reach the window and had to knock on the wall, usually startling the man awake, who would then come outside with a full scale grumble and take the empty jug in to be filled, leaving Johnny to struggle home with it. He would walk slowly along the hot and dusty road, sometimes dragging the jug but stopping once or twice to sneak his first sips of ale.

*
**

Johnny's father, Alfred Harrington, had taken over the family business in Sydney, Australia, only a few months before Johnny was born and that was the reason why they had named him John Sydney Harrington. Sydney was a great distance away from Fremantle and consequently Johnny and the rest of the family never saw that much of their father. He would usually sail in every three months or so, if they were lucky, but some years it was only at Christmas. Once he brought the family a phonograph, the wind-up type that had tin disks with holes punched in them. They often played the tunes as they didn't yet have a radio.

Alfred was a tall man with a strong, distinctive face, who always dressed in a full suit and tie. To Johnny he seemed like a very old man. Alfred was a man of morals and conviction, and he expected others in his family to be the same. He wasn't a man you could talk too. When his father said something, you had to abide by it, but Johnny greatly liked and respected him. Alfred had a penchant for saving and always told him, "Save something for a rainy day."

Johnny's grandparents were also living in Sydney at the time, and he knew that the Harrington family had lived in Australia for a number of generations by then. It left him wondering if his ancestors had had something to do with the colonization of the country or if they had been convicts. He never found out, but whatever the answer he always regarded himself as an Australian.

Johnny had many siblings, but they had become scattered all over the world and some of them he never met. The only brother he ever truly knew and felt close to was Harry. They grew up together in Fremantle when Johnny was very young, before Harry went away to school in England. When he returned, he was a man.

After his return, Harry began training to be an immigration official for the ships at Perth, and that opened up a whole new world for Johnny. Before long Harry held a post as inspector with the West Australian government. He was able to take Johnny with him on his very first voyage as he sailed the coastline to inspect lighthouses. Johnny had many trips with his brother after that.

Most of the news from their farflung family would arrive by mail or by word of mouth, and Johnny would often listen to stories from his mother or Harry about his other brothers and sisters. The oldest child was Fred, who had left for Canada at an early age, and they heard that he had a good job there with the Canadian Northern Mounted Police. But he died in Canada when he was still fairly young.

One sister, Grace, was in Rio de Janeiro, and another, Olive, had married and was now living in China. Yet another sister, Daisy, worked for the Fire Brigade harnessing horses, and there were others — Johnny never really knew how many.

*
**

From the house the boys only had to walk a few hundred yards to the school. It was a basic brick building and the kids called it the workhouse. Cluba used to walk Johnny there when he was very young and then as he grew older he went with Billy and Algi, and the other aboriginal kids. They were all good friends and liked walking to school together. The majority of aborigines were good students and there appeared to be no bad relations between their parents and the white parents.

School in Fremantle was not exactly educational or exciting; they had a very low standard. The teachers were not overly interested in what the students were taught, just their paycheques and holidays. Attendance was optional, and so as a youth Johnny did not attend much. This enabled him to spend more time with his friends and accompany his brother Harry on the trips to visit the many capes along the northern coastline. However, Harry encouraged him to go to school and so he went.

Miss Bishop, an awfully nice person as Johnny remembered, was his first teacher and he had her for two years. She was very young and ladylike, straight from England, and at times she had some difficulty with the

Australian speech and pronunciation. The spoken English was quite different where Johnny lived from the English she had learned in England, and sometimes after trying to make a point, without success, she would return to her desk and weep. Then the whole class would pretend to weep as the children loved to mimic people. Miss Bishop would often have to leave the classroom, but after a short while, she would return to resume the lesson.

Providing the children with a change of scenery, in another classroom their teacher was Jamaican. His name was Mr. Berry, and so naturally the children named him Mr. Blackberry. He did not teach them very much, a little arithmetic, a little spelling and of course, he often left them alone to read. Mr. Berry was very amusing. After giving them a problem to solve, he would return to his desk and lifting his desktop cover, he would drink from a bottle, which he said was his medicine. After he'd had his drink, he would come to the front of the class and attempt to explain the problem he had given them and then sometimes hiccup. Of course, the whole class would also hiccup and have a good laugh.

On one occasion he was very sick after someone put red ink in his wine bottle.

The headmaster of the school was a Mr. Histed, an elderly man, obviously of English descent. He had a large collection of things in glass bottles with alcohol, such as insects, snakes, and extinct animals. One could see if you watched him closely that from behind some of those bottles, he had another bottle from which he occasionally drank. It was also obvious from his breath. He would then proceed to expound on the theory that the world was round and according to nature, liquids always ran downwards and other things like that. The children would all laugh. As if they didn't already know.

Mr. Histed would also quote from well-known writers at that time and he apparently knew what he was talking about. Johnny was spellbound, never having heard such beautiful words before. His wanderlust grew, and he became increasingly curious.

One day Mr. Histed left his ink bottle open, and Johnny accidentally spilt it all over his clothes. He made Johnny sit right at the front of the room from then on.

"You're a troublemaker," he would quite often shout at the children, and sometimes he would rap their knuckles with a cane. He really couldn't be bothered with the students, but he left a lasting impression on them nevertheless.

The boys' and girls' classes were segregated, boys from girls, as was the playground. Their playtime periods were spent in a high-walled enclosure, divided from the girls by a low wall. Sometimes, the boys would kick out the bricks from their side of the outside enclosure to make a ladder to sneak over the wall. During the holidays the custodian would fill in the holes with cement, and when they returned they would have to kick them out again. The teachers always got angry, saying, "The reason for this high enclosure is so that none of you strays out into the bush and gets lost." Once more, the children would all begin to laugh, because the young aborigines knew the bush better than most adults.

Playtime at the school was unlimited and the children could return to the classes whenever they liked. Thus Johnny's education was very poor, but what he lost in education he gained in experience by meeting real people, who knew that life could be hard. Western Australia was a very hard country with its high winds, heavy rains, and extremely hot temperatures.

Like any other youth, Johnny took it all in stride, and fortunately Cluba was always there to help him with every problem or pain. She was wonderful to him and always treated him just like her own son. Her curious face had become a little plumper with time, but her heart was still as pure as gold, beating its life force deep into Johnny's soul through her inquisitive eyes.

She had trained formally as a nurse and everyone in the area, even those who hardly knew her, would come to see Cluba for the little things that bothered them. Everybody loved her. She spoke excellent English and the native language of course as well and, when Johnny was a bad boy, she used to shout at him in her native tongue. At first he didn't know what she was talking about, but the men used to tell him afterwards what she had said. Apparently, she used to curse at him.

Cluba was descended from a large family of whom many still lived off the land. Her sons Billy and Algi used to take Johnny out fishing with them and to play with the other aboriginal children. They also took him to music festivals or meetings with their elders, who were always so friendly and loved to learn new words. They used to say "Hi, Johnny, come, come," and invite him into their gatherings with open arms.

The aborigines really loved to sing and dance, and at some of their festivals they would play tunes on the didjeridu, a hollowed out branch with holes cut in it, somewhat like a giant flute. Johnny really liked playing and dancing with them and attending their ceremonies.

The young aborigines were very good to him and for him. They taught Johnny many things, not only swimming and fishing, but how to avoid the many dangers – and there were many. They taught him how to survive in the bush and find food, should he ever get lost in this vast country. It could be a very harsh country if things went wrong.

There were many places where one could fish; it was their principle occupation. They ate more fish than anything else. They used to catch it and dry it in the sun, and then cook it.

They used to take him with them on their excursions into the bush. Catching kangaroos was a very exciting game, and hunting for wild turkeys and wild dogs. The flying foxes were always something to see, and they were all just part of the countryside that was all so familiar to Johnny then. He was never afraid with the aborigines, quite the opposite, rather. They were very honest, and although they would steal anything, they would always tell you. They all had a lot of fun as boys, playing many games, even golf on occasion with wooden sticks and cricket quite often too. Racing was also a big thing, whether it was wild ponies, kangaroos, or other kids. They spoke their own language and a lot of it was sign language, so Johnny understood enough to get along.

They used to play a game called "Tidal Bore" and that was one of Johnny's favourites. At such places as Broome along the northern coastline, there were quite a lot of inlets from the ocean. When the tide came in with what was known as a bore or tidal wave, it came in with a rush. First they would build a raft made out of logs and tie it together with ropes. Then they would wait for the tide to come in and lying on the raft and holding on to the ropes, they would ride the tidewater in and out. It was great fun.

Sometimes they swam in the pools from the artesian wells, but more often they swam in the ocean. Johnny was so fond of water. They used to love going to the seaside, and playing on the shore, but they were warned not to swim out very far because there were sharks out there, lots and lots of sharks.

His friends also taught Johnny how to gather fish out of sinkholes caused by the tide. After the water had receded, they would find lots of fish left behind. They would file the head off a nail and stick it in a piece of wood and catch many fish trapped in the sinkholes with this simple tool. The aborigines were very at home in nature. They lived in thatched huts and were very aware of their surroundings. If anything at all was different or amiss, they knew straight away.

To Johnny, it seemed that there was something happening every day. Maybe one of the fellas would break his arm or break his leg and they would all scramble around. They'd get grass and patch him up, bandage the limb up with willow branches and moss. It used to heal up, too, in an amazing way. Johnny learned how to clean his teeth from his friends. They grew a plant called sorrel, from which they would break off a stem as thick as your finger. They would cut the end off and use it to clean their teeth. You'd never see a toothbrush in those days. Everyone used sorrel.

Chapter 2
THE SHEEP FARM

Johnny had many stories to tell about his childhood in Fremantle. It wasn't a big town in 1903, just a small place. There were three churches, which they called chapels, and Johnny went to all of them when he could. Usually he went with the aborigines, who generally got along well with the white people and who were quite active in the church.

It was the white people themselves who caused distrust, and Johnny was teased and insulted on a few occasions when he was called a POMME, the Aussie nickname for the English people, Prisoner Of Mother Merry England, thus POMME. There was a saying going the rounds at the time that there were three things that the average Aussie did not like – rabbits, bramble bushes (or blackberries), and Englishmen. This was only intended to be a joke to enrage the newly arrived English living in Australia; however, it may have come from the fact that they all came from England in the first place.

Church played a very important part in their lives. It was here they learned the precept that, "other people's lives were just as important as their own."

Most of the people in Fremantle attended church on Sundays whenever possible. It was difficult of course when chores had to be done or when there were very high winds and high temperatures, or if someone was ill.

One of the ministers Johnny always remembered was a Reverend Lloyd Jones, who was a very loud man with a strong Welsh accent. He was well spoken and outspoken, and never afraid to say what he felt. He was really quite an amazing man. Johnny and the other children were afraid of Reverend Jones, but they still liked him.

Another member of the cloth was the Reverend Harrison Chalmers, a Congregational minister. One Sunday as Johnny sat in the wooden pew with his friends, Reverend Chalmers started his sermon with the following words, "All ye that labour and are heavy laden, bring your troubles to me."

Johnny was so impressed with those words: to think that he could just take his burdens to a minister whenever he wanted, so naturally he did. Those words remained with him until he attended his very last church. He always thought that Chalmers was a nice fellow and very approachable.

It was at his church hall that the "Boys' Brigade" would meet one evening a week. It was an organization within the church, sort of like scouts. They would meet members of the various armed forces, who would drill them and talk about rescue operations, very useful knowledge to have in this rough country. They would teach the boys about sharks and survival in the bush. They were forever worried about the boys getting lost, but Johnny didn't get lost because the aborigines were so close to him. Still, the officers had a point because there was a lot of bush around Fremantle, and you could easily get lost in it. When you went into the bush and then came back out again, you couldn't see where you'd been as there was no track left behind. A native would go into the bush and he would be gone, you'd never see him, and you'd never know he'd been there. The white children were constantly being warned against going into the bush.

The Boys Brigade meetings were always full of lively discussions and the boys even learned about defending their country, should the need arise.

Life was hard at that time in Fremantle, and you didn't get something for nothing. If you wanted water, you would have to go out to the artesian well and carry it in. The men had dug a trench to the vegetable garden so that it got plenty of water and was always flourishing. The water would just spring up from the ground. Anybody who wanted water could come and fetch it and carry it away in buckets; otherwise you wouldn't get any.

For a quick drink the boys would use the old round tin bowls that were always around to scoop up the water, or they could use certain flowers that grew like big cups, which they would cut off and use the petals as a cup of water to go.

If you wanted a snack, you had to go and find it yourself. Money of course was scarce. Johnny felt lucky to get a farthing, worth a fourth of a penny. A penny was worth a lot of money; you could buy a big chocolate bar for a penny, but there weren't many chocolates in Australia, mostly candies like gumdrops, which were very popular then.

***

Johnny spent a lot of time with the natives and they would teach him about the various trees, what they were good for and what their properties were. Johnny liked the eucalyptus trees the best. They are tall, majestic trees that grow in stands of five or six, not far apart. Often in the summertime or autumn, Johnny would take out a blanket and sleep out overnight with the boys, under the trees. The next morning when they woke up, they would have to brush the dew off their faces, pure eucalyptus dew. It was really marvellous.

Travel at this time in Western Australia was limited to Hobson's Choice or Shank's Pony, and if they were lucky, some actual form of horse travel. Shank's Pony was a common expression used for walking. John thought it came from the tinkers who used to shank around from place to place while their ponies carried the supplies. The term Hobson's Choice, they were told, was after a tinker named Hobson who travelled from place to place on foot mending kettles and pans and household items like that. He used to have a little wind-up grinding machine that was quite admired. Sometimes he would bring certain kinds of medicine. One of them was Ellerman's Application, a particular ointment that you rubbed on yourself. Ellerman's ointment was very well used at the time.

The aborigines preferred to "walk along." The children had no bicycles in those days but they did have a little wooden cart with two wooden wheels, and they pushed it everywhere. If you had to go to another nearby town, you walked and it could take you nearly a day.

***

Johnny's father also owned a ranch just north of Perth, with many thousands of sheep and cattle, but he only visited from time to time. There were 30 or 40 people working there, and he had a foreman called Mr. Patton who was in charge of all the men. Mr. Patton was a strong man, in his prime, and he ran the farm well. He was always on horseback it seemed, and he used to ride around as if he had been born in the saddle, exercising his absolute authority.

On occasion, Johnny and his friends would walk to his father's ranch. It was a three-day trek, but for the children, there was no other way of getting there. Before he left on one of these trips, Johnny approached his mother, brandishing his little travel satchel. He proudly declared to her, "We're going up north to be cattlemen."

His mother was on the veranda, stretched out on a lounge chair, and looked up at him without much interest. "Stay out of trouble then," she replied.

The boys always had a good time when they went to the ranch. They would walk for a half a day, and then they would settle down on the track and make a meal in the shade. They would stay there until the sun had gone down and when it got cool, they would forge on. The aborigines would "walk along" and they would talk along too, partly in their own language and partly in Johnny's. Occasionally, they would catch a kangaroo and get a ride, which was great fun.

They used to teach Johnny their ways as they were walking and were always very patient and nice to him. They would put out any fires they came across, because a fire in those days was the worst thing you could find in Australia. It was a very dry country and whenever people could, they would have a moat around the house to stop the fires.

This journey to the ranch was a fascinating adventure for the young boys, and especially because the ranch had a big station where they used to watch the men shearing the sheep. They'd just go, sssssh, sssssh, sssssh, with the clippers and the sheep were quickly all sheared, and the sheep seemed to like it. Of course, after the sheep were sheared bare, they were usually sent down to the docks and then abroad to other countries.

As Johnny grew up in this land of cattle and sheep, he was becoming a tough and resilient little boy. Learning such independence at an early age unknowingly set the pace for the rest of his life. With the dingos howling, and the kangaroos hopping along through the miles and miles of cornfields and bramble bushes, it was a sight to behold. The smell of sheep and the taste of mutton were things that Johnny would never forget.

Back at home, the men used to set wire traps in a ditch beside the garden to catch the rabbits, and the boys used to sneak out at night to open these traps and let the rabbits out. Boys used to do that sort of thing then, since they had nothing else to do. It was a normal thing to raid the garden and, being a normal youth, Johnny often indulged along with other boys, in a little pilfering. The fruit was always much juicier in the other fellow's garden. On one occasion, while stealing apples from a farmer's tree, he slipped in his hurry to escape and was caught on a branch by his pants. There he hung until the farmer came to release him. He ran home with a very sore bottom.

Getting into trouble down on the docks was also not uncommon for Johnny and his young friends. They loved it on the piers – the fresh ocean breeze, the tremendous ships with their massive sails and towering masts looming over their swollen wooden hulls. It was all so intriguing, the foreign smells drifting out from the load they carried in their bellies as the sailors with curious languages and clothing unloaded their cargos.

More than once the young boys would pick up the end of a discarded cigar or anything at all that was smoking, only to disappear behind a crate to share it. The brown curly locks on Johnny's curious brow would always perk up whenever he was into mischief or just up to no good.

One day their coughing gave them away and before they knew it, one of the brawny dockworkers had picked up young Billy and Algi by the scruff of their collars, both together in one large hand. He was looking them directly in the eye, "What are you two up to now? Where's the other rascal?" he yelled, blowing their hair back.

As usual, Johnny had escaped. He had simply ducked out of sight and slipped away into the water. The boys were quietly cheering him on, "Go duck go, go duck, go."

Being wily was Johnny's natural edge and would turn out to be his ultimate forte in life. Stirring up trouble and then cleverly sneaking away unnoticed, seeing, but not being seen would be truly handy skills in later life.

*
**

On occasion, Johnny was able to visit his father in Sydney whenever he was not travelling. It was so exciting exploring the big city, a real wonder for a young child, and especially seeing his father's chief business on George Street for the first time, with the "Giant Yellow Film Box" sign hanging outside on the front of the store. The business was located right downtown in Sydney, and just across the street and down a bit was Kings Cross, a huge department store and junction where Johnny loved to visit.

Harrington "Wholesale Chemists" was the family business that had been passed down to his father. It was quite a large business where they made and sold photographic materials. There was a special paper that they used for printing, a particular tissue, and apparently they had the first rights to manufacture it in England and then they brought it to Australia from where they would distribute it to the world. Johnny never knew why, possibly because of the climatic conditions

The company had agents everywhere, in every country, connections in England, France, the United States, and Germany – all to sell this pho-tographic material. Johnny's father traveled all over the world with this business, even to Japan and China, and the stories he told Johnny of far away places sparked his curiosity like nothing before.

Many years later, this information would prove very helpful when John was in Berlin and he found there, at a firm called Kranik, this same special tissue.

Upon returning from Sydney one evening, Johnny knew there was something wrong, as the house in Fremantle was unnaturally quiet. It wasn't until the next morning that he was greeted with the worst news he could ever have received. Cluba, the closest person of all to him, had died. He had never even got to say goodbye.

Everyone in the household was incredibly upset; there were so many people who had loved her, and they were all crying and mourning in different ways. Cluba had looked after and treated so many friends and family with such warmth and feeling that most of them were still in shock; particularly as it was so sudden. He was told that Cluba had died from a lizard bite, from a type of lizard called goanna. They knew this type of lizard was considered poisonous to most humans, but the natives ate them as a delicacy. Strange but true!

Johnny missed her terribly. He didn't know what to do anymore; she had fed and dressed him his whole life and generally taken care of him. Cluba was the only one who had ever really been there for him, and now he cried and cried for days.

Everything changed after that; Billy and Algi were sent to live with their uncle in the outback — for how long, Johnny didn't know. He became very lonely and often went down to the seaside for comfort.

The stormy seas, with their never-ending salty curls pounding in, seemed to match his tempestuous feelings and draw him back to the water, day after day. After listening to the many stories down at the docks that he heard from people visiting from other countries, he remarked to his father one day, "I would like to go to England."

His father, who was in Fremantle for Christmas, looked up from his meal and sat up straighter in his chair, looking at Johnny very seriously. "Yes, I think it is time," Alfred agreed, with a deeply wrinkled forehead revealing his personal concern. He was still noticeably shaken by the death of his oldest son in Canada, but that topic was never discussed.

He could see that Johnny had become more unsettled, and the idea of his going to England to be educated appealed to Alfred, so he agreed. Johnny surmised that most likely the real reason why his parents decided he should go to England was to ensure he got a good sound education. Also, he suspected, it was a case of "out of sight - out of mind."

His father found a school for him, a place to live and arranged with the Capital and Counties Bank in London, England to pay all his school fees. He was also to receive an allowance of 20 pounds a month that his father considered would be sufficient for all his needs and for any emergencies, but this sum was to be supervised by the people where he was staying. The allowance was to cease when his education was complete, and he had found employment or married. So there he was, nine years old and off to England; it was a dream come true.

Leaving Fremantle, his feelings were mixed. Johnny's brother Harry would be the only one who would really miss him; they were real brothers. He already missed Harry, not realizing that they would never see each other again. They wrote a little, during the war, but then they drifted apart after that. Often he wondered what the others felt about his leaving, but for himself, he was determined to "make good" in this "new" country of England. Australia was rapidly becoming old to him.

At the docks when he left, everybody was shaking hands with him and saying, "Goodbye, have a good trip." His father wasn't there to see him off, and he wondered if he would ever see him again. His mother took him to the wharf and just said, "Well, goodbye, Johnny."

The scene was quiet and peaceful and there were no tears.

Chapter 3

ENGLAND – SCHOOL YEARS

Jack Wallace was a tough, breezy, sea-going man. He was an old sailor, and he dressed like one and acted like one, but he was good at heart. He was a very good friend of Johnny's mother, and Johnny had met him many times in the past. The boys called him Uncle Jack, and he used to tell them stories of when he went to school in England. He was really nice to Johnny and Johnny liked him too. They had become very good friends over the years; in fact, he was more like a father to him than his real dad as he used to teach him things and tell him what he should do. Uncle Jack made him realize that, "he had to fight," for what he wanted. He was certainly good to Johnny, and he was a role model in Johnny's young life.

Jack told him he was taking a shipment of birds and animals over to England and needed people to help care for the birds on the trip. Normally he took two men, but this time he took four boys. It appeared to be a good opportunity for Johnny to go to England, as Jack would be able to supervise him on the way over and watch over him until he was safely settled in England.

Johnny soon became entirely wrapped up in the new world around him on the ship, and his family grew to be, as they say, "ships that pass in the night." His thoughts about his family and home faded quickly.

*
**

The trip to England took about three months. It was a P&O Liner with hundreds of people on board, and below them, one third of the ship was the cargo of birds. Uncle Jack was an expert on rare birds and animals, and on this trip he was taking a very large number of them over to England. During the voyage, most of Johnny's time was spent feeding them and cleaning out the cages, with the help of the other three boys, and this kept him quite busy.

Uncle Jack was taking these over for the various zoos in England and for zoos in other countries as well. There were beautiful birds such as emus, parakeets, parrots, cockatoos, budgies, and many other species. The exportation of these exotic birds from Australia is a practice that is no longer allowed by international law. At that time, Jack Wallace also had his own private zoo at Bath, in Somerset, England, where he exhibited birds and animals.

After the long voyage, arriving in Southampton was so exciting that Johnny was trembling, and his curious eyes never blinked for a moment. Many of the passengers now lined the upper deck of the ship, and together they watched as the approaching piers suddenly burst into life. Everybody seemed to be in an awful hurry to go somewhere, rushing hither and thither.

As they disembarked, Johnny noticed that it was quite a change from the slow and easy way of Fremantle; nobody bothered about you here. No one knew you and no one cared about you. It was quite a difference.

Uncle Jack had a private aviary just off the docks, where they unloaded all the birds. From here many of them were distributed to the other countries.

After the work was finished and the crowds had left, Johnny felt completely lost.

"Come over here, Johnny," Uncle Jack bellowed towards him with a huge grin.

Johnny ran over in a hurry, and Jack gave him a brawny sailor's hug. "Not to worry," he said, "I'll take you around."

He started walking and holding Johnny so tightly around his shoulders, which were now pressed so closely to Jack's side that his little feet weren't even touching the ground. "First, we'll go to London," Jack Wallace thought out loud, as he bounded along, "and from there we'll go down to my place at Bath for a little while."

***

It was not long, however, before it was time to say goodbye to Uncle Jack, who saw him off from Southampton, where Johnny took a steam train to Victoria Station in London, and from there the underground to Kings Cross, London. When Johnny boarded the underground train at Victoria, he discarded the ticket, but when he arrived at Kings Cross, a man at the barrier asked him for his ticket and Johnny said, "I've discarded it!" (as they always did at the Kings Cross station in Sydney).

The man then asked him, "Where are you from?"

Johnny replied in his quirky Australian accent, "From Perth, Australia."

The ticket agent laughed out loud and said, "You've had a hell of a ride."

Johnny was now completely on his own.

Boarding the train again, his destination was north to Darlington, Durham. Johnny's uncle had arranged his accommodation with a couple named Ellardy, who took him in like a boarder. This was the first place he stayed in England on his own.

It was difficult to understand what people were saying to him at first, but nevertheless he always enjoyed listening to people. They seemed to be all talking in different languages, but really what he was hearing were the many different regional dialects of English. Every county in England had a different dialect, and some were difficult for him at first, but eventually, being a natural Aussie imitator, he was able to master them and quickly integrate expressions and accents into his conversation.

Seeing many new things for the first time was very exhilarating. When he stepped off the train in Darlington, Johnny saw something very unusual and beautiful coming down Victoria Road towards him. The people walking on the road were all dressed in their finery and had also stopped in their tracks to look at it. The sides of it were all made of wood, polished up and shining like a new ship glistening in the sun, and it had wooden spoke tires. The driver was a colonel or of some high rank and had a large red hat with an even larger white feather sticking out of it.

"What is that?" Johnny wondered aloud as it was going by.

A small group of passersby took note of Johnny for the first time and did a double take at the little boy who was peculiar looking to say the least. He was wearing his best travel clothes, and yet he still looked like he was straight in from the outback. His leathery dark sun-baked skin and long brown curls made him look like a native of some kind, and his little suitcase made of crocodile skin with a mother of pearl handle was unique to say the least.

"That's a motorcar," a young man in a top hat commented.

As it passed by, another man pointing his cane at it proclaimed, "It's a Rolls Royce."

"Blady hell," Johnny commented loudly in his thick Australian accent, and after a moment's pause everyone burst out laughing in wonderment at this odd child.

Later that day the same car was parked on the street and there was a crowd of children looking it over. Johnny, who was now age nine-and-a-half, had been feeling quite grown-up since he had landed in England, but when he saw the motor car sitting there, he dropped his suitcase and rushed right over with the other kids to see more.

That was the first car Johnny ever saw, but he was soon to see many more motorcars on the road. The brake on the first motorcar was on the outside and it looked so funny, as the driver had to pull this handle up to brake it. The drivers would sit on chairs in front of the engine, and they used oil lamps for light at night. It was quite exciting to experience those first motorcars. The horsedrawn carriages in general usage at the time were on their way out.

There were several different types of horsedrawn carriages then that were generally called Victorias. We see the queen riding in the most common style today, the one with four large wheels. It could seat up to four people and be pulled by one or two horses with the driver sitting at the front. Then there was the hansom cab where the driver sat up top at the back of the carriage. These cabs were always kept for the use of rich people. The poor people had to use the slow drawn ones; it was just the way of life.

Johnny often thought back in later years on those carriages as he read the stories of Sherlock Holmes.

After some time in Darlington, and having established his headquarters for the future as it were, it was back to London to start school, where Uncle Jack got him settled again, this time in a home in North Ealing with some really nice people named the Reardens. Mr. Rearden was a retired postman and lived there with his wife and son Tommy, who worked in the theatre.

The Reardens owned their own house and where they lived was called Northfields Street, because at the north end of the street were open fields. The house didn't have a number but just a name. It was quite a big house, with two front rooms, two bedrooms downstairs and four rooms upstairs. It was built of wood and brick, but mostly brick. As in Australia there weren't many wooden houses around at the time. They had a little out-house all proper and a small garden at the back. In Ealing at that time, it was a luxury to have a garden, but Mr. Rearden had acquired a bit of land and they were proud of it.

In the first year that Johnny was there, they would all go on the occasional picnic, and sometimes they would go down to Bath to see Jack at his little zoo. But suddenly the zoo closed down and Jack disappeared. Johnny never knew what happened to him. One day the zoo was just gone and the whole park had disappeared. Johnny figured that Jack probably died.

The time had now come for Johnny to take up his studies. He realized that this was the chance of a lifetime, the opportunity to increase his knowledge of the world and its peoples. He would be exposed to various subjects that he would become interested in for the future. First he went to Kensington, London, to study at Kensington High School. That's what the school was called at that time. He started around grade four, with about ten children to a classroom. Here he was to learn languages, which came quite easy to him, French, Latin, German and English, as well as math, science, history and geography.

Johnny particularly enjoyed the study of languages, because he found them very interesting. He noticed that when you learn the language of a country you also learn a lot about its people and their customs. He thought it was surprising how the way of life varied in the different countries.

The French teacher was a very fussy and finicky French woman. She was not well liked but she was a good teacher.

Their German and Latin teacher was a Miss Fischer and she was very thorough and strict. Her favourite expression was, "Du bist ein Esel!"

which Johnny knew meant, "You're a donkey!" Obviously, Miss Fischer had a sense of humour.

Miss Fischer was extremely patient with the students and taught them very well in spite of their pranks. Johnny was frequently the butt of her anger for his mischievous behaviour and for speaking French in her German class. However, after a few years they parted very good friends. Their school hours were nine to twelve and one to four, and that left Johnny time to go to the theatres in the evening.

The Reardens' son, Tommy, was a tall, strapping fellow between twenty and thirty years old and he and Johnny became very close over the years, almost like brothers. He was a "wardrobe and props" man at the London theatres, and Johnny often went with him to assist. Sometimes, when they were walking into the theatre, Tommy would carry him on his shoulders, and Johnny supposed it was to make people aware that he belonged with Tommy. Later on, he just walked in beside him.

When Johnny was very young, he used to sit him on one of the empty boxes in the theatre and give him a drink of lemonade or something. After a while some of the people got so used to seeing him that they would come over and give him tea and biscuits. To Johnny it was like being in a world of wonder, surrounded by music and laughter, wrapped up in velvet and silk with gold braids. He really had a marvellous time as he absorbed everything around him.

During these times in the theatre, which lasted for many years, he met many well-known people: He met the beautiful American singer Jeannette MacDonald, and the tenor singer Robert Keel and in later years, the young Rose Marie. He enjoyed all of these musical entertainments, because in those days, with no microphones, the singers really had to sing. They had simple electric lights, and the stage curtains had to be pulled up by hand. Johnny had to help out with the curtains many times behind the scenes. The world was good to him at this time.

Tommy, in his position as prop master, worked at different theatres on different nights. They'd set up a program for a month or maybe a week at the Eldridge Theatre, for example, and he would set up the props for that stretch, and then a month later it was somewhere else. So he and Johnny went all over the city and Johnny got to see all of the famous London theatres of the time: The Palladium, The Globe, The Empire, The Prince of Wales, Park Lane, Leicester Square, including many little theatres on Shaftesbury Avenue. Johnny first saw Harry Houdini in London at the Adolfia Theatre, and then at the Coliseum and later again at South End. Three times Houdini played for a long stretch, so Johnny got to know him very well and they became great pals.

Whenever Harry would see him, he would come over and tease him a little, and then end up sitting with him and speaking heart to heart. Johnny soon learned that Harry's mother was his whole life and when she died he became a different man, taking to drugs and drink. That was never advertised of course, but that's what happened.

Johnny thought Houdini was a really nice fellow. He said he was of German background, but all John could remember was that his real name was Weiss. Johnny wasn't very interested in people's names in those days. They laughed a lot together and those were happy days for Johnny.

There were many other celebrities on the open stage in those days, such as George Robey, "The Prime Minister of Mirth." He was later knighted, Sir George Robey. Once heard, his funny little verses were something to remember. One anecdote Johnny later told was that Robey's act once followed Marie Lloyd's onto the stage. She had been given a bunch of flowers when she bowed off. Then George came out and did his piece, and when he was finished, the audience clapped. He turned around to the audience and said, "That is what they think of me; they gave her flowers, but they gave me the clap!"

Johnny thought he was very funny, and he remembered some of his funny little stories. One went something like this:

> I once had an argument with a man, I hardly uttered a word.
> I called him a pig-faced baboon and a thief
> when he struck me, so hard I couldn't belief.
> He struck me with antagonistic violence, his injury was obviously seen.
> I had an abrasion of the oral-under gums and
> a contusion of the crane-na-meum.

It finished off with, "and a large earrecular appendage," in other words, a thick ear. That was George Robey's kind of story.

Marie Lloyd was another well-known comedian whom Johnny remembered well. Once when a banana dropped on the stage floor in front of her, she said, "The man who threw that banana on the stage can come to the stage door and he can have his skin back."

She was a great favourite with her brash banana jokes and her leg jokes. When people asked her how she was getting along, she would say, "One leg before the other and between the two, I make a good living." She had a really rough tongue, Marie Lloyd. One of her sisters had a tobacco shop in South End where John used to buy his tobacco in later years, and he would occasionally meet Marie Lloyd there.

Chapter 4
A Young Man Emerges

The young Johnny had now drifted away in time and a new young man had emerged, John. A gentle, caring teenager absorbing life and loving it, influenced by the exotic world of the theatre, which gave him an open-minded and sophisticated personality. Tommy, who was always so great to John, took him along on a lot of holidays together with his friends. Normally, John didn't have much time to play around outside of his times with Tommy because he had to attend to his studying. He often had to study into the early morning hours as his courses were so heavy.

One of the languages he was studying was German. His teacher was meticulous about his students learning grammar and studying vocabulary. However, at that time, German was just a language to John, and Hitler could have been a flower for all he knew. None of it really mattered that much to him yet.

While he was taking a course in using the transcontinental telephone, he discovered that the Gaumont British Film Studio was nearby. He took to visiting the studio often, sometimes during the shooting of films. Here John met Alfred Hitchcock a few times. Hitchcock was quite the lad then, always playing tricks on people, particularly with the phoney stage props. He had a very distinctive face even then, and he and John talked and laughed frequently over the many pranks he pulled. Alfred Hitchcock was already noted for his elaborate tricks.

On one occasion, while shooting a scene, he asked John to fetch some papers from his office. He pointed to a door across from the set. Well, surprise — when John opened the door, he was swamped with rolls of toilet paper. Needless to say, that caused a good laugh for the actors on set.

Another show Johnny saw at the time was called Chung Ling Soo. People used to laugh and call it two man shoe. The performer dressed traditionally as a Chinese man in the show and executed daring manoeuvres. At one point he held a plate up in the air and someone would shoot at it and break it. Sometimes, at the last minute, he would throw the plates in the air and supposedly catch the bullet in his hand or even in his teeth, but then one day there was a horrible accident on stage and he was shot and killed. He fell down right on the stage in front of everyone.

John knew that Chung Ling Soo wasn't even Chinese, but an American conjuror, originally from Yorkshire, and now living in the States. His real name was William Robinson.

*
**

John went on a Boy Scout trip to Nottingham, which used to be called the tobacco city. He started to buy cigarettes when he was fourteen. Cigarettes cost seven for a penny. There were only two kinds of cigarettes available, Gold Flake and his choice, Players Plain. They were always plain in those days.

When he was about fifteen, John skipped school and went with Tommy to the Franco-British Exhibition in London. All the countries were represented there. The competitions were held in an area of East London near Shepherd's Bush and near where Wembley stands today. It was called the White City because all the buildings were painted white.

John saw his first Rolls Royce engine at this exhibition, which sparked his mechanical zeal.

The young John was growing up and starting to fill out as a man. As usual, his brown curls were sticking out in all directions. Lately, they were sticking out from under his football helmet when he played for Southend United while he was attending school there. He was center forward, but he never scored a goal. Still, he remembered those as very happy times.

Southend was a very pleasant holiday resort town. Its real name is Southend on Sea, but the natives called it Southend on Mud. It had only a very little sandy beach; most of the sea shore was just mud. Still, during the summer months the town was overwhelmed by Londoners. Traveling by train, it was only a one-hour trip and they would flock in on the bank holidays. Arriving there, they took excursions to the harbour villages by means of horse-dawn charabancs that carried thirty to forty people and were drawn by a team of two horses. This method of getting about was considered "quite the thing."

At the time that the Hippodrome at Southend opened, John was still boarding with the Reardens. Tommy knew the owner of the Hippodrome, Walter DeFreese, who would let the boys in for free to go help behind the scenes. John also worked for him in the evenings, carrying luggage and stage props for the people. The extra money he earned, 26 shillings a week, enabled him to pay his way into the theatre. It cost six pence for a movie, and an opera was two shillings.

Whenever he was free, John worked with Tommy in the theatre, changing the background scenes and working the curtain contraptions. Those were truly fabulous times when he was young and eager, had no responsibilities, and was able to save the money he earned. As well, in this part-time capacity as an assistant prop man at theatres in Southend and in London, he had the bonus of being able to meet so many famous theatrical people of the time.

When they could, John and his friends would rent motorcycles, huge wooden ones. There was no such thing as a driver's license. You just went to one of the local garages where this fellow had a sideline of lending out motorcycles during the summertime for so much an hour. You could also rent a boat on the beach, and John learned a lot about boating during those summers. He and his friends used to spend many daylight hours rowing about with their girlfriends. That was the custom and it was their way of enjoying themselves.

John was experimenting with a moustache; first long then short, curled up, and then curled down. John even had a little Hitler-style moustache that was all the rage for a very short while, before he finally shaved it clean away. From then on, he was always clean-shaven.

Next to Southend was Thorpe Bay, where the two Batley brothers owned a golf course. John used to play there quite a lot and often carried others' clubs for a fee. John kept his own golf club there with the name

"Bert Batley, Thorpe Bay" on it. It was one of the first steel-shafted clubs manufactured and was a really fine club. John treasured it.

⁂

1912 was a sad year with a date to remember, the sinking of the Titanic. A fellow student with whom John was very friendly, Arthur Lawrence, was on board the Titanic and drowned when it sank. Arthur had decided to go to sea when he was very young. He applied and obtained a post on the Titanic as cabin boy.

John knew Arthur's mother very well. She had a little grocery store near Darlington, at Stockton on Tees, where he visited her frequently. She was a very nice person, a good mother, and was very proud of her son. Her husband had been killed tragically in a railway accident some years before. The death of her son was a great loss to her, and his friends missed him also.

When John was sixteen, he moved back to Darlington to attend the Engineering College. In those days there was no such thing as electric trains, they were all steam. Those first trains made for a very rough ride because they had no firm connection to each other, only a hook and a chain, and they had no hydraulic brakes. Every time the train stopped, it went crack, crack, crack.

There were wooden seats with no cushions on them. In the cold weather, they brought on the heat in big oblong metal cases about the length of the carriage. They filled them with hot water and put them under the seats to keep the passengers warm. At every large station, they would exchange them for a fresh hot unit. Later, the railways got the Westinghouse brake system with hydraulic brakes, and that changed everything – now each train halted straight away, an entirely different experience. The trains were however very unreliable, never on time. If you were due at a certain place at twelve o'clock, you would probably get there by one, if you were lucky. You could never count on arriving on time.

Back in Darlington at the engineering college, John was to learn turning, milling, instrument and tool making, and general machine practice and theory. He spent many hours at the Railway Engineering Works and some time at the George Stephenson Engineering Factory.

Mr. Jack Henderson was their instructor for engineering theory, and was he thorough. No mistakes of any kind were allowed; it had to be right. He took the young men through the many factories in this and other cities to learn the up-to-date methods of operation. They took trips to different parts of England, Scotland, and Wales. In fact, they visited the greater part of the United Kingdom. Incidentally, Jack Henderson was also the owner of the Half Moon Hotel, just across from the college. The students never had homework, so they often met up there after school hours. He encouraged their drinking, with the result that they had many pleasant evenings.

Study was essential, but it had its lighter side. One evening in the Half Moon Hotel, John looked over to see one of his fellow students, Betty Bowman, sitting at a table with a group of her friends. He was drawn to her immediately.

They smiled back and forth shyly for a while before John went up to her table and politely raised his arm saying, "May I have this dance?"

"Oh, yes," she said, shuffling her way around the table before bouncing up.

John tried but could not conceal the look of excitement on his face and in his dazzling smile that came so naturally. As he took Betty's hand, he noticed her gorgeous brown eyes looking right at him and that brought a feeling of peace over him, of complete and utter serenity; she was a soulmate at first sight.

As they danced, Betty's friends couldn't help noticing how perfect they looked together. Both of them were tall and slender, impeccably dressed, and already moving as one; it was as if they had been dancing together forever.

"I love his smile," one of the girls said with a giggle. "I'd be his wife any day."

John and Betty were soon inseparable. She was a very talented and delightful young lady, so comfortable to be with. Her home was in a village named Evenwood, just a few miles from Darlington, and she owned an old standard car to go back and forth with. On long weekends or whenever possible, they would take trips to different parts of England and Scotland, significantly enriching their knowledge of the everyday world

The beauty of the Lake District has to be seen to be believed. It was a wonderful sight to drive along the road on the west side of Lake Patterdale. In the spring you would see rows of natural flowers on the sloping hillside. First you see a row of primroses and then above them a row of bluebells, and above them a row of daffodils. It looked just like a magic carpet, a spectacular work of nature.

There were so many beautiful lakes. They quite often rented boats and rowed around the lakes in them. Or sometimes they would take a trip on a tour boat that held ten people. It would be a round trip lasting a couple of hours. The tour would take you around the big islands and then stop at one of the little inns and cafés on the island.

Lake Windermere is one of the larger lakes. It was here that the motorboat speed trials were held, and it was here that Sir H. Seagrave met his death when his speedboat disintegrated while on a trial run. It was a sad day for the entire country.

***

Betty and John used to sit for hours in the evenings, going over their work from that day and preparing for the next. Betty was far ahead of John in engineering theory. She was a real whiz at the books and could easily leave him behind; however, the practical was John's strong suit. They also practiced their languages together. She spoke quite a few, a very useful skill for both of them. They spent many days and nights together at the engine manufacturing plants, where they watched a railway engine being built and even had a finger in the pie.

They were still just good friends, both still young and innocent. She was very keen on John, and he knew that she wanted to get married, but he wasn't ready to think about marriage just then.

Darlington is considered as the birthplace of George Stephenson and of the steam locomotive as we know it today. The town's motto is Floreat Industria, Where Industry Flourishes, and that was quite true at the time. There was a huge forge in Darlington and while John was living there, they were forging the keel of the ocean liner The Queen Mary.

The engineering college was on Northgate Street and could be distinguished by the "Bulmer Stone," a huge boulder which was said locally to have been left there by a giant named Bulmer, who, when passing through town, felt something in his shoe that he removed and, finding it to be a stone, removed it and left it there in the centre of town.

The chief of police then was a man named Ben Johnson, and he used to stop in at the college to visit a relation of his. The students used to laugh at him and called him Big Ben Johnson, because he was so tall and always had to bend down to get in the doorway

The police station was on the same street as the high school and the Theatre Royal, where John participated in many plays. One such play was The Royal Divorce about Napoleon and Josephine. John was an extra in the battle scene and had to stand beside a cannon and fall on it when he was shot.

When John and Betty frequented the theatre together, they would go for a drink at a hotel right next to the rear entrance of the theatre and then sneak the drink back into the theatre. It was at this Theatre Royal, near the Inn at Middlesbrough, that John first saw such now well-known people as Charles Laughton, Elsie Lancaster, and Rupert Brooke. They were acting together in a repertory ensemble known as the Millane Stock Company and presenting a different play each week, such as the Fireman's Wedding, Murder in the Red Barn, and many other excellent plays. They were good, too.

Chapter 5

Training For War

The war that began in 1914 was predicted by Earl Haig as far back as 1912, and again in 1913. He warned the country that there was going to be another war, but the government's attitude at that time was, "Oh no, they won't fight; they wouldn't be bothered."

A clue to the German government's antipathy to England was the attitude of Kaiser Wilhelm, the last German emperor, the King of Prussia, and the eldest grandson of Queen Victoria. He visited England in 1912 and after reviewing the troops, he said, "All I have of England is my withered arm."

This negative statement shook the trust of the British population and hostile feelings began to emerge. One or two derogatory songs arose. One comical one that John sang in 1914 was called, "Where are the lads of the village tonight." It accuses the Germans of deliberately targeting Red Cross ambulances, and then tells how the British soldiers "Have gone to teach the vulture that murder isn't culture."

The song has several verses and they became more and more anti German as the song progressed. It was sung to a marching tune but many of the verses have been lost to time. John always remembered the following ones:

Where are the lads of the village tonight?
Where are the nuts we knew?
In Picadilly or Leicester Square?
No, not there, no not there.

They're taking a trip on the continong
With their rifles and their bayonettes bright
Gone to teach the vulture murder is not a culture
That's where they are tonight.

Of course, another song they sang later was, "But why, oh why, I don't want to die, I want to go home." But that came much later.

⁑

When war was declared in 1914, John was living in the Darlington district with its large number of associated industries of many kinds. This was later to become known as The Great War. John was just eighteen and being young (and against the advice of his dear friend Betty), John decided to enlist in the armed forces as soon as he could be released from his training commitments.

Even though he was still studying engineering and had about a year and a half to go, he was hoping for an opportunity to use the knowledge he already had of languages and of engineering. Having finished his training at the Royal Technical College at Northgate, he had been posted as an apprentice at The London North Eastern Railway Works, the L.N.E.R., which they called the shops. It was here he got the news that England was at war. John soon joined the reserves but continued in the shops where the work they were doing was essential to the war effort.

One of his helpers in the shops was Jordie Fly, a nice chap. First thing in the morning when Jordie got to work, he would dust the machines down and do the things that John would normally have to do, as well as setting locks in place and releasing machines, to put them into commission. He always started up the grinding machines which had to be set up an hour before work, so they would get hot. If they were cold, the men could not work as the measurements were down to so many thousandths of an inch. Jordie did all of this work for John.

Jordie had three or four children, and he spent every penny that he earned. Jordie came up to John one day in the shops and said, "I've been called up."

John was completely stunned, losing the grip on his wrench so that it slipped out of his fingers and fell to the floor with a loud clang. After all, John was the one in the reserves at the time. Right away, John said to the foreman, "I'm going to join up, too."

The foreman said, "You can't join up."

John said, "I'm going to join up. If Jordie goes, I'm going to go too."

Jordie was looking at it this way: he had a big family and he was supporting his mother. He had a poor wage at the L.N.E.R. and knew he would get a good allowance from the army.

John thought simply, "This poor bugger. If he goes, I'm going to go too," and without further thought, he did just that.

So they both went together to the recruiting office, and they got their shilling. (They gave you a shilling when you signed your name). Jordie joined the Royal Navy and John went into the Field Auxiliary. Stupid, John knew it was. He didn't have to go; he could have stayed. He had no idea at the time how serious it really was.

Jordie was sent off on one of the big battleships, and later he was drowned in one of the numerous ocean skirmishes. Poor fellow, John thought at the time, and he was a nice chap, too. Well, just the same, it could have been him.

John had had a job getting out of the engineering course. They wouldn't let him go because his training course was considered a restricted occupation. However, they made concessions, and eventually he was released. They joked that it was only because they wanted good mechanics at the front. John was released on the understanding that he was to return to complete his course after the war.

Betty and John talked and talked and talked. She said to him, "Never mind about Jordie, you just don't go." She didn't like it one little bit and was so afraid of losing him. When he left to go to the station, she didn't even go with him to see him off. She just stood on the corner, never said goodbye, no kiss nor hug, just stood there. John thought it was strange, but he knew she didn't want him to go. And he knew later that he shouldn't have gone, but being young, John felt that he wanted to see more of the world. Before long, he was wishing that he had stayed and married her, but fate decided otherwise.

⁎

When war broke out, they were all told they were in reserve for this or that. When the first division went out, there were men in their civilian uniforms, white britches and red jackets. These were men of the old British army, the old red and blues. Then there were the guards, British guards, Welsh guards, and Irish guards. They were all in their peace-time uniforms, too, and all they had was a rifle. There were no other arms to be had. They were the first division to be sent to France, with no one to back them up, only the reserve people and the few who had volunteered.

That first group of men with their horses made up the first army and they were what were called the "Thin Red Line." The people called them that because of their uniforms, with a thin red line running down the pant leg.

John was with the 2nd Division, which was eventually sent in to relieve them. In reality, they didn't really "relieve" the first division the way they had expected too, because they had lost eighty per cent of the men. They were very badly cut up.

One day, the Kaiser had said, "The thin red line, that contemptible little army," and people had begun to call the first division "The Contemptible Little Army." The first division had only two-thirds of the soldiers of John's division.

John's division was made up of reserves and volunteers, and the third division that followed in their footsteps, Lord Kitchener's Army, was made up of conscripts. "It's you or it's a hell of a change around here," they'd say, and they took you in the army almost automatically. Kitchener's Army, they were a bad little lot. Still, that was a good thing.

When they signed up for war and got their shilling, they were told that they were now "Soldiers of the Queen." Their purpose, the recruiting officer states, was "to teach the German vultures that murder isn't culture, just like the song.

John's previous experiences being useful, he joined the "Signal Section" of the Royal Field Artillery and was sent for a short period of training at Shoeburyness in Essex. Here the men learned the military method of day and night "signalling." They also learned to understand about range and elevation in regards to the firing of big guns. They studied telegraphy,

Morse code, and the use of the rifle. After initial training, they were sent to Woolwich, in London, to learn how to ride horses, saddled or bareback. John wondered why at the time.

*
**

From Woolwich, they went to Swanage, in Dorset. The men were now looking forward to a leave while the signal train that had delivered them was still there to take them to their destinations.

"John," one of the commanding officers bellowed at him.

John stood at attention, looking at him puzzled. "Yes, sir."

The officer came closer and lowered his voice, "Signalling is one thing that you are still a little bit shaky on. I want you to come with us to the mountains."

John was horribly disappointed to miss his leave, but that was that. He had no choice. He accompanied the horses by train into the mountains where they were to receive some training.

In the mountains, which were really just high hills, it was John's charge to look after the guns that were placed at intervals throughout the hills. To visit all the gun emplacements, he had to walk a few miles at night which he enjoyed, but he had a rifle with him that had no ammunition, and he was scared to death of someone actually coming.

John often used to sneak back to headquarters and have a sleep. An officers' camp was located near their headquarters where the guardroom was, and every night this bloody officer would come around, on the alert for sleeping soldiers. He caught John napping, just the once, and followed him around the guns for hours after that. It was a terrible bother.

It was quite normal in the beginning that soldiers in training would not have any ammunition, because of the shortages, but also in case a gun went off by accident. Once they arrived in France, they had a bandoleer of ammunition that went over the shoulder that carried a thousand rounds of ammunition. They were supposed to carry it at all times, but John always found it cumbersome, and when he got left on his own sometimes he thought about dumping it. He just couldn't be bothered with it as there was very little chance of ever using it in his position.

Chapter 6
FRANCE – WW I

Training over, John was eventually shipped over to France with the 47th Howitzer Battery of the 44th Brigade of the 2nd Division of the B.E.F. (British Expedition Force). They sailed from Folkestone with a full complement of men in two ships, two to three hundred horses, howitzers, other guns and equipment, and of course officers. The conditions were horrible. When John said "officers," he said it ironically because the officers knew no more than the men. None of them had ever been to war.

The officers were in uniform for the first time. They had been to the O.T.C., (Officers Training Camp), but they didn't know "A" from a bull's foot, as the expression was, nor did John.

Just loading the horses onto the ships caused pandemonium. The men were also loading guns and explosives, using all of their strength to push those big guns on board. It was really difficult work, but they had no choice. Later divisions learned from the experiences of the 2nd Division, and they devised a much better set-up, which made it easier.

But for the 2nd Division, getting these magnificent horses onto the ship was overwhelming. Six gun batteries, three batteries with six guns each. Each gun had twelve horses, six on replacement. They had to have spare horses in case some were killed and because you couldn't work horses all the time. They had to rest and have their spare time too, just like a human being. So, every gun carrier had twelve horses and that was a lot of horses. John said later that it was a hell of a ride, but it was fun. It was an experience.

After a rough crossing for men and horses, they arrived at Le Havre, France. Since the docks there were within range of enemy guns, they had to move in a hurry. From Le Havre, they marched to a small village named Harfleur. It rained continually and was cold and bitter. They had no billets, and the men had to sleep in tents – four men in a small tent intended for only two. The torrential rains continued for days.

One thing that struck John as funny afterwards was that when he needed to relieve himself, all he had to do was slip out of the side of the tent and find the first rubber Wellington boot around. You could always blame the rain for the contents of the boot. This was a common practice among the men.

It was here at Harfleur that John first heard of the game Housey, now called bingo. While they were waiting for instructions for posting, most of the "rank and file" spent their spare-time playing Housey Housey.

From Harfleur, still raining hard, the division marched on for another three gruelling days, sometimes getting a ride on one of the shell carriers pulled by horses. The marching was long and tedious. It wasn't straightforward since they had to follow the route from one village to another, and they put in three times the distance that a crow would fly. That was one of the details that no one talked about. They would walk along until they came to a little village, which would have a little pond and maybe a church and a few houses and then they might be stuck there for the rest of the day. John was struck by the outdoor urinals in the streets of France, shielded by a metal enclosure, and used by both the men and the women.

That march from Harfleur was like hell for the men. They were all soaked, and they had nothing dry to change into. Everyone was demoralized, and sleeping was a nightmare. Sometimes they had only one groundsheet, which they would try to use both to sleep on and to cover their heads with. It never seemed to stop raining and it was bitter cold. They had stopped even trying to shave. As well, they found that the French weren't very cooperative as they still objected to the British being there at all, but the men got over it. Sometimes John could not really believe what was happening.

After a few days, too many to bother counting, when John was miserable and tired, they finally arrived at a place he believed was named

Hersin. Often the men had no idea of the names of the towns they were in or how they were spelled as they didn't always meet someone from that particular town or village whom they could ask. In Hersin, he was billeted with about thirty others in what had been a winery. There was only the one building, nothing else, but they had plenty of wine to drink, and also plenty of company. Lots and lots of bugs, all sizes and colours, but no fresh water, except the rain. The men were told not to drink the water from the wells so some of the fellows had a good time drinking wine, and organizing bug races with candlelight. The next day the wine drinkers were very sick. As for John, he never drank much wine, but tired and wet, life seemed plenty cold to him.

Eventually they arrived in St. Omer, near the Belgian border, where they were issued all their fighting equipment. The men didn't know that they were on their way to Ypres from there.

"Line up, men," the commander roared. "You each have been issued a new suit, to be picked up in this tent," he said, pointing over to a large tent. "And you will each pick up a rifle, and a bandoleer of bullets over in that tent. At ease.

"That's all?" John said to the soldier beside him.

When John finally went into action, he was dismayed by his lack of equipment, but as it turned out, he didn't need it, though. When he got to the end of the line they gave him equipment for signalling; otherwise, they didn't have anything for him. He was reasonably surprised that he had no helmet, no bayonet, nothing with which to defend himself. Each man also carried a kit with a groundsheet, a water bottle, and a mess can with a handle. That was something you had to have and was part of their standard equipment. If you were working in the trench and you wanted something to eat or something to drink, you had to have a mess can, otherwise you would go without. It was common to put a mess can out to catch the rainwater.

*
**

The commanders cautioned the men on where to walk in order not to get shot down. But being in the auxiliary, they were still behind the lines. At first, they weren't getting hit, but when the Germans found out just exactly where they were, they gave them hell, bombarding them with their artillery.

For head protection they had berets, a cloth hat — in other words, they had no head protection. Most of the German soldiers had metal helmets and the Brits were quite envious of this.

The first heavy fighting they saw was at Annequin, further east from St. Omer. They arrived after the battle and found soldiers lying all over the place badly hurt. Some had their arms blown off, and some their legs, and some were blown to bits. There was nothing to be done for them as the division had no dressings, no bandages, no field equipment of any kind. Those men were left to lie there and probably died.

The Germans, on the other hand, were well prepared. They had everything they needed as they had been preparing for it. The British had nothing, at least, that's how John felt.

The soldiers of John's division walked on past Annequin for a while and found themselves standing on what had once been famously known as "The Cloth Hall" — a huge building used in the cloth industry, dating back to the 13th century. Except it wasn't a hall anymore; all that remained now was a huge patch of what looked like cement. So much for war, thought John.

*
**

Soon after that, the war began in earnest for John's division as they went into action in Belgium in September of 1915. They fought their first battle at Loos, taking part in a large British-French offensive with about 500 people. Shells exploded constantly and John had his first taste of real war. In the end, the battle at Loos was lost due to the lack of artillery power.

After they left the battlefields at Loos, the men did not know just where they were. They could only hope that the officers knew where they were and where they were going next. It turned out to be Ypres, where the 1st Division had been badly cut up. The 1st Division of the B.E.F. was so beaten up at Mons and Ypres that the 2nd Division to which John was attached was sent to relieve them. Those remaining in the 1st Division certainly deserved and needed a rest.

From there the men marched under shellfire about eighteen miles to Mons; and after a day-and-a-half, they moved on to Vimy, the famous or infamous ridge. It was here that the Canadians made perhaps their greatest sacrifice. The British and French had also been badly beaten there before them. Then on to Arras, and to a lot of places that had no name for John. They moved from place to place, and the rain was still falling by the bucket and the men were constantly soaked to the bone.

John always reminded himself that today is today and when morning comes it's another day. It would be better or it would be worse, but it was another day with new possibilities. It soon became his motto, "Tomorrow is another day."

Mons was a hellhole that John never forgot. Here the French lost eighty per cent of their manpower, the British about seventy per cent. They had walked for about three days from Ypres to Mons, to find that the trenches there were poorly constructed and not very deep. When the soldiers passed through them, the Germans could see them most of the time.

It was a very bad place – all mud and rain, sticky mud everywhere. A fellow could lose his boots to the sticky mud and when he looked up, Gerry would just "ping" and that was it.

The horrific slaughter in Mons was almost unbearable to witness. It felt surreal, forcing a new personality to emerge as John's survival instinct kicked in. Rising again and again from the blood-stained dirt, surrounded by the dead as the most awful of moments continued to occur, it felt for John as if time itself had slowed in the flash that took a human life and gave a lifetime of pain in return.

It was in Mons that the story of the "Lady of Mons" began to circulate. Some men said they saw a lady hovering over them, watching over them. Most of the men laughed about that story, but in the trenches filled with the wounded and dying, you could believe anything, even the hovering Lady of Mons.

On the trip back to Arras, some of the men gave up. The mud was so deep they'd sink into it, and they would be so weary that they wouldn't even try to get up. They just dropped in their tracks and couldn't go on, and the rest of the troops had to leave them there. It made the other men sick to their stomachs, but they knew that they had to keep going forwards, not backwards or they too would die. The stretcher bearers were carrying away the people who were wounded and would hardly even notice the soldiers who appeared to be just resting. Those stretcher bearers had a terrible time of it, manoeuvring through a trench six feet deep with a couple of feet of mud in the bottom of it and hauling a stretcher with them. In some places they couldn't take the wounded through the trench, because there wasn't enough room; it might be filled to the top with mud and debris from a blast. They would have to climb up over it, exposing themselves and the wounded soldier.

It was roughest in the beginning as the Brits were so totally unprepared for war. It was the 1st Division that had built the trenches with no proper equipment. They dug with what they had and suffered the consequences of their country's lack of preparation for war. After awhile, these things began to work themselves out as the soldiers figured out for themselves what had to be done.

*
**

Vimy Ridge was just called Vimy before the war. There was no ridge there. Well, there could have been, but they couldn't see it. It was just a field, that until lately had been ploughed up and ploughed under. All you could see across the field were the tops of what had been dugouts, and so much mud, there was mud there, nearly up to your knees. Eventually that field was called Vimy Ridge because the two lines built their own fortifications, their ridges, but in between them it was more like a ditch.

Just to get the guns into place, they had to walk along a muddy trench and dig out what had been there before, an old barn or some other structure. At first when they got there, things were very quiet. The German gunners thought it was a picnic; perhaps they were thinking, Oh well, this is nothing, we'll wait and we'll give them a chance before we shoot them up, and they didn't shoot them up! It was later when the trouble started.

Seeing an airplane flying over was still quite rare in the early years. So much so, that what actually happened was that both sides, the German and the Allies, would stop fighting and watch it go over. The blasting on the ground would slowly wane as the engine of the biplane became the only noise audible, roaring ever louder as it approached them.

"Look," one of the soldiers yelled pointing up to the sky.

"Is it one of ours?" another man yelled, crouching down as if it were a giant bird about to swallow him up. All of the soldiers' eyes were wide with curiosity while they followed the motion of this extraordinary flying machine. They could see the two men inside, their leather helmets flapping in the wind and the occasional glisten of their goggles.

"I can't tell whose side he's on. Does anyone know?" one of the gunners called.

It was hard to tell, but most of the aircraft at the beginning were used for reconnaissance and were just having a good look around.

"It's a Vickers biplane," one man would soon happily yell, but the men greeted this statement with silence. "It's British," he added, and the men let out a terrific cheer. They knew without a doubt that it was an ally aircraft when it wiggled its wings as it passed over. Many of the men would duck down on the fly past even though the airplane was at least a hundred feet above them. The pilots' orders were to fly "low and slow" back then.

The aircraft were truly a beautiful sight to see – so many different models and colours, some biplanes and some single wing airplanes which were the cutting edge at the time, but all of which were a wonderful spectacle for the eye, giving hope to the weary soldiers for a brighter future.

In later years, long after the war was over, the men still instinctively looked up at the sound of an engine, because sometimes they would throw bombs out of the aircraft, a really good reason to keep an eye on them. Everyone would run, but those hand dropped bombs were devastating when they hit their targets.

Each battery had a number of signallers who worked the Observation Post (O.P.) stations on a rotation basis. John's job was to sit up in a tree or some other high elevation and watch where the bombs landed and then signal back to the gunlayers who lined up the shot. The times and places were but vague memories for the men as the routine of fighting and bombing and misery took over.

One place John recalled quite well was the town of Bethune, thirty kilometres north of Arras, with its famous canal running through the middle. Both sides of the canal were banked up, and the Allied guns were stationed all along one side. The railway ran along the same side of the river and that's where the signal box was.

The O.P., as it was called, was in what had been a Railway Signal Cabin on stilts, complete with levers. It was quite exciting to John to see these bright yellow and orange levers, with all the wires still there. There were French signs hanging from the levers, but the signallers didn't know what they were all for. They could see that there was a place to turn the engines around.

All that was left of this cabin they were in was a part of the roof and one wall of the cabin. Two of its legs had been blown away, and the two remaining legs were badly damaged. They had to reinforce them with sandbags quietly during the night so as not to be seen or heard. From this viewpoint, John could see the German guns quite clearly. It didn't seem unusual at the time. Also from that post he could quite plainly see the cities of Lens and possibly Lille in the distance. They always had to get in and out under cover of darkness, although things were very quiet here at the time. The German Gunners, Gerrys, may have formed the impression that Bethune was of little interest to them, as only an occasional shell came their way. The British and French troops called the town of Bethune the Red Lamp City, and it was much used.

One day John was on observation duty near Bethune, between the two front lines way out in front in the town walls, between the Allied guns and the Germans. There had been a big battle three days before, but by now they had it all cleared away and it had quietened down.

For years, John never told the story about what happened there one night. He was walking around there, looking for souvenirs to be honest. Searching for souvenirs was common at this time, and finding a helmet was a real highlight. The British and German trench lines were just a short distance apart, with a no man's land in between. It was very dark that night with just a sliver of moon casting light shadows through the calm earthy air, when all of a sudden John heard a noise, a rustle coming from a surviving patch of tall grain.

Automatically, without thinking, John spoke loudly in his most authoritative voice. "Was machen Sie hier?" That's all he said, "What are you doing here?"

The other man said, "SHHH, nichts," nothing, and he disappeared. He must have thought John was an officer because of his confident tone. He was probably doing the same thing that John was doing, looking for souvenirs. The German soldier was searching in the German trenches and John was searching in the British ones. John knew he shouldn't have been there, and the German soldier shouldn't have been there either. Well, they got a souvenir, anyway, a story to tell in later years.

How different things might have been! Little things like that happened all through John's life, always so close to death and yet evading it with a comment or a duck at the right moment. Had John spoken in English, the German soldier would have taken out his rifle and shot him because John never had a rifle with him.

Chapter 7

OBSERVATION DUTY

John had a sergeant major whose name was Grey, and all the men used to call him Dolly Grey. To tease him, they sang this song to him from the Boer War called "Goodbye, Dolly Grey" and he used to get so angry, but the men would have such a good laugh. Dolly Grey was a large fellow, with a huge bushy moustache, and he was a good person. He was also a perfectionist. The men had metal buttons on their tunics that they had to keep properly polished. It was utter madness, because the Germans could see the flash from them. Everything, even the spurs the riders wore had to be polished and scraped perfect, every single one of them. Still, he was good, Dolly Grey, and well liked. John could never condemn the man, never, and he never forgot the song, "Goodbye, Dolly Grey."

To be a signaller like John, commonly called Flags, one was expected to have good eyesight and be able to judge distances by sight. They would also have to be able to transmit to the gunlayer where their shells had fallen, whether short or beyond the intended target. It usually took three or four rounds before hitting any one target.

Communication between the guns and the spotters was by telegraph. To do this, the wires had to be pinned to the side of the trenches with wire staples, which they made themselves. These wires were often broken by gunfire or other causes. To repair them, one had to feel along the wire to find the break and then with tools and wire, they would fix or replace it.

This was just another job for the signallers, all this in a muddy, cold, wet trench, and nearly always at night. This was not a nice job even by day in the summer, but in winter it was always rough.

Some of the other signallers or "the boys," in John's battery were Billy Potter, a grocer's assistant in civil life, and Arthur Kemp, who was a railway signalman. There was also Archie Allen, whose father had a poultry store, and Bill Bacon, whose father was a blacksmith. Lastly was Ralph Coffin, a water main inspector, and of course, John himself. Many other signallers would be attached to the various other batteries.

Ralph Coffin came from Shalmasford, Essex. A great big burly fella, he could almost pick up a gun and carry it himself, and they used to tease him about that. He was a funny fellow and a lazy beggar. He would always dodge the call-out if he could. Now, for instance, if it was his turn to go on duty, he'd say "I've got to see the doctor, I've got a pain here," you know, that kind of stuff. That was Coffin, he was a real dodger, and they all knew it.

To set up communication between the guns and the observation post, the signallers used ordinary bare wires that they reeled from the guns, all through the trenches and up to the observation post. It was quite a feat as the trenches were zigzag and up and down. When they were tired or just lazy, they didn't lay them in the bottom of the trench but would lay them over the top of the trench as it went much more quickly. Then of course, the wires were often broken, and they had to repair them. They would take a whole coil of wire and a pair of pliers and join the ends together. Mending wires was a big part of their job.

The drivers, the gunners, and the horses did a terrific job. The drivers were constantly on the go, driving the horses to and from the gun positions, the gunners digging the gun pits at night in all kinds of weather and sometimes under heavy artillery fire. There were often many casualties of both man and beast. The signallers' job was at times rough, but the job that those drivers and gunners did, was much rougher. It surpassed anything that the signallers had to do. They had nothing but praise for those men and horses.

The engineers were really wonderful, too. It was their place to get the trenches dug out for the men. In the beginning, the signallers would pick out an observation post that they thought suitable, but later, beginning in 1916, the officers began to decide where the observation post would be and where the trenches would be. They would pick two places, one here and one over there, and the engineers would dig deep pits in both places. Sometimes they would dig the pit or the hole in the ground so deep that all you could see was a muzzle sticking up out of it. When night time would come, they would be pulled out of one gunpit and sent on to another one. The engineers always had to be one step ahead of the men, preparing the trenches and digging the gunpits.

Then the men would just drag the guns into the next gun pit, under shellfire most of the time. It became almost a routine. It was a very confined space in the gunpit and it was very dangerous because of the recoil after the gun fired. The blast was so loud and powerful it would blow everyone's hair and clothes straight back for a second or two.

All of the men were warned that if they were forced to give up or abandon the guns, they were to disable them first. They had all been trained how to do it. On a Howitzer, there is a big barrel filled with oil underneath the gun. Just one little plug holds the oil in, so that when the gun recoils the oil takes the shock. If the little plug is removed, the oil runs out.

In the back of each gun pit, there was a trail, like a tail, with five men for each Howitzer. There is the gun layer, the gun feeder and the trail man and the people to feed the shells. When the gun was fired, the trail man's job was to run a big lever on the back of the gun so that when he opened the breach, the shell broke free or the casting moved out. This fellow at the trail, he had the worst job because he might hurt somebody. There were also the two fellows who were putting the ammunition in. They were working in such a way that there was always one going in with the shell for the gun and one going out for a new shell. Then this fellow opens the breach loader and puts the shell in just like that and then, BOOM. All in a matter of seconds! All of the men thought it was great fun at the time, and they enjoyed shooting those big guns.

50

At front of the guns was a little stick that was used for aiming. On the end of that stick was a little light at night that of course was shielded so that only their side could see it. It had a little disk in daytime that was at a certain degree, left or right, whatever it took, so that when they got the giant guns to fire the signallers would say increase your range by so many degrees and it was so many degrees left from that line and that's how they got their bearing to fire by. Many people just thought you put the thing in the ground and fire it; it wasn't that easy at all. There was a method to everything.

One officer did that one job of controlling the stick, artificer they called him. That was his job and that's all he did, nothing else. He made sure there was a light on at night time and a disk in the daytime. One stick for every gun and that was his line of sight. It had to be just a certain way, of course, and when they were moved to a new place, they would have to start all over again. It was quite complicated

When it rained or snowed, occasionally the pits filled up. Sometimes when the pitch of the guns was quite deep, and the front was up in the air and the working parts were down in the bottom of the pit, the gun would shoot out the back spraying people and dirt everywhere.

The pit itself was square, but the back of it was T-shaped because of the turret that had to be in the end of the tee. The 18-pounders didn't have that because they didn't have a recoil. They could not elevate the barrel like the Howitzer and could only fire point blank. They had a big spring and made a loud, woof, woof. All of the guns had to be cleaned and oiled every so often and have their oil barrel changed. It wasn't as simple as just pulling the trigger.

The officers often arrived with no training. John and one of his fellow soldiers were chuckling on their way over to France when the other fellow said to John, "The officers don't even know where the bullets are put," and it was true.

Some of the soldiers, fortunately, had been trained and so they knew, and they had to tell the officers how things worked. The officers weren't very nice about it, but they didn't know anything about range or line of fire. Well, John didn't know either until he'd been trained to do it in Shoeburyness and Dorset.

*
**

Everything was hard work. The trenches would be a mile in front of the guns; however, the observation post was almost level with the front line, so that they could see both sides, if possible. The trenches, the pits and the observation posts were all interlaid. Gerry knew where the guns were, but it wasn't just the guns they wanted to destroy. It was the fellow who had gotten the range, the signallers in other words.

The horses, meanwhile, had to be kept near the guns and somebody had to watch the horses as well as everything else. There were actually always six men to a gun. One man was a driver, just one man, and he would hold the six horses while he was on the front horse. He had to be relieved often. With six horses to control, with gun firing and rough territory and with no roads just rough country, it was difficult for him. Then when they went into action, they would have two drivers, so that the second one could take over if the first one was killed.

As well there were shell carriers who carried the shells, and it was tough for them too. You couldn't allow the shell carrier near the guns; they always had to be a certain distance away in case they exploded and destroyed their own guns. There were times when John's observation post was situated so close to the front line that their own infantry would cuss them, because the German gunners would be shooting at them and always trying to find their O.P.

There were thousands of men lost in the 2nd Division before Kitchener's army came on to relieve them. And they were a force to be reckoned with, these non-descript men who were called up for the army, had only three weeks training, and then were sent to France. They were a tough bunch and they learned to hold the fort.

*
**

Hill 60 was a famous hill, often cited as Hill 50, so many different armies being involved. 2nd Division had an observation post there. From this hill the Allies could see the German army, and it was a much sought after site. It was here that the drivers and gunners of what John thought was the 56th Battery of 18-Pounder Guns routed the German infantry and artillery, which retreated in confusion from "The Man in the Golden Armour." From what John gathered, the following story was a true one. At least, it was thought by many soldiers to be a true account.

On August 20 1915, during a battle in France, scores of British soldiers of the Royal Field Artillery reported that they had seen a man in golden armour. One person who heard this story many times was an English nurse, Miss Phyllis Campbell. She first heard the story from a wounded soldier of the Royal Field Artillery in a hospital behind the firing lines in France.

The soldier spoke clearly of the battle. "As our unit was defending a hill," he said, "it looked as if the whole German army was attacking at once." It was later ascertained that he was talking about the battle of Hill 60. Just as the Allied soldiers were about to give up in despair, it happened. A cloud of light appeared in front of the swarming Germans. When the light cleared away, the figure of a tall man in golden armour appeared, astride a white horse, with one arm uplifted, holding a mighty sword. The soldier watched as the attacking Germans halted, then turned around, and raced down the hill. At once the British were chasing after them, and in the confusion, no one seemed to know what had happened to the man in the golden armour.

Nurse Campbell later heard this story from another wounded soldier of the R.F.A. He told the same story, with the same conviction. However, what about the story from the German side? A German nurse, who had been a friend of Miss Campbell before the war, was now serving in a hospital in Potsdam. She sent a letter to Miss Campbell after the war. She stated that there had been stories going the rounds in a German military hospital that a regiment of German artillery had been assigned to capture a certain hill, but had failed to do so.

A German officer reported that as they attacked the hill, there was a sudden strange shape in the sky and then a huge man in golden armour appeared on a white horse. The officer said their charging horses had turned and fled, disregarding all commands and obstacles in their headlong terror-stricken flight. The German nurse concluded her letter with a simple query "Was there something to it?"

They called it Hill 60, but it was not really a hill as we generally denote them; rather it was a huge coal dump a few thousand feet wide, complete with coal dust and coal rubble. It was like a big mound, and from there the English could see all the German lines and the Germans could see all the English lines. The Germans were attacking the hill to capture that position. The Battery of the R.F.A. to which John was attached arrived at Hill 60 at a later date, and that's when they heard the story. All of the men believed that it was a true story and that the golden man was on the side of the Allies.

***

One village they stayed in near Annequin was off the main front and not of real interest to either the Germans or the Allies.

John's observation post there was so close to the front line however that they could listen to the German infantry cuss them over the trenches. The other signallers would have had similar experiences. The following are some of John's experiences as a signalman.

On one occasion, their O.P. was positioned in what had been a water storage tank, used before the war to supply water to the railway steam engines. Now it was leaning at a silly angle. The gun pits were in what had been the waiting room of the railway station. There were two problems. One was to get there under cover of darkness and leave the same way. The other was that the tower had only three legs, not exactly a secure position with Gerry firing constantly. It was well sandbagged inside however, so they had some protection. They had little trouble otherwise as it was a quiet part of the line.

***

On another occasion, the O.P. was built into the wall of a badly damaged, almost demolished chimney, about two stories above ground level. Just the front was showing, and behind it they had built a sandbagged stand, giving the appearance of a badly wrecked building. A number of partial chimneys were still standing in many of the ruined buildings and that's why it was decided that one of these should be the O.P. Well, it was not quite like home. It must have once been a college or school, as all around them, amongst the bricks and rubble, were books and papers in many languages, strewn in all directions. John used to go around and pick up some of these papers and read them when it was quiet.

This place was named Bully-Grenay. Before the war, it had been a very busy railway hub, with a really large round junction and miles and miles of tracks. The signalling signs were still hanging, and first class and second class carriages were stored on the tracks as well.

Normally in the daytime the enemy would let loose a few shots, not many, but as soon as it got dark, they hammered them. John couldn't get into his O.P. until dark, but they would have figured on that, he presumed. It was so frustrating, because at nighttime you couldn't move for the shells exploding all around, but in the daytime there was the odd one here and there and that's all.

This O.P. was a tough one. His fellow signallers all said he must have done something good to live to tell about it. Scrambling up this old chimney at night was not too bad, but when daylight came, one thing worried him. It was very close to the front line and to make matters worse, imbedded in the wall of the chimney just below him was an unexploded German Shell, a five-point-nine.

The gunners said to John, "Not to worry, it's only a dud shell."

Needless to say, he did a bit of worrying, however, apart from a few "whiz bangs", nothing much happened. In some ways, the posting in Bully-Grenay was good, and he had some good memories, but in the end, he was really glad to get out of that spot.

John never forgot that station. He was sitting up all night, feeling lonely, in that chimney with that shell at the bottom. It was a big junction with rails all over the place, and hasn't changed much today. He would always remember seeing the damaged sign hanging there, Bully-Grenay. Very often, signs were removed so that was unusual.

It was reported in 1917 that only officers did O.P. duties, but this was not true in the early days. It would have been foolish to lose a well-trained officer in such positions. John didn't have a single leave in almost two years. He could have if he'd made a fuss, but they were so short of men. They had gunners and riders, but very few observing people. When they eventually put officers on the job of observation, the same job that John had been doing, they got a great deal of credit for it. That didn't make any difference to John, but that's what happened.

Near Bully-Grenay, they found themselves in some muddy fields with crops still growing in them. They didn't have any shelter or gunpits, or time to dig trenches, and all the Gerrys had to do was shoot at them; it was insane and they couldn't do a thing about it. Men were dying all around them, and they were all crouched together trying to dig gun pits in the mud. John remembered forever how terrible it was.

After that, new troops began to arrive. Kitchener's Army arrived first, and then the Territorials followed. Eventually, the Canadians came from overseas and then the Americans and that made the difference. The Brits had borne the brunt of it during the first years, but they had only managed to stop the German advance.

*
**

They were stationed at La Bassée, and it was Christmas Day. It was a memorable town, a big town. There was this one particular row of houses lining a canal that they called the red light shop. Both the local people and the soldiers used to go there to frequent prostitutes. Once again, it was quiet in the daytime, with little shelling, but at night it was heavy again. John couldn't figure out why, but the men certainly enjoyed it there in La Bassée. On Boxing Day they were taken off the firing line for what was called a rest, and they went to a place named St. Pol, further from the front line.

St. Pol was a little country village just like many in England. There were miles and miles of countryside with a wide stream running through it. It was quiet and away from the front, and it was here that John began to understand why he had been trained in bareback riding.

The rule, strictly enforced, was that when the batteries were out on rest, it was the duty of the signallers to look after the horses. To groom, water, feed, and exercise them. They were there for three days and each signaller was put in charge of six horses. As they had no saddles, you may imagine just what it was like riding one horse bareback and leading the other five horses with a rope. They often did this at a gallop in order to give the horses some exercise. Apart from the fun of it, this was the only time the horses had any exercise – with the exception of when they were pulling the guns in or out of the gun-pits. The horses were very excited but John's bum was very sore.

When they said the soldiers were to rest at St. Pol, what actually happened was this. The men went out one night and rode a long way and stole some of the Gerry's food, right out from under them and brought it back for a feast. There was no camp in St. Pol, just a large piece of felt on the floor of the stables. John never saw any officers at all. The officers had gone to a quarter mess somewhere else. The men never saw them and that didn't bother them. No, that was good. They had plenty to drink and plenty to eat, and that was quite a change.

The soldiers had a great feed up, and filled their kit bags full of food to save for later. Everyone was so happy about going back into the line again, loaded down with extra food. Suddenly, heavy shelling began, and they were caught off guard. Some of the poor buggers never got back at all; John didn't know just how many and a lot of the men had their kit bags full of food that they never had a chance to eat. That's too bad, eh? said John later.

Chapter 8
LIFE ON THE FRONT

The Canadian soldiers were very good, according to John, and they deserved all the credit one could give them, especially at Vimy. Vimy was just one big mud hole, that's all it was. The Germans had blown up all the bridges and all the dams. All the roads were blown up all over the country. It was all mud, mud, mud, mud. John sometimes went months on end before taking his boots off.

You didn't notice it, in an odd way. There was so much going on around you, you didn't want to notice it. Yes, he had trench feet, swollen and bleeding and painful. They had few officers there to supervise them. They just had to put up with it. There were no doctors on the line to tend to them. Of course when you really needed it, they would take you in and put a new bandage on. That's all they could do, as they had no equipment. When they gave them their new uniforms, their third uniforms, there was a little pocket on the side and sewn in the pocket was a bandaid and a pill with iodine in it. That's all you had, just one little bandaid. The men had a few chuckles over that. But it was nice to take your boots off. Still, there were lots worse off than John, he used to think, lots worse off.

John never had a tin helmet. The soldiers were never issued one in those days, and they had no earplugs either, none of those luxuries.

For the sake of morale, the public back home was never told about any of the hardships the soldiers were suffering on the front. Back in England, they were "keeping the home fires burning."

*
**

At Noeux-Les-Mines, on the route to Arras, they had a quiet time. The woods around the town made a very fine cover. The village was the centre of a large coal mining district. Of course the people who lived there, the coal miners and families had been moved out. The Brits would set up an observation post in one mine and another one in a different mine, and then when one was hit, they would switch to the other one.

On the roadsides could frequently be seen a small wooden box on a post. It was like a small church, with an open front containing an icon, a small figure of Jesus Christ inside. The roadside shrines were very refreshing to a weary soldier. They had some very large ones as well, and the French would kneel when they went by. Some of the English, well, some were very rude and John noticed with dismay that they used to spit on them.

It was here that John saw his first German observation balloons. One thing that seemed strange to him was that the Germans had quite a number of these observation balloons in the air, at which the Tommys, or infantry, down below in the trenches were having a fine time taking pot shots at. They used to have some fun doing that, great fun. One felt sorry for the men in them, when the balloons collapsed. Alas, poor Gerry. The fortunes of war, as the saying goes, "All's fair in love and war."

The infantry fought very hard, but they were badly hit because they were in the front line. They took some ghastly blows in the trenches and many men died there from the heavy shelling. It was appalling to watch but it always made the surviving men, who weren't in shock, want to fight on harder to stop the murderers. The trenches were in the shape of zigzag and every so often a shell would fall on the side of the trench, blow it in, leaving an open space that you could see through. They would have to fill those empty spaces in again, with rocks or mud.

During the night the men on the front had to string the barbed wire and that's when the Gerrys would always strike. If anything shiny was showing, they would shoot at it. It was tough work. Quite often, when a group of men would gather for a work assignment, horrifically, one of them would just drop down, shot dead.

In Noeux-les-Mines, their observation post became known as "The Hole in the Wall." Here, one had to crawl in and out at night, through the cellar window of a large hotel that had been destroyed. John crawled in through this window night after night, and then one evening he accidentally caught his arm on a sharp piece of glass and ripped the skin. He never felt it and he didn't even know – until he got down into the bottom of the observation post and the fellow that was with him said, "Hey what's happened to you"?

John said, "Nothing why, what's the matter?"

He said, "What's wrong with your arm, look at it?"

That's when John saw all this blood. "Whoa," he said surprised and then laughing. "I must have scratched it," and when he took his jacket off, he could see it wasn't very serious. He had the little square bandage in his coat, so he pulled it out and stuck it on and that was it. John carried that bandaid on his arm until he was wounded, never took it off as there was just no point.

Fosse 8 was a huge heap of coal dust and clinkers from the mines that were situated between the two front lines. The Gerrys seemed to have a lot of fun pumping shells into it from time to time and for no reason whatsoever, except to annoy the enemy observation post by making the air dusty, almost unbearable. They were just being a pest. They seemed to know when the Brits were going for lunch, and the Germans would shoot their shells into the top of Fosse 8, not in the middle but on the top, and the coal dust would spread all over the place. There's another name for that spot in the official record, but that's what the men called it, Fosse 8 or Ditch 8.

The town of Festubert had apparently been the centre of a thriving farming industry. On the roadside beside a pile of bricks that had once been a farmhouse, was an old style threshing machine, riddled with holes of all sizes. It used a steam engine to run the long belt that drove the machine. It was here that John's division first met the Canadian Infantry. They were a lively crowd. They were as eager to learn about the British, as the men were to learn about Canada. They said they came from places like Medicine Hat, Red Deer, Moose Jaw, and Kicking Horse Pass. At the time, John thought they were pulling his leg, as it were. They were great fellows once you got to know them. They gave each of John's crew a pack of cigarettes, Aladdin's, which they greatly appreciated.

Festubert was a lovely country town with lots of farmers and many of the elderly farmers were still on their farms. The fields were filled with rakes and combine machines still standing there, and in those days, most of them were pulled by horses. The houses were very pretty and many had thatched roofs.

The streets were full of glass. When the Canadians were about to leave, they decided to ruin the place by blowing out most of the windows. It was never clear why. Nevertheless, the town of Festubert remained a pleasant memory for John.

Life at the front line had its funny and sometimes tragic sides.

On one occasion, while having a brief spell of relief, they were sitting around in the gunpit shooting the gab. The men were eating rice out of their mess tins, as rice was often all they could get to eat (and it was not very popular), when suddenly a whizz bang, a quick firing small German shell, burst overhead and to their horror and consternation, what did they see? Lying in one of the mess tins was part of the gunlayer's hand. One of the crew, Art Barker, a Cockney remarked, "Blimey, hav'nt yer got a spoon, mate," and they all laughed. When John looked back on it, he would think about how terrible it was to see that poor fellow's hand lying in a pan of rice, and yet they had laughed about it. It was just a freak accident, but they lost a good gunlayer, a good man.

The men survived on rice and hard biscuits, often all they could get. The transportation of food in those days wasn't regular and the men ate what they could find, occasionally stealing chickens or pigs from the people because they couldn't get any other food. But rice was the principal foodstuff.

The horses were tethered in long lines near the guns, so that the guns could be moved in a hurry when they were under heavy gunfire. On more than one occasion, a German shell burst among a line of horses. The result was carnage. It was a terrible sight, and bad enough for human beings, who could be helped, but nothing could be done for the horses.

Their screaming and traveling around killing each other was a sickening sight, really horrible. Not only that, when they lost their horses, they lost their power to move the guns. When the Germans realized they had hit something, they would continue to pound that same spot and very often wipe out most of the guns. It was no picnic.

The Germans had a small shell about the size of a cup. It was more like a can, but it was filled with nails and pieces of metal, so that when they exploded the metal pieces spread out over a large area. They were deadly, quick and very sharp. You couldn't hear them coming; you would see the shell burst and then you would hear it being fired. It traveled so quickly that it exploded before you could hear the shot. You couldn't avoid it.

One of the worst sights that John ever saw (and he saw many) was when a live shell exploded in the barrel of a Howitzer gun, killing all five of the gun crew and their officer. The cause could have been faulty ammunition, careless inspection in the manufacturing, or carelessness in the handling. It was not the first time it had happened.

The usual routine when they got to a fairly quiet spot was to organize a latrine and a garbage dump, often making use of a shell hole. On this occasion at Bully-Grenay, their cook was taking the garbage out to one of these shell holes and was returning to his kitchen, such as it was, when a Whizz Bang burst overhead. He heard the boom and immediately flattened out on his tummy but received a small splinter in his rear end. When he got back up, he was covered with mud on his face and his behind was all blood. The men had to laugh about it, and the remarks that were made were unrepeatable of course. They said, "What is he going to do when he gets to England and has to get bandaged up." Yeah, it wasn't nice, but they thought it was quite funny. Whizz bangs had become a way of life.

He was a lucky man but it was tough luck because the wound was serious. It was a big piece of metal and he was badly hurt. They rushed him to the casualty clearing station that was also luckily nearby. Eventually, he was sent back to England, or Blighty as they used to say. The war was finished for him. John wondered what happened to him when he got back and the nurses had to dress his behind. He thought it would be very embarrassing.

The casualty clearing station (C.C.S.) was where the stretcher-bearers used to send the wounded; it would be a temporary hospital under a big tent somewhere behind the front lines.

One night while on sentry duty, John was walking around the gun pits when all of a sudden, immediately over his head, there was a burst of friendly gunfire from a battery of 18-pounder guns. One never knew just where the guns were at any one time. It scared the daylights out of him, and he thought that for a minute that he had had it.

From the O.P. in Clarency Woods where they were stationed, John could see in the far distance a church steeple or spire leaning over at a very strange angle. It could have been a German O.P. and they were taking no chances, so he gave the gunners the range and they had lots of fun shooting at it. When it was quiet, they used to cheerfully take pot shots at it. They never knocked it down either. It was still there when they left. It was near here that John met his Waterloo, his "Pons Assinorum."

Now this is how it happened, at a place named Givenchy. John was returning to the rear, towards the guns from the observation post and had met his relief, Corporal Art Kemp. They usually met about half way between the O.P. and the guns, with each man making sure that the lines of communications were intact and discussing anything that might have happened. Normal procedure.

They were just sitting down there in the middle of the trench. Kemp was holding one end of the wire and John was pinching them together where the line had been broken, tying the two wires off. They had just fixed one and were going on to the second one when suddenly, poof, there was an eerie silence and they saw a flash. A shell burst overhead, probably a whizz bang, and being in the wrong place it wounded them both and that was it. They never fixed those last wires.

It was just getting dark when they were hit. John and Kemp lay there all that night, because the lines of communication had been destroyed and they could not contact the guns. However, after it was noticed that John had not returned for awhile, the signaller at the guns, not hearing from the observation post, surmised that something had happened. So a search party was sent out to find them. They didn't find them until the second night. There was just so many trenches, they didn't know which one they'd been in. It was up to the two signalmen to find their own way, to pick the trench between them. You couldn't always use the same trench; some would get blown in and you would have to find another way back. They constantly changed their route because, if you had just the one track, the Germans would soon know there was one track and they would target it. The signalmen always had more than one. And they always zigzagged. You'd go one way one day and you would go back the next day and the track from the day before would have been destroyed. It was never simple.

Their comrades never knew where John and Kemp had fallen; lots of men died that way when they couldn't get back or got lost. Being wounded, they couldn't move themselves, and so they would just lie there and die. The other men couldn't come and look for John and Kemp in daylight or they would have been seen. Something, like a shiny button, would give the enemy something to shoot at. No, they couldn't take that chance during the day. John and Kemp had to wait until the next night before they were found.

John was never sure later just how it happened, but they did find them and eventually they got them both back. They were both taken to a casualty clearing station and that was the last time that John saw Art Kemp, or Kempy. He was a Cockney fellow, and a real comic. He would joke about all kinds of things that would make everyone laugh. He'd say "How are your plates of meat?" Meaning, how are your feet? Or, "How's your loaf of bread," for your head. That's the way he talked. According to John, he was quite a character, and a real nice fellow, but in the end, John never knew what happened to Corporal Kemp. Apparently, John was out like a light and the first thing he recalled was being at the casualty clearing station, and all bandaged up.

At the C.C.S., John was left on a stretcher that was to be his bed for some days. They had him all patched up with bandages and made comfortable. A whole batch of men stayed lying there for a day and a half, or maybe it was two days.

John was still numb when a medical orderly, another Cockney fellow, came to him and asked him, "Would yer lyke some fish and chips, mate, or would yer lyke bangers and mash?"

Thinking that the orderly was joking and trying to cheer him up, as it were, John said just to humour him, "Yes, I would like some bangers and mash, please." Imagine his surprise when sometime later the man appeared with, believe it or not, a plate of sausages and mash. It tasted really good and just how he obtained it John never knew, nor did he ask him.

Little did he know that it would be many days before he would have another solid meal.

After a day and night approximately, John, with many others, was put on a Red Cross train. As there had been no doctors at the C.C.S., their bandages had not been changed and would not be removed until they arrived at the hospital. On the train, the stretchers were placed three in a tier, one stretcher above another, about ten tiers to a coach and an orderly walked between the rows to feed the men and look after them as best he could.

They travelled for about three ghastly days and nights. (John didn't count the days.) For all of the injured men, the jolting, bumping and swaying of the train was enough to think about. The food was bad, soup and cold at that. The French trains had no platforms between the cars, just a coupling, so each carriage was separate. Because the troop trains were coming and going every couple of hours, the hospital train would often be bumped to a sidetrack, where they had to wait until the troop train had gone by. Because of these delays, it took them a long time to get from the casualty clearing station to the hospital.

What John remembered mostly when they finally arrived at their destination was the smell. Most of the men were immobile and had no choice but to do it in their pants as they lay there. He imagined the train was an awful mess when they took the men out.

Some of the wounded weren't even on Red Cross trains; they were just on cattle trucks with canvas over the top. They just didn't have the equipment in 1915-16. The British hadn't been prepared and the French weren't prepared either. Conditions were terrible, but still John had lived through it. At night, you could hear the fellows shouting and screaming with their pain, and John always felt bad that he couldn't do anything for them. The orderly would come along and mop their brows and wet their faces and that's about all they could do with one orderly to a coach. That man must have been pretty worn out by the time they got to the hospital.

At long last, the train arrived at the Second Canadian Field Hospital at Le Tréport, France. John was still wearing his uniform. Incidentally, this field hospital was the only Canadian unit to be awarded the 1914 STAR. John did not recall how or when he arrived but when he became conscious he was lying on a pallet, not a bed. There were no beds there at the first. The first thing that he noticed was that the walls of the hospital seemed to shake. So he thought, I must be on a ship, and he even seemed to hear the waves of the ocean.

A pretty nurse came up to him and said, "That's the wall of the hospital," and chuckled a little. "The whole hospital here is entirely under canvas."

She gave John something to drink and said to him, "How are you, honey, feeling good? I'm going to undress you now," and that was the reception he got. John was so happy to be in her hands that he didn't give a damn what happened; he was so worn out, it all felt so bizarre.

His wounds had not been touched since they'd been bandaged. The original bandages were still on his leg, and he was still wearing a pair of leather army riding britches, parted down the side. They didn't take those boots off him until he got to the hospital at Le Treport. His leg must have been a mess, but he didn't see it anyway.

For meals, they came around twice a day with a bowl of soup. At least, they called it soup, but again it was more or less just cold water. The wounded men had to eat it because they had to have something to keep them alive, but they were constantly thirsty and hungry. Once, though, they brought John some grapes to eat. They were so delicious.

The next thing that John recalled, he found himself lying on the operating table completely naked and covered with a yellow kind of dye, possibly picric acid. When they came around the table to look at him, four doctors or surgeons were all looking down at him. He couldn't see his toes; he couldn't see anything. All he could see was yellow paint all over his body and smell that strange odour. The surgeons were discussing whether to remove the leg or not when John uttered his last few words to them, "I would rather die than lose my leg."

Chapter 9

ENGLAND AND RECOVERY

One of doctors was holding a mask over John's nose and mouth with little drops of liquid falling in it; he found out later it must have been ether. The doctor said to John, "Keep still." Then he added, "Now count, count."

John kept counting, and he knew that he had this cup over his head and he could hear the little drops falling down onto his face, and it smelled awful. They thought John was out because he wasn't counting, but he was still counting in his head. The surgeons were discussing the news that they had just received by cablegram from England, saying that Lord Kitchener's ship had that day been torpedoed and he himself was drowned. It was the 5th of June, 1916, and John was listening to the whole story.

When he came out of the operation pit and returned to the ward, he heard a gramophone play the "Destiny Waltz," and his emotions went wild. John reached for his leg, and with a huge sigh of relief, he felt it. He then looked up at the nurse and whispered, "Lord Kitchener has drowned."

As the nurse straightened him out on the cot and tucked him in securely, she replied boisterously, "Oh no, where did you hear such a thing?" She didn't believe him and John chuckled until another nurse came by and they chatted a bit. Then she came closer and asked him curiously "How did you know?" They thought that John was dreaming until the news was announced on the radio. The nurses still wondered how he knew about this.

It took him a week to reconcile himself to the surroundings. He couldn't sit upright; he spent his time lying flat on his back, not a nice feeling. When he woke up, he had a splint on his leg, and it was still numb. It remained numb even after he got to England.

John's stay at the hospital was a really good experience. He was treated like a king and he would never forget the wonderful treatment that he received. No person on earth could have wished for more. The attention of the doctors and staff was wonderful, in spite of the fact that the whole hospital was under canvas.

The surgeons, when they'd examined him, discovered that he had a severe gunshot wound to his right leg and also a compound fracture of the whole right side. His leg had been split open right down the front, almost the whole length of the leg and all of the bones had been shattered and misplaced.

They also found a splinter of metal embedded in his skull, just at the hairline on his forehead. It was a thin strip about three-quarters of an inch long, and shaped like a top hat. This had not even been detected at the C.C.S. and it caused some complications, but they took it out, and left a hole where it had been. He was lucky it hadn't penetrated. Afterwards there was a scar but no damage. All was well that ended well.

In later years, John often thought what good doctors they were. It could have been so much worse, and he knew he was very lucky.

⁎⁎⁎

Life was funny sometimes. In one corner of the hospital under the tent was a Canadian lad who awoke and asked, "Was I left here to die?" The nurse, who was Australian, casually replied, "No, you were brought in yesterdie."

All of the wounded soldiers within earshot laughed heartily at that, it was so funny. That nurse was quite a character and seemed to be in charge of the hospital. She was broad and brassy, just like the young Canadian lad had been. When she came to see them, John had difficulty understanding her though, despite the fact that they were both Australian. It had been a long time since John had heard Australian.

It would have been about two or three weeks that he was there at Treport. Not very long because they would try to clear out most of the wounded soldiers as quickly as they could because so many new men were coming in daily.

The nurses must have been tired as they worked hard. You could see it in their faces, which were drawn and haggard from putting in so many hours. John could hear the trains coming in with wounded every day, all the time, and they were all full.

Then it was time to go and they strung John up in the railway carriage. They put him in a Thomas Splint, which was an apparatus that went around his leg. It had a ring with a knot on it that kept the leg suspended. Down at the bottom was a piece with a hole in it that they could put a key into and open to adjust it. John was hanging as if he were in a hammock. When he got on the train going from the hospital to the boat, he swung back and forth, and back and forth. It was very exciting but in a bad way, as his genitals were squished into the splint for that long stretch and no one could make it stop. He was very uncomfortable and unhappy.

As he was suspended there, every so often John would see, as if in a dream, a doctor came along to adjust it. John never realized then what would come of this leg injury. He was just happy to be alive.

After being patched up again and able to be transported once more, he was put on board the hospital ship Saltar strictly for wounded people. They had a very rough crossing of the channel over to Southampton, England. The men were all on stretchers, and John was swinging backwards and forwards so much on this splint that he was scared that he was going to fall out – but he didn't because he was fastened to the bottom of a track.

On arrival in Southampton, the wounded soldiers were given a quiet reception. Very efficient, no noise, no fuss, no bother. Everyone was very nice and there was plenty of food. Candies and cigarettes, treats like that, but you know John never felt like having anything. He was just so tired.

Three trains were waiting for them in Southampton. Almost immediately, they bunged the wounded men into the trains one by one. John was loaded onto a Red Cross train along with the others to be deposited in Wrexham, North Wales.

They cleared that train out in no time at all, the serious ones first. John wouldn't have been too serious from their point of view so he would be one of the last ones. Incredibly, John felt very little; he remembered watching things happen around him, and feeling pretty rotten. But he never felt much pain, not until he got to Wrexham, and then it was different; he started to feel it. He was the last one off the train.

John was then taken to a hospital named Croes Newd, which means New Cross. It was a very small hospital with three wards. His ward was named "Boscombe Ward," and contained about fourteen beds in just a little narrow room with no partitions. He didn't remember much about the first few months, as he must have been under sedation, but after a few more months he was able to understand what was going on around him.

It was a really quaint country hospital. The chief doctor was Dr. Evans. He was very nice, elderly and very human, a jovial fellow, too. He and John got along well, a good thing since John was there for some months. When they finally took the splint off, John just sat straight up and then fainted. It took him three weeks to get his foot out of the bed after that. He couldn't bear the pain. Every day for many months to follow, John had a dozen or so tubes, the size of your finger, protruding from his leg to drain the green pus from within.

All the doctors and staff were very good to him as were the local people. As John had no kith or kin that would be visiting, he had frequent visitors who took a delight in taking him out in his long bath chair once he was able to be moved. They gave him a very warm welcome and even the local rector made many frequent visits.

One particular young lady, Miss Maisy Love, took great pleasure in taking him out. She would come every weekend, when weather permitted, with this big wooden-wheeled chair that had a large arch in the front to protect his legs. She would push him out for long rides in the wonderful countryside. Maisy also took him to the local cinemas and other events, once they let him go. She was really fond of John and he liked her also, but the thoughts of getting married never entered his head. He was always left wondering why afterwards; they might have been very happy.

John used to tease her about her funny name, Miss Love. She even came to London to see John later when he was in Roehampton, and he was such a dumb fool that he didn't follow it up. When John was in the hospital, he wasn't concerned about women at all; he was only concerned about living.

Another patient there, Tommy Howe, changed that somewhat for him when they became fast friends. Tommy and John became known as the "Brothers Twist," and a small group of them on the ward were known as the "H" Gang. They seemed to be always in trouble, doing everything they could do to get something for nothing, scrounging anything. They had a lot of good times together, and on a number of occasions they went to London to listen to the bands in Hyde Park. Well, not really to listen to the bands, but to show off their "hospital blues." The blue hospital uniforms marked them as wounded soldiers, or sailors or airmen. They were a handy way of attracting girls.

Those good times ended when John had to leave Wales because of complications; his wounds were getting worse instead of better.

John was transferred to Queen Mary's Military Hospital at Roehampton, on the outskirts of West London. This hospital was actually a very big house with many extensions that was donated to the government by Mrs. Wilson, wife of the president of the Wilson White Star Steamship Line.

In the ward at Roehampton, there were about 26 beds on each side. There was one fellow who had been a postman, or an official in the post office in civilian life. Then there was a soldier who was brought in one day but was still unconscious. During the night-time he started peeing in his bed and the stream was going right over John, right over his bed. At that time, there was another fellow in the bed on the other side of John, who used to have to pee in a bottle. Both his legs were damaged and he walked with a stick. He would never get any better than he was at that time. A shell had blown him into a hole where he was covered in dirt. His legs were too damaged to be helped.

He was a quiet fellow, a typical English butler type, and he behaved that way, even in the hospital. He used to come and talk to John and they used to laugh about the fellow who pissed over the bed. Oh, they would laugh about that, but then the poor fellow hanged himself in the toilet.

As for John, three doctors in Roehampton worked on his leg and altogether they did seven operations. Seven times they cut it open, and I tell you, he suffered. In those days, every day, they put him in a big bath with oil and other ingredients. He would lie in the bath for a specific amount of time while an orderly or nurse held his head up out of the hot mixture. When he got out, the liquid dried and caked. That sort of treatment he was told was to set his joints. It was painful, but he got used to pain after awhile. Strange as it may appear, at first when he got hurt, it hurt so much, but he began to realize it was just a sore leg. You'd think he was maybe dying when he was actually lucky; there were lots of poor fellows worse off than him.

*
**

In May of 1918, a mighty offensive by the Allies had brought an end to "The Great War," as they were now calling it. A very fragile time followed for many people, and for all of the nations involved, the recovery. For Britain it was a quiet time. All of the lost men were noticeably missing in the colleges and clubs and the workforce. Indeed, that "lost generation" was obvious everywhere you looked.

At times John felt guilt-ridden that he had survived while so many others had not. The harshness of war had changed him in so many ways. He was no longer a scrawny teenager but had transformed into a tough young man, both in body and in mind. Even his voice had grown deeper, acquiring a new gentleness and understanding.

John now felt that he had a duty to rationalize his existence after surviving the war, and so after his discharge from Queen Mary's Hospital, he arrived back at Darlington to finish his engineering course,

Unknown to him at the time, a 25-year-old, black-haired rebel known as Adolf Hitler had also been fighting in those same bleeding fields of France. Hitler, who was from Austria, had volunteered for military service in a Bavarian regiment. He was a runner between company headquarters and the guns or trenches, and was wounded twice during this time.

Adolf Hitler also had a mission after the war ended, but it was not a peaceful one. While almost everyone was slackening off, just trying to bring back some normal in their lives, Hitler was becoming obsessed with his plan for Germany's "Thousand Year Reign."

After Germany's surrender in 1918, he was convinced that they had never truly been beaten, but stabbed in the back by socialists and Jews in their own government. It was then he decided to become a politician.

⁎

Back in Darlington, Betty was on cloud nine when John appeared at her door one afternoon, with his cane in one hand and a bouquet of flowers in the other. After a long glance towards each other, he took his hat off and one of his little curls popped up revealing the new scar on his forehead, she threw her arms around him and squeezed with all her might. John couldn't believe his eyes. Betty had also transformed from a bubbly school girl to a stunningly graceful woman. John had lost his balance by now, but she was holding him up and wasn't letting go. They quickly took up where they had left off, both still enjoying the theatres, clubs and shows, but mostly just being together.

⁎

What followed for England in the 1920s was a time of toil and reconciliation, yet there was a distinct contentment that was very fragile. John still had an insatiable appetite for news from all over the world, and he became more aware of the politics going on around him. The nation was focused on getting back to life as they had once known it. The general public wanted nothing to do with the "war machine," and military budgets were slashed. Many officials were warning of a future war, but their words fell on mostly deaf ears.

A free and easy feeling swept through the people now, and the age of romance and courtship was at a peak. Betty and John went away on many weekend getaways and got considerably closer during these quiet post-war years.

In the evenings, John took on a job as a part-time teacher of bookkeeping and shorthand and worked as a typewriter mechanic on occasion. He also became a reporter and photographer for the two newspapers in Darlington, the Stockton Times and the Northern Echo. The first photos John ever took were at the Scottish Exhibition, which was around 1922. His first camera was German, and it had delayed action. He went up to Scotland with a crew of four or five people who at the time were all working for the newspaper, the Northern Echo, and it was only one of many trips he would take with the same group.

John acquired his first receiving set for his home, on which he would listen to the BBC news regularly. On occasion they were talking of the German revival and how the Germans were ahead of Britain in their science and military technology. This brought on talk of war and the need to re-arm, mostly from Churchill, and no one else seemed to be listening, but John was. Having survived the horrors of the first war, it became particularly important for those wounded soldiers to prepare to defend themselves early on against any attack. It had become instinctive; ex-soldiers were now paying much closer attention to politics, even if no one else was.

John was successful in obtaining a Journeyman's Certificate or a Membership of the Associated Society of Engineers (A.S.E.), considered quite an achievement at that time. The A.S.E. was later known as the Associated Engineering Workers, A.E.W.

They had a fairly big graduation class, 45 or 50 of them. That gave him a journeyman's privilege to do practically any job in engineering. However, he was still teaching office skills and reading at Bale's Commercial College.

Eventually, John secured a post as supervisor with the British Thomson Houston Engineering Firm at Rugby, Warwickshire. It had taken him some time to adjust to his new body after the war. His right knee was fused solid and he never bent it again. Still, he got around fairly well. He used to jokingly say that he had a wooden leg, and who really knew? John sombrely realized there were many things he would never do again, such as swimming and driving, and never again would he run. Sometimes in the summertime John would go to the golf course and talk to the pro there, Artie Steel.

One day Artie said, "You sure like to play golf," and he gave John a couple of sticks to play with. He also mentioned, "John, you have a natural swing," and that made John feel so much better; at least he could still play golf.

John was keen to learn of Germany's politics. At first the country had collapsed after the war and was in a state of turmoil – economic, social and political. Mobs of communists and revolutionaries roamed the streets. The young unknown, Adolf Hitler, joined the German Workers' Party and quickly became the sole leader, renaming the party The National Socialist German Worker's Party, or N.S.D.A.P. And so the Nazis were born.

Hitler's ruthless words in his hectoring voice had an alluring impact on the German people and he soon became very popular, his name well-known among the German elite. That gave Adolf the confidence, during this time of economic chaos, to attempt his famous "Beer Hall Putsch" in 1923, which was an attempt to seize power in Munich.

It was reported that Hitler had organized a meeting in the Bürgerbräukeller or beer cellar, a commonly used gathering place for his newly formed Nazi Party. Those attending included the Munich police chief, the president of Bavaria, and the general of the current army. It was said later that Hitler then lured these three men into a side room and forced them, at gun point, to sign a document declaring that they had joined him and General Ludendorff in overthrowing the current German government.

Historians later noted that Heinrich Himmler, who in the future would become the chief of Hitler's SS or Defence Corps, was already a supporter and helped to barricade the doors to the Munich beer cellar for him. Two of Hitler's other famous future marshals, Hermann Goering and Joseph Goebbels, were also reputed to be with him during this famous incident.

The officials involved exposed their blackmailers as soon as they could and revoked their signatures. Hitler's coup d'état had failed, but it wasn't long before the Nazis held a march in the streets to rally support again. As they marched towards the city centre, they came upon a line of resistance and shots were fired. Chaos broke out, and sixteen people, mostly youths, were killed. The newspapers reported that Ludendorff continued to march on through the bullets and was arrested.

Everyone else, including Adolf Hitler, quickly ran off. Hitler was later caught, and in 1924 he was imprisoned in Landsberg Fortress for almost a year for high treason.

This was Adolf Hitler's second time in prison, but this time he was treated much better, with comfortable confinement. Even photo opportunities were allowed in the prison's large lunchroom that he shared with his fellow Nazis. The same room it is said, where he dictated his notorious book, Mein Kampf, (My Struggle).

Hitler's autobiography put him at the head of his movement, the Führer, to become leader of the world. It was a guidebook for the Nazis to occupy the world and destroy all other societies in their path. And it was full of hatred for the Jews.

Upon his release, Adolf Hitler found that most of his comrades had scattered and left him isolated. Herr Goering, Himmler, and, Goebbels had moved on. It was discovered that Julius Streicher, who was an elementary teacher and an early recruit from Nuremburg, and who was thought to be one of Hitler's rare intimate friends, had just been charged with child molestation.

Stubborn as he was, Hitler never gave up even though no one was listening to him. He continued with the Nazi party under different names, as the National Socialist Party had been outlawed in most of Germany. He gradually talked his way back into the hearts of his cronies, and in 1925, as the German economy improved, the National Socialist Party and the Communist Party were both legalized. Once more, Hitler became the commander-in-chief of the Nazi Party, and it started to regroup.

**

John put his newspaper down undaunted; it was one of those evenings when he was just relaxing with Betty in the kitchen of her little flat. The year was about 1926. The radio was buzzing with the news that Fritz von Opel had gotten his rocket-powered car up to a speed of almost two hundred kilometers an hour.

"Two hundred," John repeated out loud as he slouched over the table, half daydreaming while he watched Betty reading. Her curly reddish-brown hair was circling her face so perfectly, and her lips were sweetly moving as she read the local newspaper, the Daily Telegraph.

She looked up at him, brushing her hair back, and said, "Here's an advertisement for a German speaking clerk." Betty seemed to know, as soon as the words came from her lips that nothing would ever be the same, that she was probably going to lose him again.

John raised his eyebrows nonchalantly and then he sat up a little straighter, his eyes opened wider. "What else does it say?" he asked curiously.

"Not much else," she said, reading it out loud for him, "Full-time position for a German speaking clerk, and then an address, that's all. Rather a mystery there," she said, "I wonder what it's for?"

Instinctively, Betty tried to change the subject. "Do you want to go out tonight, maybe to the Comet, or a theatre?"

"Sure," John quietly agreed, already deep in thought about this mysterious ad in the paper. The next day he put in an application.

Betty and John were so happy together and becoming quite settled. Life was getting back to normal, not only for them but for many others after the first war, with a new generation of children once again playing in the streets. They both had good jobs; Betty was a teacher now at the college and John was happily working as a supervisor in Rugby. John knew that Betty wanted to get married but even though he loved her, he was young and still wanted so much more out of life. He wanted to travel and see the world, speak all of the languages that he had been learning for so many years in college and high school and even as far back as his early days sitting on the docks in Fremantle, listening to all the travelers' stories. He felt as if he were born to travel the world, and that was why as a child, he had left most of his family behind in Australia. He still felt very alone and needed the love that Betty gave him, but the call to explore was beyond his control.

Almost nine months went by and he had completely forgotten about the application that he'd made for that post. It was a just another Wednesday morning, when John received a telegram to report to St. James, London at once. It was quite a shock.

He was in the middle of teaching two girls to use the Gorton profiler machine, when a man came down from the office and tapped him on the shoulder.

"Here," he said, looking over his glasses and passing a piece of paper to John, "Telegram. You have got to go to London."

"What for?" John said, quite intrigued, "What's this all about?"

"I have no idea, John," he said, shrugging his shoulders, "But they have sent your fare for the train to London, and you are supposed to go pack right away." He left grumbling, and that was it.

John didn't know what he was in for; no one told him anything. He was really curious and wondering what it was all about. Until he reported to the address in London and discovered that it was the headquarters of British Foreign Office.

At St. James, John was asked a few questions in German and then told to report to their Foreign Office doctor. Dr. Lancaster just looked at him and said, "You will do fine; go next door and get your photo taken and report back to St. James." He directed John to the next building.

Here he had his photo taken. John asked the aging photographer, "What is this all about? I still have a job at Rugby?"

The man told him, "Not to worry, that has been taken care of. Just sign this passport and you can be on your way."

He placed all the documents together and told John, "Here is your ticket to Berlin. When you get there, you are to report to the Consul General at the British Consulate on Tiergarten Strasse."

John was almost speechless. "Berlin," he said in disbelief and, looking down, he noticed it was a one-way ticket. He was trying desperately to contain his excitement as a million thoughts exploded in his head.

"Wind up your personal affairs at Rugby," he was instructed by the man.

This was on Wednesday and by Friday he would be working in Berlin. Quick work. They must have been in need of someone in a hurry, John thought. No one had asked his age or where he was born, but he assumed his background must have been checked. He was eager nonetheless, his daring side had not yet been quenched, and adventure still held a special thrill for him. This was to be the start of a new life, a new education.

***

Leaving London, however, for John was like leaving an old friend and once more he was leaving his faithful girl Betty. It wasn't at all like the first time he had left her ten years earlier, when he'd left for the war in France and she had cried and cried, and spent every night trying to talk him out of it. This time she was very quiet and left the choice to him, which was a far scarier feeling for John, who now realized with his painful leg that she had been right the last time and he shouldn't have gone.

He felt a little unhappy about it, and guilty leaving her at this time but with his life before him all he could think of was, I must travel and see more of the world and its people. He was too impressed with his new appointment to think of their friendship and love.

When he boarded the train at Liverpool Station in London, Betty was there to say good-bye and deep inside they both knew that life moves on. There were no more words left for them, just sorrowful gazes of possibilities abandoned. They kissed good-bye, not knowing if they would they ever see each other again, and that was it.

Chapter 10

BERLIN 1926 – A NEW WORLD

From Liverpool Station, John went to Harwich or, as some called it, Parkstone Quay. This is the port of departure for people going to certain parts of Europe. It was the crossing point of the North Sea to get to the Hook of Holland, the gateway to Europe and also the station for the trains to Berlin and further on. The really rough crossing reminded John, with a cold shiver, of an article that he had read in 1907. It was about the wreck of the S.S. Berlin, which was shipwrecked off the Hook of Holland with the loss of many lives.

There was no trouble however and at the border, the inspector did not even open his passport. He just handed it back to John with a smile, and that was that.

While boarding the train in Holland, he saw that a very large crowd had gathered on the station platform and a man with a very thick Irish accent was telling a nasty bad joke. He was so loud that you couldn't help but hear him, and John was listening just like everyone else. Just then, a well-dressed gentleman standing nearby came up to John and said, "Hello there, where are you going to tonight?"

John looked right at him, but, with the long overcoat and wide-brimmed hat, he did not recognize the singer at first. Nevertheless, he replied with a smile, "I'm off to Berlin, and yourself?" Just then, the man lifted his head and John got a better look at him, realizing it was Richard Tauber, a well-known singer in the theatre-land of London.

They had never met before but John instantly recognized him, and having sensed John's recognition, his large expressive mouth flashed a huge smile and he said with a nod and an outstretched hand, "Richard Tauber, it's a pleasure to meet you."

John was a little overcome with star lustre but held out his hand, "John Harrington," he said. "The pleasure is mine."

Richard Tauber had a presence about him that was hard to disguise, even under a large coat. He made a flourish with his arm as if he were on stage and replied "And, yes, I am also on my way to Berlin. Have you been there before?"

John said "No, I haven't," with such enthusiasm at the approaching adventure that nothing else needed to be said.

"Ah, your first time! What brings you to Berlin then?" Richard Tauber asked, looking John right in the eye.

John innocently replied, "I am going to work at the British Embassy, under the consul general there now, a Lord Van Sittart."

"Oh, really," Tauber said with interest, his voice lowering an octave. "A friend of mine is going to be taking over that job soon, Captain Foley."

John shook his head in surprise, "I don't know anything about that."

"Oh, he's a great fellow," Tauber said. "You'll like him."

On board the train, John felt quite honoured to be sitting with this famous Austrian tenor about whom he had only read. John had seen his picture in the paper a few times, but those photos did not capture the handsome and debonair side of this well-spoken man, or so John thought.

They talked about Captain Foley for a while; Tauber knew him fairly well, apparently, and John didn't know until afterwards that Captain Foley and he were very good friends. Of course, John didn't know any better at that point, and he talked about things that he probably shouldn't have.

As they relaxed in the comfortable first class coach, Richard Tauber was very helpful to John in many ways, correcting his speech, and explaining that he might find the version of the German language that he had been taught at school would in many instances differ from the German language spoken.

Richard Tauber looked him square in the eye and said, "Time and experience will now have to be your teacher."

Later in the train's dining car, Richard Tauber was looking more distinguished than ever in his white suit jacket with bold silver buttons, and soon the other passengers were milling around him, smiling and stopping to chat. To John's surprise, Tauber waved him over to join him at his table and the maitre'd quickly shooed the people away, returning with a menu. Without even looking, Tauber ordered prawns and they were huge.

"Perhaps you would like to try fish served the German way," Richard Tauber suggested to John in his amazing and robust stage voice.

John thought it might be something that he ought to know, so he said, "Yes, of course." Imagine his surprise, when the waiter came along pushing a small kind of cart containing a great big bowl of water with fish swimming around in it.

John was horrified and murmured, "What the heck is this for?"

The waiter said, "Choose the fish that you would like," and he gave him tongs to pick one out with. John couldn't believe it, but he did pick one out, and it wasn't easy. Richard Tauber was having quite the chuckle over it. John thought, "Well, that's okay, the worst is over, that will be fine now." He thought they would bring him a nice fish and chip kind of thing, you know. More surprises were to come when the waiter served the fish. It was well cooked, he thought afterwards, very well indeed, complete with the head, tail, fins, and innards still attached. The waiter stripped it open for him and took the insides out, right in front of him. Well, John ate it, and it was very good. Tauber was amazed that he had gone through with it, as he understood the British way of serving fish.

At the frontier at Osnabrück, the inspection of passports and luggage took place. With John's diplomatic pass, the inspector did not even open his passport. He just looked at it and smiled. Richard Tauber disappeared into the unloading area as quickly as he had appeared. John suspected later that his meeting with him might have been arranged, since he was a very good friend of the soon to be Consul General, Captain Foley.

Arriving in Berlin at the Alexanderplatz Bahnhof, or the "Zoo Station" which was what they called it, John was met by one of the staff of the passport division. Thomas was a good-looking young man, dressed formally in his evening suit and impatiently waiting with his top hat in his hand. He rushed towards John and eagerly shook him by the hand. "This way, John, we have a ride waiting for you," he said.

Outside, the Berlin air was crisp and fresh, with the faintest whiff of diesel fuel in the background. John felt right at home. He was even happier when he saw the large black Rolls-Royce with its majestic fenders, silently waiting next to the man whom he was following. John stood there for a second, enjoying the moment and admiring the beautiful vehicle and the immaculate care that went into its sleek glistening finish, until the door was opened for him and he was abruptly shuffled into it. Thomas went to get in the car a little too quickly after John, and there was an awkward moment when John's stiff leg got in the way, so that in the end Thomas sat in the front seat.

He looked over at the driver saying, "Frank, this is John Harrington. Back to the consulate with us then."

Thomas turned halfway around in his seat, "John, this is Frank," he continued his introduction, waving his arms back and forth between the men in an introductory fashion. "He is our consulate driver, and you'll get to know him soon enough," he retorted, crinkling his forehead, "you can be sure of that."

"Hello, Frank nice to meet you," John said with a huge grin on his face, already full of wonderment with the sights and sounds of this famous city, Berlin.

"If you need to go anywhere, you just let me know," Frank responded with a fleeting smile over his shoulder.

He raised his voice as he forcefully hit the gas pedal and began to swerve his way through traffic, "They keep me pretty busy here, but not always." Frank was a tall man, judging by the way his chauffeur's hat, with his neatly trimmed black hair sticking out from under it, was almost touching the roof of the car.

John was quite surprised when Frank, who looked decidedly British, with his long face and generous ears, gently pulled the limousine up to the British Consulate building on Tiergarten Strasse and loudly spoke in a new deeper voice, in perfect German.

"Hier sind wir, das Passkontrollbüro." They had arrived at the Passport Control Office.

John was confused and said, "Is this the British Embassy?" He was thinking it looked rather small for that.

"No, no" Thomas said. "This is the consulate where you will be working. The Embassy is over on Wilhelmstrasse, but we go over there sometimes and you'll see that soon enough, too."

It was late in the day and most of the consulate staff had gone home, except for Miss Avery, whom John soon got to know very well. As they walked through the empty wickets and past the desks, they could see her standing at her usual post, clipboard in hand. Her office was at the very back of the room and was open to the front, giving a complete overview of all the desks and the reception area. The three walls behind her were extensively lined with filing cabinets; a few were placed in front where she could hide from view for the occasional preening.

"Miss Avery, this is John Harrington, our new passport clerk," Thomas remarked, in an obvious hurry to carry on. "Miss Avery runs the show out here at the front," he added.

John stopped in his tracks. Passport clerk, he whispered in his mind, with an outstretched hand towards her. This was news to him.

"It's a pleasure to meet you," he said and they both eyed each other up very nonchalantly, instantly forming equally wrong conclusions.

At first glance, Miss Avery appeared highly organized. Even at the end of a busy day, her thick brown hair was neatly tucked up in an interesting knot, with never a single hair out of place. She was an attractive, broad-shouldered woman, with just a few wrinkles around her unrelenting green eyes, giving away her age. Around five years John's superior, he thought. Miss Avery's lips curled up at the edges, as if she were trying to smile, but had forgotten how.

In due course, she lifted her hand to shake his. "We'll get you settled in tomorrow," she said, as Thomas was urging John onwards.

He took John past a number of doors and into a little office, "You're with us now, John," he said, as he patted him on the shoulder. "Here is your desk and this is where you work."

John was speechless; it was much more than he had expected, "This is really nice," he exclaimed in surprise.

It was just a small office, but it had two crimson leather lounge chairs and a small table in front of a heavy oak desk and chair. John was immediately drawn to the window, where he gazed out with relief at being able to see outside.

"All right now," Thomas said, "let's get your quarters squared away. We have a pension assigned to you."

That first night, John was settled in a room on the second floor of an old hotel and then on the same night they came and moved him down into a cellar room. After one night there, he was out for blood. He demanded decent accommodation, and he was moved back upstairs in a hurry.

On his first morning in Berlin, John stepped out of the hotel, looking very smart and feeling very stylish in his new suit. It was the latest thing, with a double-breasted vest under the single jacket, which was a mesmerizing deep indigo blue, adorned with a beige silk handkerchief in the pocket. It fit his handsome body like a glove, having been recently tailored for him in London. John reached into his pocket for a cigarette as he took a deep breath of the unfamiliar air. The sun had only been up for a few minutes and yet the city was already buzzing with activity.

Before John could even get the cigarette package from his pocket, Frank, who had been waiting for him to come out, pulled up in the consulate car and leaned out.

"Good morning, sleepy head," he said in his rough German, with a playfully receptive look on his face.

John didn't completely understand what Frank had said; he wasn't used to the Berlin dialect yet. "Yes, I slept well," he said quietly in response, while getting in.

Frank let out a deep laugh as he sped away.

"We will have to work on your German, I see," he finally said in perfect English. John's feelings were a little hurt, but he was already listening intently and trying to pick up the Berlin accent. Frank was to become very helpful to him over the following years.

"May I smoke?" John asked.

"Of course," Frank replied, looking over at John long enough to gain eye contact.

Then Frank bulged his chest out. "Did you hear that Herr Himmler is driving a taxi now?" he asked out of the blue.

"No," answered John, somewhat puzzled.

"He has a chicken farm too," Frank said in a way, as if everyone knew that, while looking over his shoulder and hoping for a response.

John nodded his head and opened his eyes a little wider. "Really," he said, with a puff of smoke, embarrassed to admit that he didn't know much about these things. One thing John soon learned was that Frank got around, a lot, and was constantly gathering information. "Not to worry, you'll pick it up fast," he said as John barely got out of the car before he zoomed away.

John stood on the sidewalk in front of the consulate building, finishing his cigarette and admiring the lush lawns just inside the huge wrought iron gate that he was about to enter through. Behind him loomed the beautiful Tiergarten Park with the fog snuggling against the huge majestic trees; it was breathtaking at this early hour. The consulate looked very quiet from the outside and John was sure he was early. He found out differently when he entered the front door, and the office was buzzing with typewriters and people talking, for at least three steps that was, and then everything got quiet. All eyes focussed on him as he entered the restricted area, and his cheeks began to redden a little. There were a few people waiting in line to be served, and the numerous empty desks were now all filled with girls, good-looking girls.

John could hardly believe his eyes as he walked past their desks and back towards his office. A few of the girls whispered, "Hello, hello," and John smiled back at them, shyly nodding, "Hello."

He could see Miss Avery standing at the back with her clipboard, wearing her well-fitted, fawn-coloured ensemble that was to be her trademark. She took a few steps forward with a very stern look on her face, and the girls went back to work right away, click-clacking on their typewriters. John went straight towards his office with just a nod and a quick "Good Morning" to Miss Avery, which, he could see, brought a look of great relief to her face.

He sat in his new office for a little while, not sure what to do with himself and began playing with the telephone which had three buttons on it – white, red and green. He got up and was looking out of the window when a man came to his open door and knocked on it.

"Hello, I'm Jimmy," he said, holding his arm outstretched for a handshake. "You must be John."

"Yes, hello," John replied anxiously, feeling completely at a loss.

Jimmy was wearing a formal suit with a bow tie, which did not match his scruffy head of thick blonde hair. Even in his new suit, John immediately felt underdressed for the occasion, whatever the occasion was.

"I work right next door," Jimmy exclaimed, pointing towards the hall.

John wanted to ask him a million questions but never got the chance before Jimmy continued, "Captain Haysley wants to meet you now. I'll show you the way."

They went upstairs and into another part of the building where it was much quieter. And, as John followed Jimmy, he could see from behind that his back pocket liner was pulled out and the cuff of his left leg was upturned a little. Noticing that seemed to give John his confidence back.

In the waiting room for Captain Haysley's office, was a very small, delicate-looking woman with extremely red hair working at her desk.

"Margo, this is John Harrington, the new guy," Jimmy said. He turned to John and patted him on the shoulder on his way by, "She'll take care of you."

"Hello, John, take a seat then," she snapped, in a way that made John step back a few paces. He nodded back at her, not really wanting to sit down as that might show off his stiff leg. A green light appeared on her telephone, and she yelled loud enough at him to be heard from the other room, "Okay, knock and go in now."

Captain Haysley was sitting at his desk, surrounded by newspapers and files. He leaned forward out of his chair, offering him a strong hand to shake, saying, "Come in John, come in."

He plopped back into his luxurious office chair with a thud. Captain Haysley was quite a stout man, but he held it well. He was neatly dressed in a rather plain uniform, with no flashy medals, which instantly put John at ease.

"Sit down, John," he said, as he leaned towards the ornate wooden box on his table, "Would you like a cigar?"

"No, thank you," John replied politely.

"I thought you smoked, don't you?" asked Captain Haysley a little surprised.

"Yes, on occasion," John answered with a smirk, wondering how he knew that.

"Well, it is pretty early for a cigar, we might as well have a sherry then," the Captain stated with a laugh as he got up from his chair. "It's never too early for that!"

In the corner behind two file cabinets, just barely out of view, was a little wooden barrel that was apparently full of sherry. As the captain poured the sherry, John's eyes scanned the room, and he noticed on the other side of the office that there was a shelf with two radios on it. One was all in pieces, all laid out for viewing, and so of course John instantly walked over, wanting to inspect it.

"You like that, do you?" Captain Haysley asked, as he passed the glass to John. His silvery white hair gleamed, as the sun from the window streamed in on it. "We'll have to get you one of those sets right away," he said. He lifted his glass, "To your arrival."

They both stood quietly, thinking for a moment. Captain Haysley was a reserved man who never said more than he needed to.

"Do you speak German," he asked John, in a butchered attempt at the German language, to which John started prattling away with ease.

"Ich habe seit vielen Jahren Deutsch gesprochen, zum ersten Mal als Junger gelernt..." I have been speaking German for many years now, I first learned it...." John was about to go on, when he noticed Captain Haysley waving his arm in the air.

"That's enough," he said with a smile. "You can be my eyes and ears around here now."

John looked at him, bewildered, "I really am not sure what my actual position is here at the consulate; I heard Jimmy mention I was a passport clerk and this is the first I have heard."

Captain Haysley sat down again and took another sip of his sherry. He looked at John and then looked at the wooden box on his desk, "Oh, what the heck," he said reaching for it, "nothing goes better with sherry than a good smoke. Here take one for later."

"John," he eventually said, letting out a large puff of blue smoke, "your job is hard to describe, and to say you are a passport clerk, yes, is correct. However it also involves many other avenues, private affairs of the consulate."

John's ears perked up, and one of his little brown curls was on the verge of popping up, just like a sneeze about to erupt.

"It will take time," Captain Haysley said, "but eventually I want you to feel free to mingle with the people of Berlin, find out what they are talking about, but most importantly, don't forget that you work for me and no one else."

The captain squirmed in his chair a little, "I want you to report back to me every day. Regardless." He spoke with a great urgency in his voice that was mysterious, and did not allow for questions. "When I am not here, Atkinson will be here; you'll meet him later."

Captain Haysley took his last sip, and his intense, slightly bloodshot eyes were focused directly on John when he said, "I also may have you run a few special errands from time to time."

He leaned back in his chair and with one eyebrow raised, he reached for his newspaper saying, "But for now, Miss Avery will assist you with getting set up at your post."

Miss Avery snapped him up right away as he strolled into her area, "You're here; let's introduce you to everyone first," she said to him, in her matter-of-fact voice.

"Line up, girls," she bellowed like a drill sergeant, which they did in a hurry. She was the chief of the girls there and took her job very seriously. Miss Avery turned out to be a watchful mother hen to all of them, as John instantly noticed when a clumsy girl caught her knee on the desk and Miss Avery was very solicitous.

She loudly introduced each girl, going down the row so fast that no one could possibly remember. John smiled and nodded, "Hello, hello," he said.

Miss Avery stood back, "There you go, John. These are my girls and if you ever need to talk to them, you can go through me," she bluntly stated as she signalled the girls back to their positions.

One last "Hello" was all that John could say, before Miss Avery was starting to show him around the front office, now full of distracted girls.

She was explaining to him, "You'll be doing this and you'll be doing that," but John wasn't completely paying attention, as the girls were teasing him behind her back, and they all looked so darned pretty. They began whispering names for him in German that he didn't understand and were having a really good laugh over it. John smiled at them with exuberance, even though he felt crushed at his own naiveté. Miss Avery was annoyed with all of them and she literally put her foot down with a bang.

Miss Avery kept walking and explaining the system. "I have to make sure the girls get all their cards in every night."

As it happened, when someone came into the office for a passport or a visa, one of the girls would give them a card and they would fill in their name and address and all the requested details. Then, they would go to another girl, who would ask them a few questions about their home life, their job, and things like that. Then that girl or Miss Avery herself would pass the card on to John or one of the other clerks, and he was to go through their records.

On that very first day, he was introduced to the "Black Book" – the referencing and updating of which became one of John's primary duties when he first arrived at the British Consulate in Berlin. The Black Book was used to keep all the records and information regarding people who they knew had Nazi sympathies or were well-known officials of the German government. There were also known secret agents and other sources of information, trying to get visas and passports. Denying these people was something that was strictly enforced, for obvious reasons. People who were pro-Nazi did not get a visa. They were all named "Katz," and they had five or six hundred odd cards under that name.

If the card was doubtful or if he wasn't satisfied, John had to investigate by finding somebody to go and talk to them, and personally request more information. The bottom line was, if he had the card, all he had to do was sign it, but when all was said and done, the chief or his personal secretary was still the only one who could give the final say. John did the filing and interviewing and then the recommending.

They had a room filled with nothing but cards from the previous years. No one had ever kept any proper record of them all. Miss Avery stood with John in the middle of this little room crammed full of boxes and file cabinets of various sizes. One wall was entirely made up of small, long drawers designed to hold these particular cards, and they were stuffed full and overflowing.

"This has to be sorted out," she said with a sigh. "It has just gotten out of control."

John eyes widened with interest as he began to tackle that first job, sorting through all the cards. Arranging them by name and then chronologically, he found out there were huge gaps in the information and that there was still a lot that was needed to be known about many of the people. As the organizing job drew to an end, he thought of the many interviews he could hold and interesting people he could meet.

Many of the individual cards were already marked as suspect or possible German agents, and all of them were entered in the official Black Book, the ongoing ledger that was constantly being updated. This took awhile, but he did get through them eventually, and he removed everything else that he didn't want. That's what he was strictly told to do, and so all of those detailed records went to the paper destroyer.

*
**

Miss Avery knocked on his office door, and John sat up in a hurry, clearing his throat and tidying his hair, but that one stubborn curl popped out anyway.

"John," she said with a pause and then entering, "I wanted to make sure you remembered we are meeting Captain Foley upstairs tonight."

"Yes, yes I do," replied John, relaxing a little. "I am looking forward to it," he added with a crooked smile.

Miss Avery shuffled around the room a little bit and then stopped with her hands on her hips. "I need you around here, John," she just blurted out. "You're the best clerk I have, and I hope it remains that way."

John just raised his eyebrows and tilted his head, feeling humbled, and didn't know what to say; he tried a few times but nothing came out. Finally, Miss Avery puckered her lips, "Okay then," she said, and gave a big nod before she left the room. John wasn't sure if that was a compliment or an insult, a favour or a command, and so he decided to just leave it be.

Upstairs in the consulate was a large banquet room that was used for entertaining on various occasions. John had never been invited up to this hall before, but today it was different; they were meeting Captain Frank Foley, who was to be the new Consul General in Berlin.

Stepping into the large banquet room, he suddenly felt much smaller in stature and yet wealthier in status. The richness of the décor was captivating, and the fantastic gold frames on the large pictures hanging high on the walls demanded his immediate attention. The long plush burgundy curtains led his eyes down to the mingling people, everyone dressed to the nines in their very best attire.

Among the guests John spotted Jimmy and some of the other clerks eating the hors-d'oeuvres off to the side and so he joined them while they were deep in discussion.

"Of course, the top man before Captain Foley was a Lord Robert Vansittart," one of the older men was explaining to a new clerk. "He was the consulate general," he continued, lifting his shoulders higher and swaggering a little.

"What a milksop," he added quietly.

"Hello, John, you met him, Lord Vansittart, didn't you?" he asked.

"Once when I first joined up," John replied as he leaned over to pick up a cracker.

"Well?" Jimmy urged a response from John.

"He did seem to be more interested in public ceremony and in being a popular figure, than he did in being consulate general," John replied with a pause. "At least that's what I thought."

"All pomp and ceremony," John smiled at them, "but he was quite a nice fellow though."

Another clerk interjected, "The girls used to call him pumpkin or something; it was a funny name because he was a big fat fellow." There was a little chuckle, and the men turned towards the buffet table in unison and continued to eat a little more.

The older clerk would not let it go and carried on, "In the end though, Vansittart was not very efficient in the office and didn't run the place well, and things happened."

"That's when Captain Foley was thrust in," another clerk commented, stuffing a little sandwich into his mouth.

Just then, Captain Foley and his wife entered the room, and the clerks quickly lined up, looking wonderful in their finery. As Captain Foley progressed down the line, he shook everyone's hand and already knew every man by name.

"Hello, John," he said quietly in English. "It's good to meet you," he continued in a rather rough German accent, which caught the ear and the eye of the other clerks nearby.

Captain Foley immediately reminded John a little of himself – or the person who he strived to be – with his unusual accent that no one could really place and the look in his unflinching eye that said he was a man capable of carrying the weight of the world on his shoulders, without any doubt.

"It's very nice to meet you," John responded with the greatest respect. Even though he knew very little of his new leader, the uniform and Captain Foley's expression alone made him feel that he certainly deserved the respect he was held in. He could see instantly that Captain Foley was only about ten years older than himself and that he had a truly unique and wonderful smile. The corners of his mouth would squarely turn down, as if in a frown, but you could still see the sweetest smile coming right through the middle, full of mischief. An amazing and mysterious man as it turned out, a man with an interesting history and an even more spectacular future that was soon to be revealed.

As they socialized, John could see Miss Avery talking to Captain Foley, and so he joined them. "Our clerks here are some of the best going," she said, looking around. "They have been specially trained and are highly qualified."

Her voice raised slightly, "It is starting to get busier though, and I think we might need more staff soon," she stated firmly.

"Indeed," Captain Foley commented. "We will be getting a lot more clerks for you, Miss Avery, as many as we can."

Miss Avery was happily surprised. "Oh," she said, a little flustered and slowly turned to John. "This is John Harrington — you have met, yes? He is one of my best clerks." The two men both nodded at each other in reply.

Captain Foley cleared his throat, "You are no longer just a clerk now, John; you are an agent, I could use you in the field with that wonderful German accent; it's so valuable."

John was ecstatic but was trying hard not to show it; he now had an official excuse to explore more and mingle with all the people of Berlin. Miss Avery was not very happy about that, but how could she really complain with the news that there were many others coming to join her team.

A small crowd had gathered, but for some reason Captain Foley looked directly at John with an expression that resembled a very stern, fatherly look, before he stated point blank, "Don't forget now, No Sex." Captain Foley shook his head, "You can do a lot of good here, John. All of you can," he said looking around, then raising his voice a little. "Just be careful though; it can be very dangerous."

The room became oddly quiet in an uncomfortable way; it was apparent now to John their very strict rules about having relationships with German women were to be taken seriously.

Just then, John noticed a reflection in the men's widening eyes and was overtaken by an enchanting smell that suited the fashionable lady he was surprised to see suddenly standing beside him. He had never met her before but was instantly enthralled at the way she was stealing all of the men's eyes.

She started to explain to John, "The Germans don't like us to mix company." John shyly turned towards her, face to face, and she said, "You are tall and good looking." She pretended to brush the wisps of hair away from his face, "That will be difficult for you."

John could feel the heat coming from his red cheeks. "That will be a breeze," he coolly exclaimed, and everyone burst out laughing.

The "no sex" rule had been explained to all new staff members as they arrived in Berlin. It was a criminal offence for a member of the embassy or consulate staff to have sex with a German National. To have sex with a Jewish person, one would be immediately returned to England and maybe sent to prison for a period of time. They even had to sign a paper to that effect, stating no fraternization. It was considered a very serious offence to break this rule, for many reasons, mostly security. It was considered a breach of diplomacy.

Chapter 11
BERLIN – THE ROARING TWENTIES

Berlin in the twenties was the most absolutely fabulous place to be, and John could not believe that he was really there. It was the brim of cosmopolitan society in Europe, with people from all over the world gathering there to compare notes on fashion and culture. Entirely new cultural identities were burgeoning more quickly than one could imagine. The city had become rich in talent from every walk of life and in every language. The modern age was at its leading edge here in Berlin, right now. Airplanes, cameras, telephones, typewriters — the list was endless, and it was all changing so fast it seemed to be going faster than its footstep in time could even be recorded. Decadence came right along with it and the newest and the most outrageous ideas and actions were accepted for the first time ever. There were hundreds of places to get a drink and have fun — pubs, nightclubs, theatres, opera houses.

There were dozens of night clubs alone — Russian, American, Irish clubs, jazz and blues clubs, homosexual and lesbian clubs, and even the more extreme, private erotic clubs.

The most accomplished of architects were there, and artists and sculptors were all drawn in by the electricity of the time. Berlin had always been an extraordinary city with a long and interesting history, visible in the highly ornate buildings and grand statues throughout the great city. An historical city had become the centre of all that was avant-garde.

Berlin was the envy of the modern world. Sought-after geniuses in engineering and every sort of technology resided in this flourishing city. Everything was the newest – the cars, the cable cars, even the household appliances. Berliners had also become leaders in literature and science, with so many brilliant minds living there – Albert Einstein in physics, Max Planck in mathematics and Werner Von Braun in aerospace, just to name a few.

John embraced the Berlin nightlife at every chance he got. He loved it all, especially the theatres and the nightclubs. He would report back to Captain Haysley of his adventures and the people that he met, and the captain was always grateful to know.

They were keeping an extra close eye on German politics at the time, because after the First World War the government in Germany was shattered, and there was no one firmly in charge. The 79-year-old Paul Von Hindenburg was an aging, out-of-touch president, and the two main political parties, (the Socialist Party or SPD and the Communist Party or KPD) were profoundly divided.

Most Germans, however, really had no patience for politics at this time and especially the Berliners, but Adolf Hitler, the small, dark-haired leader of the National Socialist Party with his speeches and newspaper stories was not to be ignored.

Hitler was living the high life himself at this time, entertaining top officials and building financial bonds. He seemed to be enjoying himself, although at heart he was a loner and teetotaller. Meanwhile his supporters were doing the dirty work for him, clearing out the opposition one by one, at first hidden from view in dark back alleys but leading up to assassinations on the street.

Every chance he got, John was out and about walking around, a habit that he had developed at a young age when going "walkabout" with his aborigine friends in Fremantle. On one particularly delightful lunchtime walk, he discovered an apartment building that had a For Rent sign in the window. It was an ornate stone building with a huge wooden doorway that towered over him. It led into a block of four buildings, a quadrangle with two towers in front and two at the back called the garden house.

John had to check at the consulate office first as they had told him they were going to find him somewhere else to live right away, but he was tired of waiting and thought he should look into it himself. He was lucky to run across this little suite at 33 Kluckstrasse; it was very cozy and secure.

The block had only one entrance. Here the caretaker had his quarters, from which he could see everyone who entered or left the building. Each owner of a suite was given a double-ended key, which you inserted, turned and pushed through to the other side of the door, where it was removed once you were inside. Thus, only the one person with a key could enter or leave, taking the key with him or her. It was quite a common practice in Berlin where security was concerned.

John acquired a suite on the second floor of the front south tower, facing a small park. Mr. and Mrs. Hammersmitz were the caretakers and occupied the suite below him. They were a very welcoming older couple, charming in their own right. Anna was always so eager to please. Whenever John would come in she would say, "John, would you like to stop for a coffee?" There was always a luscious smell of something cooking or baking in the background, and John quite often joined them for a coffee and chat. Anna would get excited when he did and rush around to get him some cake or biscuits. She loved to talk and, although she was only in her forties, she looked like an established grandma. Her long grey hair was carefully tied up in two braids neatly arranged on the back of her head. She was a little overweight and small of stature, yet full of exuberance. "How was your job today?" she would say in broken English.

The sound of her voice would always make John beam inside, "It was a very good day, Anna," he would usually reply in German, to make her more comfortable.

Even though Anna liked to learn new English words and John was always eager to teach her, he wouldn't always correct her, because he enjoyed her broken English-German mix; it made him feel more at home.

Anna's husband Horst was a brawny man with steel-blue eyes. He had a pale complexion and was heavily wrinkled for his age. His hair, mostly grey by now, was perfectly straight and would stick out in all directions with just a touch or even a near touch. Horst never spoke much, but was always happy to see John. He would read the newspaper more than once each night, and their radio was always turned on, another of Horst's favourite pastimes.

They were announcing another street fight in the Charlottenburg district when Horst looked up from his paper and over his glasses, "What is this city coming to?" he said in his hoarse voice.

"We are very lucky to have good jobs; I hope they are paying you well over there at the consulate," he remarked as his eyes opened wider to look at John, forcing his bushy eyebrows up onto his forehead.

⁎⁎

As it turns out, John's first confrontation with the consulate staff was over money. Miss Avery was the pay clerk, which kept her very busy in addition to her other chores. This day Miss Avery, prim and proper as ever, said to John, "I'm going to give you your pay packet, and it will be in German currency." Marks.

So he thought about it for a little while, and then he thought, the heck you are, so he went upstairs to the paymaster directly and told him, "I want my pay in English Sterling." Pounds.

The paymaster replied, "No, this is a new policy — you are in Germany now."

John pointed out that he had been appointed in England, and he was working for the English government; therefore, he should be paid in sterling, and, he was duly paid in sterling. This did not please Miss Avery at all. She didn't like changes in her plans, whereas John thrived on it. He got the feeling that she never liked him very much after that, but still they managed to get along. John thought that as a newcomer she had assumed he would not know the difference in the value of the mark and the pound sterling. The official rate at this time was four marks to the pound. However, under certain conditions, on the Black Market, one could obtain German marks at the rate of 12 or more for a pound sterling. In later years, this went up considerably.

⁎⁎

Miss Avery was from a much higher class than John, an important distinction at the time; in fact, most of the girls there had been to Cambridge. She had had a distinguished career with the Foreign Office, and it showed by the way she always held her head high when she walked and by the way she moved very slowly and purposefully. Most of her staff had been specifically trained for their jobs, but John had had no training at all. She wasn't completely sure where he would fit in, but these were peculiar times in Germany. She knew his language skills would be useful and sure enough, it wasn't long before John was telling her stories of the outside world on a daily basis.

Some of the British staff from the consulate went to the different nightclubs and they enjoyed showing him around in the beginning. Quite often, John would go to his local pub there, which was French and called Esteman's. John used to call it a pub as did the other Brits, but actually they were Bierstube or beer houses. There was not much else for them to do in the evenings and so he went out a lot to his local Bierstube. Quite often they would sit for hours telling their war stories and solving the problems of the world. One night the Destiny Waltz played on the radio while the men were telling war stories and it reminded John of the time when he woke up after his surgery in WWI and that song was playing in the background; when he realized he was still alive and had kept his leg. His emotions flared up again and John had to leave the pub. Later that night he had horrible nightmares with cold sweats and ghastly visions of unimaginable scenes. He moved around a lot more after that trying different clubs and bars, to avoid the war stories.

At the north end of Berlin, John discovered a very fine nine-hole golf course. As golf was his special sport, he went there whenever he could. It was quite near to the North German Radio Station, Nord Deutscher Lloyd, which was quite a landmark and he was to find it quite useful in the days to come.

The golf course was also located on the edge of a town called Siemens. There was a big factory there, which had been built in 1918 and was manufacturing electrical parts and equipment. That factory was later moved to a small town about 500 kilometres south in Bavaria. Siemens, or Siemens-Stark, as it was known, was a completely self-contained town on the outskirts of Berlin. It had its own churches, schools, stores, everything, including an internal railway system and a broadcast station. It was a complete town for all the people who made this equipment.

It was here at this golf course that John made many friends over the years and had the pleasure of meeting many important and interesting people. One such person was Fräulein Gerta Hoffman. It was a warm and sunny afternoon as John was sitting on the balcony of Berlin's oldest golf and country club with his friend Otto, whom he had met at the club weeks before.

"Such a noble old building isn't it, this clubhouse?" John said as he put his beer down and reached for his pipe. He was thinking that it must have been very old with its rock walls, two feet thick and furniture that seemed to be from the stone age, even the roads leading up to it were all the size of horse trails.

"Yes, it is wonderful," replied Otto, when a group of young golfers sitting nearby all let out a huge laugh at the same time. They were having a jolly good time telling stories and laughing, while enjoying their refreshments in the afternoon's sunshine.

The cocktails were flowing and everyone enjoyed drinking them as they watched the last of the golfers return from their games, and were they a sight to see! Some happy, some sad, all wearing pants with puffy short legs and oversized golf caps, some with large pom-poms on top.

"How silly they look," John whispered to Otto, even though he was wearing a special golf suit himself, with matching checkered socks. But John's was tailor-made, which made him appear considerably more distinguished, at least he thought so.

Neither John nor his friend had anywhere to be, and so they ordered another drink and a meal. Soon most of the patrons had left, leaving just two ladies at the table next to them, whom Otto soon convinced to come over and join them.

After a brief introduction, John could not seem to keep his eyes off Miss Hoffman. It was as if the moment their eyes met, destiny took over, and their actions were beyond control. She looked back at him with her stunning hazel eyes, enticing in their intensity. Her pale complexion was perfection itself, and it made him want to reach out and touch her, over and over again.

He could see that Gerta was taller than most girls, taller than most men for that matter, and with a good solid build, yet she was so very agile and feminine that it made her appear smaller. In reality, she did physically look down on many men when conversing and that had made her male relationships tricky, but not with John, who was comfortably taller than her.

Gerta was not a real beauty in the traditional sense, but so unique, so mysterious – the most exotic person he had ever met before.

"Fräulein Hoffman, I love your golf dress," John commented. "I noticed it immediately when you arrived, and I must admit it is the prettiest one I have ever seen."

"Gerta, please," she said to John, as she jumped to her feet. "Just call me Gerta," she repeated as she turned around on the spot. "Do you really like it? I designed it myself and then had my seamstress make it for me," she expressed with pride, while sliding her sunglasses down off the top of her head to pose. Then she lifted her sunglasses back up again to see everyone's expression clearer in the fading light.

"Extraordinary," John replied, as his eyes were slowly scanning her body from top to bottom, his heart beating a little faster than normal. The dress was very nice, deep green and white velvet in a typical "shirtmaker" style of golf dress, met at the waist with a band of sorts, to give the appearance of a sporty two piece. John's eyes followed down the pleated skirt to her knees, and then her legs — ooh, they were exceptionally nice all the way down to her short little white socks. When he looked back up to her delicate leather gloved hands perched on her sunglasses and the deep red lipstick on her full lips, it felt like love at first sight and he knew he was in trouble. He tried to hide it at first, but instead the magnetism grew as did their friendship.

That evening they went for a romantic walk on the greens and were watching the stars twinkling in the moonlight, when suddenly Gerta realized that John had a limp. Her compassionate nature swung into high gear and she instantly felt sorry for him and wanted to wrap him in her arms, but instead she asked him, "Do you want to come home with me, back to my flat for a coffee?"

John was so torn; he knew he shouldn't, but he desperately wanted to anyway. In one ear he could hear Gerta, "Come on, Johnny, come with me home, please?"

But in the other he could hear the words coming out of Consul General Captain Foley's mouth, "No Sex!"

Her flat was on the top floor of a brand new deluxe apartment building that had been designed by the "well-known and often talked about" architect, Albert Speer. While John balanced his little coffee cup on his knee and leaned back in the big lounge chair, he realized that hours and hours of talking had just slipped by in a flash. He remarked on her lovely abode and how fortunate she was to have such a nice place, when Gerta casually replied, "He is a friend of my father's."

"Who is?" John asked, the little cup starting to jiggle in its saucer as he sat up, "Speer?"

"Oh, yes," Gerta said. "My father has known him for some time. My father is Heinrich Hoffman, you may have heard of him." A troubled look crossed her face and then she seemed to get mad at life itself, saying "Heil Hitler" with a little sarcastic move of disgust, then flung her arm straight up in the air while stomping her foot down, imitating the Nazi salute.

John was now totally perplexed; he had many other things on his mind a few moments ago, which were now entirely shattered. "Your father is Heinrich Hoffman?" he asked almost in a daze.

"Yes, and lately he has become quite well known as Adolf Hitler's personal photographer," Gerta told him.

John could have been knocked over with a feather, "Is this true?" He finally managed to get the words out of his mouth.

He could see the look of utter dismay on Gerta's face, so he slipped his arm around her shoulder and they sat down together on the sofa.

"Yes," Gerta said, while shaking her head. "I don't tell anyone that usually; I don't know why I told you, but I try to stay out of my father's affairs. I really don't like politics at all. Except for the suffragettes, of course, but no one really cares about that now. They think it's just a big joke, and so does my father, truth be told." Her sad eyes looked up at John. Gerta took a breath, exasperated, "Besides, there is nothing my father can do; he must always do as he is ordered."

"Oh my god," John said, standing up again, not really sure what to do or even whether to stay or go. His emotions were wild with intrigue and happiness and sadness, but fear took over.

"Where are they now?" John asked, as if feeling their physical presence in the room.

"Oh, they are down in Munich, right now," she said with a sad laugh, wrapping her arms around her body. "You see, this is why I don't talk about it very much."

John could feel her loneliness and hear a faint desperation in her voice. He leaned over with both arms to pull her up off the chair, as a few tears rolled down her cheek.

"That must be so difficult for you." He held her in his arms and didn't want to let go, and she didn't want him too either.

"Thank you so much for everything, Gerta, but I really should leave now," John said apologetically, "I have to work tomorrow."

Gerta could read the fear in John's movements, "Of course," she reluctantly said.

"Will I see you next Saturday?" She asked passionately as their hands touched at the door.

John could not help liking her, she was so very friendly and they got along so well. Gerta was such an incredibly fine person as an individual, and he knew she was a good golf player, which meant a great deal of fun for him. He was very attracted to her.

John leaned over and gave her a long gentle kiss. "Yes, my darling Gerta, I would love to see you next Saturday. Shall we tee off at two?"

John was so guarded, he could hardly wait to give the news to Captain Haysley, or, did he even want to say anything at all? Oh, why was life so confusing, so trying. This all seemed so trivial when he went back to work and remembered the severity of the situation.

Of course, John immediately reported to Captain Haysley about his chance meeting with Fräulein Hoffman and that her father was Hitler's photographer. "We are planning to golf together next Saturday," John said with a sheepish smile, "If that is okay?"

Haysley looked over his glasses, "This could be a tricky one, John. Are there any guards around her or any sign of authority, even in disguise."

"Well, there wasn't that night," John said bluntly, and seeing Captain Haysley's worried expression, he added, "Oh nothing happened, we just talked."

"Well, what do the other golfers think of her?" Haysley asked out of curiosity.

"I don't think they know who she is," John said. "None of them seem to have put the connection together, and she is purposely trying to stay incognito, she 'wants a new life' was how she put it."

"Okay, see her again, but be careful man, for god's sake." Captain Haysley was looking older suddenly, from concern that was obviously sincere. "We'll take this one day at a time."

The week would not go by fast enough for John, who was completely infatuated with Miss Gerta Hoffman. He kept thinking of when they had met and the silent electricity that formed between them, so powerful that it actually seemed to lift her skirt once.

✳
✳✳

It was about this time that John also had the pleasure of meeting and knowing Fräulein Eva Braun. She was at this time employed as a postal clerk, literally selling stamps in a post office quite near the consulate building. John had occasion to visit this office almost every day during the week, as one of his duties was to post the various passports that had been granted that day.

"Good afternoon, John. How are you today," Eva would say, with a hurried smile and generally a no-nonsense look on her face, while stamping the large envelopes and piling them off to the side.

John, in his usual way, never rushed around women. Preferring to slow down and absorb all of their wonders, the fragrances, their soft soprano voices, their shining hair, their fashionable outfits ... John loved women.

"Today is a wonderful day," he said with a huge unrelenting smile, "for wonderful people like you and me." He couldn't help himself from staring at her lovely auburn hair and her figure, which was very good indeed.

She could feel the energy of his eyes on her and joyfully spoke up. "Maybe we should go on a date sometime. What do you think?"

"Wouldn't that be lovely?" John replied, and he really meant it. "But my boss would not be happy," he added, shaking his head.

"Neither would mine," Eva laughed. "No dice, but it would be fun," she said as she handed him the receipt. "I collect foreign stamps, you know," she added, touching his hand when he reached for the paper. "If you ever have any, don't throw them out please; save them for me, would you mind?"

"No, not all," John said. "I will try to bring some in for you every day when I come in."

John always thought that Eva Braun was "quite the girl," never imagining for a moment where her amazing yet tragic life was about to lead.

✷✷

The following Saturday, Gerta waved John over to the crowded table of young golfers all yammering away about their games. "Everyone, this is John" she said with a smile. "He's a friend of mine."

Everyone stopped talking for a second and then all at once, or so it seemed, they all said "Hallo" back to John, and two of the men reached out their arms to shake his hand. "Guten Tag, John."

One of the men stated, "I have seen you here before. Are you a member?"

"Yes," John beamed. Golf was his favourite pastime and it showed.

They sat down, as Gerta commented, "John used to play golf in Australia when he was a little boy, didn't you, John."

"We did," he replied as he lit a cigarette. "But golf was not quite the same as it is played today. We just had curved wooden sticks for clubs and balls made of 'Gutta Percha' — that was really raw rubber, and they were not even round." John laughed, as he exhaled a large puff of smoke, and everyone listening laughed along too.

"As little boys were told to 'Play golf, to keep our heads to the ground' and to swim, to keep our heads above water." Everyone laughed again and he was off to a good start.

Gerta and John played a lot of golf together after that and became very close. They kept their relationship a secret for both of their sakes, except as golfing partners where they just had a lot of fun.

✷✷

Siemens Town had built a number of small factories all around the golf course where they were playing, and thus John could keep an eye on what kind of installations they were building. Factories were his specialty, and he realized they could possibly be producing weapons.

Gerta was free with the information on where Hitler and her father were at the time, and even though John would not seem to notice, he always did. This became a good excuse for him to stay with her, only as far as excuses were needed when it came to reporting back to Captain Haysley.

After all, John wasn't exactly an old fella yet and he was enjoying himself, and she was a nice girl. She'd accompany him to the golf club and after playing a round of golf, they would always sit under the same tree. They would talk and she used to cuddle up to him, and John would have to say, "Now look, that's enough Gertie, not here." But she was difficult to resist.

Chapter 12

LISTENING IN –
TELEPHONE LINES

John's official position in 1928 was still listed as passport clerk, but it entailed a lot more than that. His assignments became more varied as his skills in the language and understanding of the people in Berlin increased. At the consulate they kept him busy every day, at first with smaller errands and odd jobs. There was never a dull moment.

One day, as John approached Margo, the red-headed grenade outside of Captain Haysley's office, she quietly said, "Go on in."

John suddenly felt worried. "Is everything okay, Margo?" he asked.

She shook her head no, and then it sank lower. "Not really," she answered, motioning him into the office. "You'll see."

John knocked on the partly opened door, and Captain Haysley bellowed, "Get in here, Harrington."

As he entered he was surprised to see Jimmy and one of the other new clerks already in there. "And close the door, behind you," Haysley continued with a snap in his voice.

"Can you believe this Hitler fellow," he yelled.

"Who does he think he is!" Captain Haysley was shaking the morning paper in the air. "Have you read this, John?"

"Yes, I have," replied John, nodding his head in total agreement. Looking over he could see that Jimmy was starting to look a little worn down and was becoming sleepy sitting in the comfy lounge chair drenched in the sunbeam, thus leaving the new guy to take the hurricane.

Captain Haysley yelled louder, "That is the third judge this month who has been murdered in the streets; this is out of hand now." He paused and his voice became solemn. "Churchill is right; we should be re-arming." Then, under his breath, but still loud enough to be heard, he said, "That little browbeater Hitler is merciless. He's behind all this, I just know it; he's making his own laws."

John sat down and so did Captain Haysley, but then he was on his feet again. "He's been in jail twice you know. How can they trust someone like that? Do they believe everything they read?"

It seemed he just had to get that off his chest. John tried to calm him down by saying, "That's right, Churchill has been warning us of this fellow for some time now and I think he's right, we do need to keep a close eye on him."

"That's for damn sure," Haysley countered, looking a bit calmer for a moment. Both he and John had survived the horrors of the first war; they had that in common.

Jimmy sat up now. "Well, they certainly are ahead of us in their science and military technology," he pointed out.

Both Haysley and John glared at him in silence and Jimmy sat up straighter, as if he'd been slapped in the face. All four men were quiet for a little as the severity of the situation was starting to become obvious. It was time for action.

"I have these dossiers on Adolf Hitler here; have a look," Captain Haysley said, pushing the folders forward on his desk.

At this time, the Nazi movement was rapidly growing. In the front of the file was a picture of their outspoken and powerful leader Adolf Hitler, who was now combing his hair off to one side and was constantly shaving his little black moustache in the square fashion that was to be his trademark. (Probably to hide his embarrassingly pointed nose, John thought as he stared at the picture).

Not many realized just how active Adolf Hitler had been while traveling around Germany the past year. With his arm straight up in the air stiff as a board and with determination streaming from every fingertip, he was yelling hypnotically, "Sieg Heil," or Hail Victory.

His goal was to join the large numbers of small reactionary groups all across the country together to become his Stormtroopers, the Sturmabteilung, a paramilitary group. These SA soldiers were the ones who were all given brown uniforms left over from an African campaign in World War I, and in their mass numbers they had become known as the Brownshirts.

The SA were starting to be seen in large groups, especially at party rallies where they would all raise their arms straight out, mimicking their leader and yelling, "Sieg Heil! Sieg Heil! Sieg Heil!"

Captain Haysley got the attention of the group after a moment and changed the topic, asking the men, "Do any of you know someone in the telephone department here?"

Jimmy was shrugging his shoulders, and hesitantly John replied, "No, not yet."

Captain Haysley was calm now and, closing his eyes, he leaned back in his chair so hard, resulting in such a loud crack that they thought it would break. "Captain Foley has informed me that the German government is able to tap into certain telephone conversations," he said, now opening his eyes wider than usual. "They appear to be listening to whomever they want, and they can do it any time they want," he said with frustration.

Haysley continued talking before anyone else could comment. "The Embassy has a few agents that they dangle out there as possible spies to distract the Germans, and they have all reported that their phones must be tapped, but they are not having much luck in solving the situation."

John's forehead crinkled a little in determination, and he firmly said, "I haven't thought very much about the telephones here in Berlin, but I sure will find out for you. I did take a course in Transcontinental Telephone once at the Foreign Trunks Telephone Exchange in London," John said, turning to look at Jimmy.

"That was near the Gaumont British Film Studio, where I met Alfred Hitchcock on a number of occasions," he added conversationally. "Yeah, he was quite a card, always playing tricks on people, particularly with the phoney stage props. When you went to shake hands with him, he would pull a banana out of his pocket and shake it, and then laugh."

"All right, enough" Haysley said robustly, but with a little smile, rarely seen. He stood up and came around the desk, "Well, someone better figure out how they're doing this telephone tap, and soon" he declared.

"John, I want you to work with Jimmy until you figure this out," he ordered.

"That's all now, step to it," he said firmly.

*
**

At least three or four other men had the same position at the consulate as John and Jimmy. He never really knew exactly who or how many, but they worked together quite often in the beginning. Jimmy was one of the fellows whom John got to know quite well. He was from Weybridge, England, and still had family there, under a different name. They were really nice people, and John stayed with them for a few days once.

Like most of the men, Jimmy liked to be seen as a gentleman, and wore a high collar and tie. All of the men in the consulate office would dress up, wearing white shirts with collars and ties, and gold or silver sleeve garters to keep their cuffs clean. They were also proud of their education and loved to brag about it, but Jimmy wasn't like that. He was somewhere between the rest of them and John at the other end, who never liked the high collar and tie but always preferred to wear the more modern suits of the day.

Later that day, after their discussion with Haysley, the men gathered in one room where a telephone had been taken apart into every little piece and displayed on a table. The men had their heads together and were combining their knowledge. "It could be in the telephone itself," one of them said. "There are many different models."

There was silence until John put the question forth again. "Who would know someone in the telephone department?"

One of the fellows said, "Peter over at the Embassy switchboard, he might know of someone."

"No, we already asked him," Jimmy said, much to John's surprise.

He turned to John knowledgeably and said, "The British Embassy has quite a large international telephone exchange here with a few different operators. Be sure to have a tour of it next time you're there."

Another fellow interjected, "I overheard this chap in the pub the other day say he was a supervisor in the telephone exchange, but I don't know him."

"Would you recognize him?" John asked.

"Oh yes," he said, "he was quite the blowhard — I'm sure I'd recognize him if he was there again."

So, that evening, a group of clerks went out to the Irish pub – a rowdy and very lively nightclub – to search for the elusive man. They had a good time there, and they had to drink a fair amount while they waited, but the results were good and he was able to point out the man.

John went to the club night after night until finally he was able to meet and become a friend of a man called Mehnrich, who, as they had expected, was an engineer and supervisor with the telephone department. He and John both had engineering in common and a bond was soon formed.

"When I was in training in Darlington," John said to him, "we toured all sorts of production plants." Mehnrich listened intently to all of John's stories.

"Once we went to Darlington Forge to witness the forging of the rudder for the Queen Mary, and then we went to Glasgow later to see the rudder on the stocks and then we saw part of it again at John Brown's Ship Building where they built the side of it up.

"Then it was on to Newcastle-upon-Tyne to the Parsons Turbine Works to watch turbines being assembled and then back to the Darlington Rolling Mills to watch the wrought-iron railway lines being formed. From there we went to Birmingham to learn how small tools were made, which was very interesting. Then to Sheffield to see stainless steel cutlery being formed and on to Rugby to learn how magnets were formed."

Mehnrich was fascinated and had many stories of his own. He was full of questions, "I wish I could see all of those places you've mentioned. What a wonderful experience."

"Well, maybe one day you will," John replied. "I would love to see the telephone plant where you work," he added with ingenuous curiosity.

John smiled and continued with his college stories, "You know, once we went to Derby for a visit to the Rolls Royce Factory. You know, that place was more like a dairy than a factory. Everyone wore white shoes and white coats, and on some instruments they wore white gloves. In some places they even had to cover their heads! Can you imagine," he said.

"I even remember one industrial town called Middlesborough. They have a story that it was the only town in England where they will not serve beer to a woman," John paused.

"But she can get stout," he said looking Mehnrich in the eye, and they both had a good laugh over that.

Back at the office, they were having a really hard time trying to figure out the telephone taps, with no good news at all, but John persisted and after a period of time he asked Mehnrich outright to let him visit the telephone exchange.

At first Mehnrich said no, but eventually with some persuasion, he said he would. "But only if you go in as a mechanic," Mehnrich said.

"Can you get me a uniform or overalls to wear" John replied eagerly.

"Yeah, okay, I'll see what I can do," he agreed. John was elated; this was the first step.

The telephone exchange was huge, and John was being shown around as a neighbouring mechanic. At one point he was left alone with an adorable, chubby little operator who was really friendly and would answer all his questions. It had to do with the different lights on the telephone that would light up, red, white and then green.

When you picked up the telephone, it would light up a white light in the exchange and also the white light on your telephone would go on. Then, when they were connecting you, a red light would go on until the connection was complete and a third light, a green light, went on every time that your call went through; you didn't have any power over the system of lights. It was just set up that way.

It turned out that, during the first stages, the lines were like sisters and you could hear anything until they got the green light. That was how the operators could pick their favourite telephone numbers and covertly listen in.

"Good job there, John," Captain Haysley said, as he raised his arm in a toast to him, their two little snifters almost full of sherry. John was savouring the icy burn of the sherry on its way down his throat and into his chest, when Captain Haysley removed the glass from his unwilling hand and quickly put both the glasses away, into a new more secretive location but still behind the file cabinet.

John looked at him curiously, "What's the rush?" After all it was Friday night, and Captain Haysley did not seem to have a very active social life.

"I have much work to do upstairs for tonight's party," he said. "I'll see you on Monday." John took the hint and left, feeling a little dejected that he wasn't invited to the party.

After work he arrived at the front door of the apartment block where he lived and met Herr Jacoby from the flat above his, who also was arriving home from work and was in a very good mood.

"Guten Tag, John," Herr Jacoby said, as he was moving about the sidewalk in slow dance steps. He was seemingly full of energy, even though the tweed suit on his short square body was looking all crumpled after a long day's work.

"Good evening," John responded with a smile, stopping to light up a cigarette, and for a little chat. He asked him politely, "You're off for the weekend now, Herr Jacoby?"

"Yes," Jacoby sang the word with a little roar, embarrassing John somewhat.

"Hey," he then said, straightening up, "Would you like to join me, John?"

He looked up into John's intrigued eyes, "Old Hammersmitz usually comes with me, but tonight he is busy. How about it, would you like to join me at the Russian club?"

Chapter 13

THE RUSSIAN CLUB

Her stunning red lips appeared through the fog of the thick, pungent cigar smoke of the Russian nightclub for a long moment before she did. "What a beauty," John quietly said.

Jacoby looked over, "Now that's a real dish," he laughed loudly, with one eyebrow raised as her sleek body came into focus. The shimmering dress appeared to be weightless, almost part of her skin, the quivering dangles all over drew your attention to every inch of it.

The band had quit playing the Charleston, but the song was still going on in the minds of the exhilarated dancers who were now mingling, catching their breath, and searching for their drink and a smoke.

The room was full of flappers, young girls being free, wearing make-up and short skirts, smoking and drinking, and most importantly, they had bobbed hair, cut short in rebellion against the age-long-era of not being allowed to have short hair. This trend still remained in less liberal places around the world, but this was Berlin and there were not many rules at all, if any. They watched as the beautiful woman passed by their table, reaching for her semi-long cigarette holder on the next table over. Following close behind her was a handsome man, tired and panting hard in his pale blue shirt with the sleeves rolled up and his jacket slung over his shoulder. He just wanted to sit down for a moment, but Jacoby leaned forward from between two lively, robust girls and grabbed him by the arm as he went by.

"Freddie," he said, "I want you to meet John. He's my neighbour." He motioned towards John, and Freddie stopped in his tracks, still trying to catch his breath.

"Guten Abend," Freddie softly said with a large sigh, raising his hand towards John.

"It's a pleasure to meet you," John replied in perfect High German, while extending his hand and making an effort to stand up from behind the crowded table.

"Speak in English, Freddie," Jacoby spoke up, his large round face was all red and appeared slightly swollen, and, with the lipstick kisses on his cheeks, it was hard to take him seriously.

"This young man works in the British Consulate right here in Berlin," Jacoby said, when one of his female playmates suddenly turned his head for a kiss. Almost forgetting what he was talking about, he suddenly piped up with a huge smile, "He's in the passport office there and so if you ever want to leave our beautiful Berlin you should talk to him." He laughed and raised his shot glass. "Vodka."

Freddie shook his head, "Not right now," he said smiling, looking down at the table full of glasses of varying sizes and noticing the second bottle of vodka was almost empty, the official way of telling the time in the club.

"I have no intention of leaving Berlin," Freddie said. Opening his arms wide and motioning as if to give everyone there a hug, "I love it here, everything is going so well for me right now. As Lili would say, 'It's the cat's pyjamas.'" He turned with a longing look for the girl in the shimmering dress who was now coming towards him.

On the huge elegant stage, there was a nice looking girl in very simple clothing, which was very unusual in the Russian club, compared to the flash and fanfare normally going on. She stood alone and was slowly starting to sing louder and louder with the most spectacular voice. At first no one really noticed, but the sound was so breathtaking it became hard for John to focus on any conversation, especially over the buzzing crowd noise, which was also starting to hush under the spell of her voice. She was one of many new entertainers, singers and dancers who were arriving every day in Berlin, from all over the globe. It was such a wonderful time and place to be alive.

Jacoby shattered the peace, in his usual boisterous and yet pleasant way. "Johnnie," he sang out, while waving his hand in the general vicinity of Freddie, "Freddie here and his brother Karl make uniforms for the army.

He just got a new contract to replace all those old brown uniforms that were left over from World War I, and to make them some new ones."

Jacoby stopped to take a sip of his vodka before continuing. "It's about time, don't you think," he added, shrugging his shoulders and focusing back on the girls' legs.

John tried not to show that he found that information overly interesting. He had now worked his way out from behind the table, squeezing past the luscious blonde who was sitting next to him, and was standing up next to Freddie. Both men were about the same height (around six foot), and their good looks and well-tailored suits were attracting the attention of every girl who went by.

Freddie instinctively smiled back at John and could not help noticing the one distinct curl that had popped out of place on the side of his forehead, exposing a peculiar scar.

The beautiful girl with the gorgeous lips and body was now fondly caressing Freddie in a sensual and yet respectful way. Freddie gently grabbed her around the waist and drew her nearer. "This is my wife," he said, "Mrs. Lili Solinger."

She looked John up and down so fast it was hardly even perceptible, except for the reflection of her approval behind her lovely smile. "It's a pleasure to meet you," she said with a deep voice in almost perfect English, while wearing her unlit cigarette like an accessory before slowly easing it towards her mouth.

"Unlike Freddie, I love to travel and so we just might leave Berlin for a holiday one day." She looked John in the eye as he leaned forward to light her cigarette; his lighter was always at hand.

Lili Solinger snuggled back into her husband's side and, for a moment, there was a silence as the singer continued to mesmerize the crowd.

John noticed a group of young men off to one side who were quite drunk and laughing very loudly, while trying to roll their sleeves back down to get their suit jackets on. They were enjoying themselves greatly and hadn't been paying attention to the cute girl singing. John suspected they were homosexuals; after all this was the Kurfürstendamm area. But this particular club was not like that, and their gay behaviour stood out. It was a first-class club, a private members' only club, well-known for its truly unbelievable band. They had every reason to feel safe at this club. The band struck up a loud introduction, and a cabaret show of glamorous girls appeared on the stage, singing and dancing. The feathers were flying off and before long they were half-naked, another sign of the late hour. The highly energized crowd were gathering closer to the dance floor, and Freddie and his wife followed with a nod and a smile backwards, "Auf Wiedersehen."

Just then a few Brownshirts, strolled through the club. No one really cared. They were just two young men in uniform looking around and trying not to be conspicuous about it, or so it seemed to John, who noticed everything and was constantly on the lookout. He became uneasy, for no particular reason, but just out of habit he ducked away, and as they approached he eased the voluptuous girl who had been eagerly sitting beside him all evening to her feet and gave her a long kiss until the Brownshirts were well gone by. It was after all something they had both been wanting to do all night.

Jacoby lifted his glass for a toast. "Prost!"

John held the girl at arm's length, his deep ocean blue eyes seemed to look right into her soul, luring her, and scaring her a little, both at the same time.

"I am so sorry I must leave now," John said to her and glanced over at Jacoby, who was actually paying attention. But before he could protest, John added with a shrug, "I have to work tomorrow, but it was fabulous." With a little kiss on her cheek and another quick apology, John was off.

Outside, the two Brownshirts were having a run-in with the large group of gay men. It looked like trouble could break out momentarily, so John took off in a hurry. Whistling as he went, John crossed over the little bridge that led to his apartment. He was appreciating how much he loved walking and what a beautiful warm summer evening it was for Berlin, when he tripped a little and grasped hold of one of the majestic elm trees that lined the Tirpitz Ufer Canal, a huge canal that winds its way through the city.

Streams of moonlight were shining down like floodlights through the trees as he went on, swerving and humming the last song that he had heard playing in the club, getting louder and louder all the time, "Oh, the shark, babe, has such teeth, dear. And it shows them pearly white, do do doo do, do do do... it's Mack the knife."

John had his arm outstretched and was touching the trunk of each tree as he passed them by when suddenly one of the trees appeared to be swinging in the breeze. He lost his balance and grasped hold of it with both hands to balance himself, and it started swaying back and forth with him.

The feeling of death, of limp tendons and muscles in the human body, is undeniable in one's bare hand, and that straightened John right up. As he jerked his arms away, his legs went weak underneath him, and he stumbled backwards across the little sidewalk to rest his back against a small brick building before he slid down it to the ground.

He sat there for quite a few minutes trying to grasp what had just happened. He focused on the man's face and could see a deeply entrenched look of horror staring back. It was an awful sight, and now that he had confirmed it was a dead body hanging there he felt nauseous.

He had seen enough in his first glance to know that the corpse was just a young man in a nicely tailored suit. He could have been coming home from a club just like himself, John thought. He gathered his wits and scrambled back on to his feet again, never looking back, except for a brief moment to see a silhouette of the poor man's legs swaying in the dark.

It wasn't far to his apartment where he stumbled in and rushed up the stairs, heading right for the telephone to call the police. He told them where to look and then shakily placed the heavy black handle down on its cradle.

It was time for a nightcap, just a little shot to calm his nerves. John wasn't normally much of a drinker, but it was too late for that, and seeing his first dead body in Berlin had been quite a shock. He ran his fingers through his neat hair, leaving it in chaos. John was now worried that his British accent might have come through to the police officer he had just spoken to. He had almost mastered the dialect of the typical Berliner but because he spoke so many languages and their various dialects, it got a little confusing sometimes when he was drinking and self-control was much more difficult.

He was muttering to himself while he reached over for the newspaper, but quickly fell asleep in the chair before having read the headlines.

Within no time he was dreaming the worst of dreams; he was back walking through fields of dead bodies again in France.

Like a gun going off, the telephone rang so loudly that John's body was lifted a good foot off the chair from fear, and he had the telephone receiver in his hand in a fraction of a second. Confused and not yet awake, he answered softly, "Hallo."

A lively young man's voice was on the other end, a South German accent from Bavaria with an Oompah-pah ring to it, and for a moment John felt better again until the young policeman's words confirmed his worst fears, and left an impression he would never forget.

"Herr Harrington," he declared, "there is nothing to worry about, sir. It was only a Jew."

"Danke," John simply replied, which he thought was adequate for that time of the morning, and then he just waited for the policeman to speak.

"Well, goodnight then," he said, and John muffled a noise in response that sort of resembled a word before hanging up.

"What," he thought so loudly that he gained clarity. "What," he yelled out loud, before he started to cry. He put his head down between his legs, feeling sick again. "How could this be? No more bodies, no more wars, please."

He looked over at his pipe on the table; his old friend was his first and last hope at this moment. He lit it and slowly exhaled an enormous puff of smoke. It soothed his soul immediately as if calmness itself had been injected.

There was a newspaper on the table and he glanced over at the headline: "The Nationalist Party growing stronger, party leader Adolf Hitler speaks to all." John's head bobbed again and he nodded off.

The following morning, John's hand trembled as he shaved and combed his hair. He was thinking about this new nemesis, Adolf Hitler, who no doubt was also waking up about the same time and not far away. John pictured Adolf reaching for his tooth powder with a morning grimace and neurotically trimming his little square moustache, which was very distinct and still quite bushy, and then wetting down and holding back that nuisance chunk of square bangs that would just not stay to the side.

*
**

John walked to work every morning in Berlin. He enjoyed the change-able seasons and harsh conditions which you always had to be ready for. The air seemed so fresh with the continental airflow, even though Berlin was quite an industrial centre. This day was a typically hot, rather sticky, summer day and John was dressed for travel. He looked quite dashing as usual in his fitted suit, as he strolled along down Kluckstrasse and past the location near the canal where the dead body had hung the night before. Not even a glance, he thought, or the slightest change in step. He couldn't chance that someone might be watching. Walking at a normal pace, John was able to conceal his stiff leg, but any faster and it was impossible to miss the limp. He hid it well when he wanted to.

"Guten Morgen," good morning, he would say as he passed others on the street, or just nod and smile. There was something about John's smile that would win your heart immediately. He had learned over the years and through all of his travels, that a smile means the same thing in any language or country.

Kluckstrasse where John lived was a continuation of Bendler Strasse, divided by the Tirpitz Ufer Canal. So he just went straight down his street every morning and would end up on Bendler Strasse, which was the street where the German High Command, the German War Office, the Secret Service Office, the Air Force Command, the Admiralty, and many other government offices were situated. Of course, this meant that many of the top German officers soon had an office there. Goering, Himmler and also Admiral Canaris were a few.

John's morning walk always took him past these impressive build-ings, and the street would get busier and busier as he went, with all of the staff going to their various posts. On this particular morning, as he was approaching the War Office, John could see a short distance ahead of him that Hermann Goering was getting out of his spectacular beige convertible limousine and was about to proceed into the building. People on the busy sidewalk had slowed their pace to allow him through. He had an entourage of three men behind him, scurrying to keep up with their boxes and papers.

John had recognized Hermann Goering instantly. He was a well-known personality, famous as a World War I fighter pilot in the Richthofen Fighter Squadron. He was also a notorious collaborator with Adolf Hitler.

John's first impression of him was different from what he had expected from seeing his photo in the newspaper. Herr Goering was shorter than he would have guessed and quite a stocky man. As John got closer, he couldn't help but notice the peculiar angle of Goering's sharp chin as he lingered before entering. Goering looked very official in full uniform, which really suited his broad body shape and his oversized square head that was adorned with neatly manicured dark hair and short side burns which curled upwards.

On the doorstep, Hermann Goering turned to the crowd, his numerous medals glistening so brightly in the morning sun that it was hard to look at him. He beamed the friendliest of smiles at the people gathering on the street, which turned sinister the moment his head turned towards the building. He gave one last glance, right at John, with an evil look on his face that seemed to look right through him, as if John were invisible. Just another secretary or clerk, he probably thought, or so John hoped, just a nobody.

This was not unusual for John; in his first year there, he had made an art of blending in with the bustling crowds on Bendler Strasse. He took notice of every detail he could about the German officers and their staff. He knew that everyone at the consulate would find the fact of Hermann Goering's visit interesting. They used to talk of his addiction to morphine and the latest news was that he was in Sweden being treated for such.

As John continued to walk down Bendler Strasse, he would quickly end up at the beautiful Tiergarten Strasse, a road that went for miles in either direction and encompassed a huge park in the middle, Tiergarten Park. Tiergarten translated, means animal garden and there was a large zoo in this spectacular natural area, which John thought greatly resembled London's Regents Park or Hyde Park in Sydney. There were also quite a few well-known people who lived there on Tiergarten Strasse, such as Werner Von Braun, who was known to be experimenting with miniature rockets from the family villa there in the Tiergarten.

The British Consulate was located right there, at 17 Tiergarten Strasse. It was a graceful white building, three stories high, with a tremendous number of windows on every floor. It was quite stately, not only in its location but with the extensive lawns all the way around it and the nine-foot-high railing to enclose them all.

John quickened his pace as he entered the majestic front door, not wanting to talk to anyone yet this morning. He said, "Hi, hi," and nodded at a few of the girls who had arrived early and then whisked away to his office in the back. He was unusually tired and confused after last night, and just wanted to put his head down for a few minutes. He turned on his wireless and closed the door, hoping that would keep everyone out, and he closed his eyes for just a second or so it seemed. For the first time there, he wanted to go home; he missed England and his college sweetheart Betty. He hadn't even thought of her in some time but now he missed her terribly and drifted to sleep dreaming about their last meeting.

*
**

A loud noise woke him abruptly, and he could hear Captain Haysley's words from yesterday repeating in his mind, the curious reason that had brought him into work today.

"You'll be off to Leipzig tomorrow with Jimmy. It appears that someone has a British passport there that we didn't issue."

It turned out the reason was that there was a chap in Leipzig with the same job as they were doing in Berlin and he was a friend of the German national in question. He'd given the German a passport on his own without going through the proper channels. Jimmy and John were sent to find out why, and they did. They never found out what happened to the Brit after that and felt rather bad, but most assumed he would be sent back to England and disciplined there. They were very strict in the department.

Jimmy was moved around a lot after that and ended up in Munich, so he and John didn't often meet up again. John was mostly on his own now in the field. On one occasion he had been directed to deliver a small package to the British Embassy in Frankfurt and to bring some important documents back to Berlin. He had the package hidden away inside his black leather briefcase with its art deco clasps. It was brand spanking new and he was proud of it. Somehow it made him feel more important, special, to carry such a nice case at his side.

As he slowly walked towards the consulate car, he watched his reflection becoming clearer in the giant fenders of the Phantom II Rolls-Royce before he knocked on the window and got in. Frank was expecting him, wearing the chauffeur's hat as usual, which nicely hid his bald spot.

"Good morning, Johnny. Where are you off to, today?" he asked, in a rough morning voice, as if he'd been yelling all night. His usual big grin from ear to ear was beaming back at John, who noticed that Frank always seemed to be wearing the same black suit, but there was never a wrinkle or a spot on it. John wondered how he did that.

"The train station," replied John. "Official business," he murmured, looking sideways out of the car window.

"Oh," Frank replied, becoming curious. "I see," he said, looking over his shoulder with his wide inquisitive eyes in hopes of getting more information out of John. Frank was a real talker and always had some news to share. Frank had been exceedingly helpful to John when he'd first arrived in Berlin, giving him hints on Berlin dialect, and they got along well after that.

There were of course many slang expressions, and Berliners had a habit of cutting words in half as it were. For example the word Bleistift, pencil was sometimes shortened to Blei, which means "lead" and that would have seemed really odd if John hadn't known what people were talking about in the first place. It could be a very serious error if said at the wrong time in the wrong place. There were many other examples. In Germany similar to England, each area north and south speaks a different dialect and John soon mastered them.

"I have to deliver a pair of gloves to Frankfurt, can you imagine that?" John replied with a smile. "They belong to some bigwig's wife or something, and she left them behind."

"Oh really, I've heard that one before," Frank said, his voice getting quieter with each word.

"What was that?" John asked him, getting louder.

"Must be really nice gloves," Frank chuckled, as he looked over his shoulder again to see the look on John's face.

John nodded back with a sheepish grin. He felt a little embarrassed about his mission, realizing that he didn't know the whole story, and that Frank probably knew more than he did.

"Here we are," Frank said, as he pulled up in front of the train station and squeaked to a stop. "Have a good trip, Johnny," he said, while lighting his cigar.

Shortly after, John was standing on the platform waiting for the train. He was holding tightly onto his briefcase with the important package inside, and in his other hand he was holding onto his handkerchief and his transport papers; they didn't have tickets then, only papers. As he stood there, someone bumped into him and he felt a tug on the case. When he turned, he saw no one out of place but his papers had slipped out of his hand and fallen down onto the railway track.

The train was right there in front of him and the piece of paper had fluttered down between the track and the wall. John stared in disbelief at the predicament he was in. It would not have been very easy for him to jump down the little wall and get back up again with his stiff leg. Just then, a lady appeared beside him and quietly said, "Shall I get it for you."

"Oh yes," John replied so thankfully. So, she climbed down on the track and picked the papers up. Handing them to John, he thanked her again but when he looked up, she was gone. The hair on his neck stood up, and he wondered who she was, and if she had been sent to keep an eye on him. He looked down at the briefcase still firmly clenched in his hand.

On the train, John always enjoyed reading the newspaper; the German press was bulging with news on the latest theatre or opera productions and how Germany was now a growing nation.

Reading closely, John would feel uneasy when he saw requests for young men to join the Jugendbund. Adolf Hitler was building himself a deadly little army. He had started forming the Jugenbund almost ten years earlier. It was a group for young men between 14 and 18 years of age commonly known as the Hitler Youth. This organization was the initial training step for their future advancement to Stormtroopers. It had remained small until recently and was now rapidly increasing in numbers. Their training focused on physical strength, war tactics, and anti-Semitism. Their academies were eventually to become breeding grounds for "Aryan Supermen," who would devotedly fight for the Third Reich.

Chapter 14

AGENT HARRINGTON

Funny little things were happening to John all the time now. When he arrived at the British Embassy in Frankfurt, he felt that he was being watched again. After climbing the steps of the building, he snuck behind one of the pillars just in front of the door and went out of view. Moments later, a man and a woman rushed up the stairs and in the door. They didn't see John, but he caught a glimpse of them. He had seen the man once before at the office in Berlin and felt greatly relieved.

John strolled in behind them, staying out of view while he watched their bewildered faces. He stole away into the desired office with a slight chuckle. He was having mixed feelings and knew that he was part of something much bigger, no longer just a spectator. The thought of espionage and being a spy out in the field intrigued him.

The man sitting in the office looked up and said, "Agent Harrington, I assume."

John beamed with a confused enthusiasm, "Yes, here is your package," he said, pulling the box out of his briefcase. He knew by now that it was more than just a pair of gloves as the magnet he quite often carried in his pocket was sticking to the box, and it had the distinct weight of a heavy handgun.

"Good job then," the man said with a smile and handed a large envelope back to John.

"Take this right back with you now, and don't delay; this is very important." He looked at John intently, then nodded his head as if to say goodbye.

John had always been an undercover sort of man, always behind the scenes, and this felt just like when he was a young lad in Australia, sneaking around being nicknamed "duck" and leaving everyone wondering where he went. It all seemed so perfectly normal for him, but now he wanted to know more than ever what was really going on.

That was first time he realized that he was being sent on a covert mission, but he was sent on many "errands" after that. Quite a few involved trips to the British Embassy in Berlin, which was on Wilhelmstrasse, close by many of the German government buildings. The Embassy was a beautiful building built in 1868 that used to be known as the Palais Strousberg, a palace no less in its majesty and named after the railway tycoon who had it built. It was quite a distance away from the consulate or passport office, and on the occasions when John was working in between the two places, Frank would usually drive him. He always had something to say. "Did you hear what Hitler is up to now?" was one of his favourite topics.

The second time that John went over to the embassy was a simple case where a young man and his fiancé wanted passports to England, but someone at the embassy wouldn't give one to her. John was sent over to talk to them and find out the reason why.

John found out that they had friends somewhere in England they wanted to visit, and that it was these friends in England who were the suspects. Well, he couldn't tell the young couple the real reason why the passport application had been denied, not then or later. He couldn't help those people, despite the fact that he really wanted to; they were really nice young people he thought. That case struck a nerve for John and he felt bad about it, so from then on he decided to get even more involved with his interviews, and to try to find out more information or other ways to help people whenever he could, especially the Jewish people.

John still frequented his favourite golf course whenever he was able, and Gerta Hoffman had become his desired golfing partner. Hours and hours they spent playing golf, and for one whole year they played off a tee into a secluded glen that was covered with trees all around. It was so beautiful.

It became their magic spot, hidden away from prying eyes, the silence matched only by the aroma of wildflowers in the air. They always took a break there to have a picnic or sit on the bench and talk. Gerta often said to John, "I would like to go to England. Would you or could you get me a visa?"

"I can only look into it," John replied honestly.

"We could go back to my place for the night if you'd like,' she said with her hand on his good leg.

"You know I'd like to," John answered in anguish. "I will probably be fired or killed, or who knows what would happen if they catch me staying over with you."

"Oh I wish we could both just run away to England, and we could get married and live happily ever after." Gerta's head slumped. "I don't think I will ever have a normal life now, living in the shadow of my father."

John sat quietly, not really knowing what to say or do. He was a little stunned at Gerta's blatant words. Usually, their secrets were too big for each other.

"I want to marry you, John. We could move to England."

John smiled back at her with longing in his eyes, but he knew it could not be. "I just cannot, Gerta, I am so sorry," and nothing else needed to be said.

Gerta persisted, nonetheless, "I could give you money, one thousand golden sovereigns." She smiled seductively, "Or anything that you might desire."

John put his arm around her and hugged her for a while,

"Oh Gerta, you are far more tempting than any amount of money. You are so alluring; this is torture." John closed his eyes from the heartache growing inside. "I would love to go away with you, my dearest, but I just can't, not now."

"No one loves me; I must be a horrible person." Gerta started to cry.

John kissed her tears away, "That's just silly, Gertie, everyone loves you. I love you, and our friendship is one of the best things in my life right now. I just wish that our circumstances were different."

Soon she had resigned herself to the fact and began apologizing for her forwardness. "I must sound desperate," she said ashamed. "I just want to get out of here so badly and see the world, and honestly, John, you are the first man who can seem to accept me."

"Don't be silly, you're a wonderful woman, any man would love you," John replied with a huge smile, meaning every word of it. "I hope we can still play next weekend or perhaps even sooner." John was trying to console her.

Gerta thought about it for a moment and replied, "Well, Father is coming back to Berlin on the weekend, and so I will need to be here for him, but I might be free for a little while." She looked away to hide her tears.

"Saturday then, at two."

They remained good friends. The fact that her father, Herr Hoffman, was Hitler's official photographer proved very useful for John, as he was able to know through his daughter just where the big chief, Hitler, was appearing on certain days and with whom.

✻
✻✻

Captain Haysley was always interested in John's news and sat intently listening to him. Shyly, John talked of their conversation, "She made me many tempting offers, including marriage. She's such a nice girl."

"That's completely out of the question," Captain Haysley roared.

"Of course," John said nodding in agreement. "She wants to go to England. Do you think it would be possible to get her a visa?"

Captain Haysley rubbed his forehead as if he had a headache building and shook it in disbelief as he waved John towards the door.

Just the thought of marriage had sent John for a loop. Deep down he still had thoughts of his student friend Betty, whom he had left behind in England. He did not know then that she had already married.

One other real reason was that the marriage would have to be performed by the Consulate General, John's boss, or his deputy — if he would permit it. John's career would have been finished. He would be discharged and sent back to England without a reference. It would be a case of people watching him instead of him watching other people. Still, it was a very trying situation.

Days later, Captain Haysley reported to John in a very serious voice, "It's official; Gerta and her father are on the 'black list' as suspected secret agents."

John was crushed and knew he had no way to help his precious Gerta out of the country.

"I think you should stop seeing her now," Captain Haysley said to John.

John was in a momentary daze, "Yes, yes," he replied. "I'll just see her one more time to say goodbye."

*
**

The golf course was still John's favourite place to be, and Miss Gerta Hoffman was a fabulous companion. And she really liked John a lot, and he her. More than once she had said to him, "Johnny, I wish you'd marry me."

This naturally was out of the question, because of what Fräulein Hoffman did not know, nor did her father, the fact that they were on the black list. Gerta really would have been a good Nazi agent. So it was "no dice."

Nevertheless, they still had some good times both alone together and with lots of other golfers and friends. Also, the area all around the golf course had now become a big production zone with all of the factories located around its circumference, now bustling with activity and workers.

Even though he had been told not to, John still took the time whenever he could to go golfing with Gerta and other friends and to try to gather information at the same time. In that sense, golfing provided both business and pleasure for him.

And in the end, John learned lots of things there. They never got caught either, never. He didn't know why, but then of course Gerta used to say things to him like, "I can't come tomorrow because my dad and I are going to Hamburg," and that's what interested John the most in the end. He knew then that Hitler would be there too and he was able to pass that along. But it was very risky.

After John and Gerta left the course one day, he noticed a black car with two men following them. John had seen the men earlier at the golf course and wondered who they were, but now he really wondered why they were being followed. Later, in Gerta's apartment John knew it had to be the last time that he would be there with her; it was far too dangerous. He said his farewells and ducked out the back of her building in the early hours.

Chapter 15
THE CONSULATE STAFF

Occasionally, John would encounter Gerta Hoffman at the golf course after that, but they no longer had their two o'clock rendezvous. Then one day she was just not there; she was gone and no one seemed to know where she had gone. It was a complete mystery.

At the consulate, Captain Haysley was looking at John confused for even mentioning Gerta, "Are you joking, man? You know this relationship could get you killed."

The tides of time were turning over now, and there was an odd feeling in the air, like a welcoming rain to a dry crop, which might suddenly turn to hail and destroy it.

The power hungry Heinrich Luitpold Himmler with his little round spectacles, often made the news, especially since January of 1929 when Hitler appointed him leader of the SS, the Schutzstaffel or special police. Originally called the Ordnertruppen, they were started as a small group of very strong men that Hitler had created himself back in 1920 to be his personal bodyguards and to protect him during his speeches and rallies. Since that time, the SS troops had grown considerably in numbers. They could be picked out quickly by their eerie pitch-black uniforms, with ties and black caps that had a skull and cross bones symbol on them.

It was obvious now that the Nazis were on a "secret mission" to destroy and kill as many communist party supporters in Berlin as possible. The press was still able and quick to report every bit of this action that they could: the hangings, street shootings, and gang attacks.

Later on in 1929, that fateful year, the stock market crashed, and life as they knew it started to change. Berlin was the largest manufacturing centre in Germany and was funded mostly by foreign investments that immediately stopped. Eventually most of the factories closed.

Unemployment became rampant and families went hungry everywhere, as the world tipped into the Great Depression. People had no jobs and no money, and they were miserable and forlorn. They became radical and rowdy in the streets. The citizens of Germany needed a saviour, a miracle, or at least a job. That was how Adolf and his National Socialist Party got their foot in the door.

*
**

Back at the British Consulate, it was getting busier all the time, and John was now heading out and conducting interviews on a steady basis.

One afternoon John went up to Captain Haysley's office with his report. "He's not here today," Margo said looking up with no other explanation. She pointed down the hall, "Atkinson is in his office today though. You should stop in and see him."

John knocked on the door.

"Enter," came the reply.

Shyly, he said, "Hello, I'm John Harrington."

"Oh, hello, yes, I know who you are. Come on in, I'm Atkinson," he said, jumping up from a completely bare desk as if it had just bit him. "Come on in, sit down, sit down," he said, nodding his head towards a chair in the corner.

John looked over at the rickety wooden chair and then looked back at him with a wrinkled brow. Atkinson leaned forward, way over the desk to shake his hand. "It's about time we met, John. What can I do for you today?"

As John reached his hand out for a shake, Atkinson snapped it up prematurely, giving it a vigorous shake. He was a very large and powerful-looking man, who seemed to be ready to leap out of an airplane at any moment or luge down a hill. His jetblack hair was immaculately manicured and greased back, which somewhat distracted from the lengthy scar on his neck than ran from his left ear lobe curving forwards to disappear under his shirt. A story never told.

John cautiously remarked, "I have a report for Captain Haysley, but I am sure it can wait." After receiving no response, he said, "A young couple came into the office today and applied for visas to England, but there was nothing on file for them, nothing at all."

Atkinson replied, "Right, usually Haysley takes care of that, but he's away all week. You might as well go and check it out yourself," he said with a teeny smile that revealed a missing tooth on the bottom. Atkinson walked over and gathered up a stack of manuals off the shelf.

"Follow me, we just got a whole load of supplies in," he remarked, as he rushed past John and then out the door, fumbling with his heavy load. John followed in a hurry, and soon Atkinson unlocked a door, and they entered a room that was completely lined with shelves, all fully stocked.

"This is my warehouse," he boasted, as a huge smile emerged that rarely showed itself as John found out later. "Anything you want, you just come to me, and if I don't have it, I can get it."

He was still grinning as he walked around to the different shelves, "I have uniforms and work suits," he stated. "I heard you bought yourself some overalls," he said, trying to contain his laughter. "Sorry I didn't get to you sooner."

Not waiting for an answer he carried on, "Sugar, real coffee, cigarettes, you name it."

John was surprised and impressed with this discovery. "I can use these work suits," he said in disbelief at all these supplies.

"Absolutely, just let me know what you need. Anything that might get us some information is worth it," Atkinson's voice became serious. "You know, to entice these people you're interviewing or people like them."

John spotted a shelf with brand new radios on it and longingly looked into Atkinson's eyes, which were always waiting for a request, "Could I have one of those radios for my apartment?" he asked

"Sure, you should have one already," Atkinson remarked, as he reached up for one. John walked back to his flat that evening a new man, with the radio and a few work suits under his arm. It was a breezy afternoon and he rushed there, hoping it would not rain.

Passersby were chuckling at the large radio he was carrying, and he couldn't help but think how Berlin was such a pleasant and friendly city to live in.

As mentioned, Bendler Strasse was a big street where all the German officers were, and once you crossed over the other side of the Tirpitz Ufer Canal you were on John's side, Kluckstrasse; that's where the servants lived. At the end of Bendler Strasse in those days, on the right-hand side of the street, was a big dynamo, an electrical generator, that was producing a lot of the electricity for Berlin, and on the other side there was the Shell building, the motor oil people. It was a hub of German official and commercial activity. Even Hitler had a place in the Chancellery nearby.

That dynamo, in-between Bendler Strasse and Kluckstrasse, used to start up at five o'clock every night. This particular generating station made the power for most of Berlin and the special generators made a lot of noise every night right from 5 o'clock, GRRRRR. This really irritated John because the English news used to also come on at 5 o'clock, and he couldn't listen to it because of the noise. It was one of his major pet peeves.

Shell Berlin was a really huge place and, of course, lots of people worked there. John liked it because he could go and mix with the people and talk with them about the factory. He began to augment his wardrobe, with even more suits and overalls, and he also purchased various outfits to blend in with the public. John was like a sponge, gathering up information everywhere he went; there was just so much to see and hear, and according to him, it beat working in the office.

The British consulate was always full of surprises, and John met another really interesting person there – Alfred, the caretaker. It seemed as if he was always in the building, day and night, but in reality he had a wife and a teenage daughter at home.

"Are you still here, Johnnie," Alfred asked him one day as he entered the empty lunchroom, which seemed to be Alfred's unofficial office or at least that was where he spent most of his time. He took up his usual pose with one arm draped over the end of the motionless mop. His blue work shirt was dirty as if he had been working in the yard, and his leather newsboy cap was tilted a little off to the side.

Alfred greatly resembled Von Hindenburg, and the staff used to tease him that he had "peaches for cheeks." You would honestly think it was Hindenburg standing there. Alfred was a very nice old fellow, and John got along well with him.

"This is such a nice room," John replied. "The sun shines so beautifully in here this time of day, and it is just far enough away from the clatter up front."

"Yeah, I love it here, too," Alfred said with a rather rough German accent that made John inwardly question his loyalties.

"Where are you from, Alfred, here in Berlin?"

"Not really," he said, looking at John and wondering how much he could tell him, "I've moved around a lot over the years. When I was little, we lived in a small town, here in Germany that was quite near the Dutch border, but then my parents split up and I went with my mother to England. That's where I went to college for carpentry and that was where I learned to speak such good English." He laughed a hilarious sounding laugh and looked intently at John, clearly trying to read his reaction, but he couldn't, and so he continued, "But, I came back after the war to find my father. Alas he was gone, no longer alive."

Just then a group of girls from the front office came into the lunchroom, giggling and acting surprised to see the men there. "Oh hello," one of the girls said, stopping in her tracks and looking directly at John. "Are you coming to the party tonight, too?"

"Party?" John said, trying to produce the cutest, most innocent expression he could muster in the hopes that she would invite him.

She lowered her head a little, "I guess not then," she apologetically said. "It's pretty hush-hush if you know what I mean. We just came in here to have a bite to eat before we get changed." Her attention was drawn away by the other girls already getting in the party mood, as they were playing in the long curtains that adorned the stately windows, wrapping themselves up in them as tight as they could and then unwinding in a hurry.

"Come on, kids," she joked, and smiled at John as she walked away and joined them at the table. "Let's eat now."

Alfred turned to leave the room; he had blended in so well that most of the girls hadn't even noticed he was there. John looked at him in confusion and disappointment. Alfred shrugged his shoulders on his way out, and John heard him say, "Come on outside, John. I'll show you another very nice spot to watch the sunset."

The intoxicating aroma of freshly mown grass was all around them, as the two men sat together on a large wooden bench behind the consulate building. Alfred had been busy mowing all day, and the lawn looked beautiful even with the German offices and the German Press Club in the background.

Alfred reached down to loosen the laces on his work boots before lighting up a cigarette, while John stuffed his pipe full of tobacco.

"I love this spot," Alfred said, the sound of his words seemed to be riding along on his breath of smoke, as his dark brown eyes turned towards John.

"Yes, thank you for bringing me here, this is a great spot," John said and really meaning it, as he put his match to the bowl and a flame instantly jumped upwards. "Do you know anything about this party they're on about," he asked after letting out a huge puff of smoke.

"I know, of course," Alfred said.

John knew very little about their parties. When he'd first arrived in Berlin he had been quite surprised to learn that select staff went to some rough weekend parties in the big hall above the consulate, with both German and British officials in attendance. He thought it was probably because the consulate was right next door to the German Press Club. He was never invited.

"They're not normally for the consulate staff though," Alfred said, vigorously nodding his head no. "They're just for the officers and officials. And just about every weekend, there is something going on here. They do a lot of entertaining."

"Why here?" John asked curiously.

"Oh, it's out of the way a little, I suppose," Alfred said, "away from the bad press. I mean, the attachés have to relax, too, and they can't just go to the pub." He laughed and shook his head, "and sometimes the parties can get pretty big with all their big generals and aristocrats and maybe that's why the office girls are going tonight — someone fun to talk to."

"Gee, I bet Miss Avery gave them a long speech before they left," John said, starting to laugh, and Alfred roared out loud. They both sat and enjoyed their thoughts and their tobacco for a quiet moment.

"Do you stay and see the officials at these parties," John asked, really interested in what he was missing out on. "Do you think I could get in?"

"Oh, yes, I stay, I have to stick around," he said. "After all, someone has to clean up when they're all finished," he grinned at John.

Then Alfred looked around nervously as if telling him a secret, "But, of course I can't go in; I have to hide in the background so no one sees me. I wouldn't want to anyway." His eyes widened, "There are too many high officials for me, German government people, chiefs of police. You never know who will be there.

"You can't go in either, not without an official invitation," Alfred continued regretfully. He tried to break the news gently, looking very apologetic, "They have them printed weekly and, sorry to say, I'm pretty sure they won't be inviting you."

John pretended to look perturbed, in a very comical way.

Alfred took on a funny look, too. "If you're not an officer or a big wheel or haven't been to Oxford or Cambridge, you're not one of the select few."

"Huh," John said sarcastically, trying not to show the big disappointment he was really feeling. And, of course now even more so, he really wanted to go to the party.

Alfred let out one last puff of smoke and stood up "Well, I have my own chief waiting for me at home who I have to answer to first, and she's a five-foot-two knockout named Ella," he said smiling at John. As he straightened his body out, a split second of excruciating pain flashed across his face.

John smiled back at the gumption Alfred had for his age, which seemed very old to him then, and as he was walking away he noticed Alfred's limp, which was on the opposite side to John's. He wondered how he got it, and thought, "We'll look quite the pair if we ever walk side by side." John wanted to ask him what had happened, or if and where he had fought in the war but was too afraid to. Slim as the chance was, Alfred could have been in the German trenches where John had fought; they could have caused each other's malady, their permanent limps.

Not that it would have mattered to either of them, being compassionate souls, but it was still very personal. John never really knew how much he could trust Alfred or not, and so he was very careful what he said to him, but he did know one thing for sure – Alfred was a lot smarter than he looked.

*
**

The following day, a group of the male clerks had gathered in the hall, and Thomas called out, "Do you want to come for lunch with us, John?"

"I'm coming," John replied, gathering his coat and scarf up in a hurry, "Where are we going?"

"Over to the German Press Club," Thomas replied. "It's not far from here, we can walk there. You'll like it."

Chapter 16
THE PRESS CLUB

Bendler Strasse and the Press Club were actually back to back with the British Consulate, strange as it might seem. They were divided by two large lawns. The consulate lawn was, of course, enclosed by nine-foot high iron railings, but the Press Club's railings had been removed for use as ammunition in the First World War.

John found out it was a commonplace thing for some of them at the consulate to be invited in to the Press Club for a drink and a chat. In fact, in those early years, they did not even need to be invited, and they went quite frequently. It was a great place for lunch during the week, and there was nothing else quite as close if you hadn't brought your own.

The Press Club was a plain brick building from the outside, with only a small decorative sign over the door, but inside it was just lovely, very comfortable. It was always warm on a cold day or cool on a hot one, and the service was fabulous. At the front area of the club was a high glass case with all kinds of foods, and you could pick whatever you wanted. They had everything to drink that you could imagine – hot drinks, tea or coffee, wine or mixed drinks, and fortunately, John's favourite drink, beer.

Of course, various German clerks and officers were always there, sitting at their own group of tables near the rear. They filled the room from the back forward in an orderly fashion as they arrived, and sometimes there were very many of them and they got quite loud.

John didn't drink a lot, but whenever the opportunity arose (which was most days), he would have a Pilsner. It was always served in a tall glass, with a big stem on it and you couldn't put much in it. That was a little disappointing to him that wherever he went he'd get the same small glass.

Once in awhile he used to horrify the fellow who ran the café there at the Press Club. He would sit down with his paper and say to the man, "Tea, please."

The man would usually reply, "TEA, vat's dis?" Then he would give John tea in a glass, and he used to lay on the shtick. John used to think it was funny.

After a short while he became a familiar face to the German officers, and they would talk to him from time to time. It was here at the German Press Club, where John was once again fortunate to meet many interesting and well-known people with whom he had quite a few informative talks on many subjects. It was here that he got to know Herr Erwin Eugen Rommel – a healthy and happy young officer, who would become Field Marshall in the Hitler regime, and with whom John would spend many hours.

There was always something interesting to report after an extended Press Club afternoon, but right now the topic of the day in Captain Haysley's office was politics. By 1930, the Nazis were trying to attract the young college men eager for some action to join their army. The Bund Deutscher Mädel had also been formed as a similar group for German girls. Then came the Jungvolk for even younger children.

Adolf Hitler was becoming more acceptable to some of the German people, with his passionate speeches on patriotism and prosperity. He was beginning to receive generous royalties for his book, Mein Kampf, and would spend it on lavish election campaigns.

Germany's political situation had worsened. President Paul von Hindenburg was now in his eighties and without any real power; and yet, in 1932, Hitler ran for President against him and lost. It was in that election, however, that Adolf Hitler actually gained support and that was when the National Socialist Party, or the Nazis, became the largest political party in Germany.

Hitler promised the people a great economic recovery. First a radio and then a Volkswagen for every household, and that was just what they wanted to hear. He promised them new laws to promote peace and order, to curb the fighting in the streets. Meanwhile, his SA troops had grown to almost half a million soldiers, and many of them were the instigators of the increasingly horrific street brawls that had many Berliners frightened to go out at night.

John was very suspicious of everyone, even the people that he was working with at the consulate. There was something unusual about Captain Foley, too. When John first got there he had learned that Foley's wife was a German national, as was his secretary. Then, of course, there was Alfred the German caretaker who also had a German national wife.

The funniest thing was that the fellow who was the chief telephone operator on the main switchboard at the British Embassy, Paul, was also a German. This was the international telephone exchange, their main exchange for the whole world, and Paul had a brother who was a German Air Force officer.

Isn't that strange, John was wondering. What the hell is going on here? He didn't know whether to complain or inquire, so he kept quiet.

*
**

It was a good thing, too, and it may now be told that Captain Foley, who was later promoted to the rank of major, was the Chief of the British Secret Service for the whole of Germany, the head of MI6.

The passport control office where John was working was considered to be the secret service headquarters, with Captain Foley as chief under the cover of Consulate General. This was not known generally but was suspected by some. John had no idea at the time as no one had actually told him yet. It was just another enigma of his time in Berlin.

Every time John went into Captain Haysley's office, he saw a new shelf with another interesting gadget on it, and this time it was full of cameras. There was the common Leica model that was quite popular with tourists and, indeed, John had one just like it himself. There was an interesting movie camera that John fondled affectionately and a few miniature cameras that instantly caught his eye.

Captain Haysley was leaning back in his chair and casually had one foot up on the table. "That Captain Foley of ours is quite an amazing man, you know," he said to John, without looking up from the report he was reading. He knew John was also curious, when he reluctantly stepped away from the cameras.

"It says here that he was born in 1884 at Burnham-on-Sea in Somerset," Haysley said gazing off into the distance. "That makes him 49," Captain Haysley said in surprise. "Land sakes, that's only five years older than me. I thought he was much older." He put his head down and went back to reading the report.

"Well, you're both old men to me," John joked, who was already in his mid-thirties and some days feeling every second of it. He was picturing Captain Foley in his mind, what he had seen of him so far – which wasn't much because he was usually in his own office and area at the rear of the consulate. Every now and then, however, John would see him running around in the common areas. An energetic man, Captain Foley had such a mischievous smile that always made life seem full of fun and games, which wasn't the case at all in reality. If one looked closely, there were the rings under his eyes portraying that he really did worry a lot more than he let on.

John appreciated Captain Foley's humbleness, in that he was not one for fancy dress or flashy uniforms, but like John himself, he just liked to wear a suit and blend in.

"It says here that he was in the Intelligence Corps in the first war," Haysley stopped reading and looked up at John standing there.

"Really," John said, exuberantly. "Is there anything else we should know?"

Captain Haysley read on, "Foley was educated in France, where he became an accomplished linguist, fluent in French and German.

"Then, in World War I, he was a Captain in the Hertfordshire Regiment, where he had an impressive record and was mentioned in dispatches. He was then wounded in the chest during a German attack and sent back to England to recuperate before returning as an Intelligence Officer, on the staff for the British Army on the Rhine, with the mission to recruit secret agents there."

John was quite intrigued, "Well, that's something to know, isn't it, and he's right in the middle of it now, here in Berlin."

Captain Haysley chuckled, "Yes, right in the middle of it. And speaking of that," he sat up and changed the topic, looking John directly in the eye. "I hear that Hermann Goering is having a photo taken nearby today.

Perhaps he will come to the Press Club later." He paused and raised his voice a little, "You do know he has just been appointed the president of the Reichstag?"

"Yes, I read it in the paper," John replied, nodding his head.

Captain Haysley's orders were never direct; he would give hints about what he wanted John to do. Those were peculiar times in Germany.

"I'll be there," John said on his way out of his office. The German Press Club was now one of his favourite places to mingle with German people and find out what they were talking about.

He left right away, and pulling on his long coat as he went out the door, John briefly looked back towards Miss Avery, who seemed more curious than angry today. The crisp, cool air of Berlin winters was something you quickly became proud of and had to embrace, otherwise it was miserable; but the German Press Club never let you down, it was always cozy and warm.

An empty room greeted John as he entered, with the exception of Teddy, the regular bartender, and a fetching young woman, whom John had never met before. She must have been brought in to help, John thought hopefully.

"Ah, hello, Johnnie, I thought I heard someone come in," Teddy cried as he appeared from behind the counter.

"What can I get for you today, tea?" he said laughing loudly as if it was a release from the stress he seemed to be under.

"I'll just have a Pilsner, Teddy, and maybe this sandwich right here," John said, pointing to one of the many beautiful plates arranged behind the glass.

"You must be expecting a big crowd today," John said, trying not to look overly interested.

"Oh yes," Teddy said quite enthusiastically, "Have you heard? Hermann Goering has arranged a photo session in the back garden here, and I am sure he means to stop in for a beverage after!"

John smiled back innocently, "Perhaps I should be on my way then."

"Oh, I don't think you have to worry," Teddy said with another big laugh, turning in a hurry to carry on preparing. "We all know you by now."

John had almost finished his sandwich and had the newspaper strewn out over the table when the door slammed open with such a crash the light fixtures shook. A black glove emerged followed by a black cape that for a split second looked like a giant bat entering the room, and then Hermann Goering's head appeared above it adorned with a helmet. He flung off his huge black cape as he strutted into the room, momentarily slowing to toss it backwards to the first man behind him, who was at the leading edge of a large crowd of people coming in.

Goering shot a little smile at Teddy, who was nodding and bowing at the same time, and then suddenly he spotted John sitting there in the corner all alone. He did a complete stop and turned towards him. The whole crowd of people behind him also came to an unexpected screeching stop.

He walked right over to John's table, much to John's dismay, and with a big flourish, loudly said, "Ach, der Engländer, Sie haben ein Bier, aber kein Fräulein!" You have a drink, but no girlfriend," and then he laughed loudly, causing many others to laugh. Goering shouted to the waiter, "Kellner," and waving his arm in the air, said, "Eine Flasche Wein, bitte!" He turned and walked off to their favourite area where the highly decorated tables awaited them, complete with frothy pitchers of cold beer. A huge chattering group of people followed him, with everyone from photographers to generals.

A bottle of wine arrived at John's table, and he had to pay for it. This type of occurrence with Goering happened to the British staff on more than one occasion after this. To John's way of thinking, the WWI flying ace was nothing more than a boasting bully; always wanting things his way. He was a "One Man – Man."

Soon the Press Club was overflowing with people, all very well dressed in their finest uniforms and fanciest attire with all of their medals and ribbons displayed on their chests. John felt extremely uncomfortable, but no one even noticed him after that. The beer was flowing and the glasses were clinking, and before long it seemed like everyone was talking at once. It got louder and louder, but John could still distinguish one voice telling a story. It was Herr Albert Speer, an extremely good-looking young man whom John did not recognize at first. He was still on the verge of becoming a well-known and very busy architect.

"When I met the Führer for the first time," Albert Speer said, "he told me he didn't like the Reichstag or the Chancellery buildings. Hitler yelled at me, I don't like them, burn them down, destroy them." Everyone around laughed at the possibility, and the two soldiers near the door, upon hearing the name Hitler and then the cheer, stomped their feet and raised their arms, yelling "Heil Hitler." A split second passed where the crowd looked at them, and they were a little embarrassed – and then it was noisy as ever again.

Another gentleman in a naval officer's uniform was standing next to Albert Speer and said to him, "Hitler wants to rebuild Germany, and it sounds like he wants to start here." The crowd cheered and clinked their glasses again. John got a better look at the man and discovered it was Captain Wilhelm Canaris, a well-known naval expert who was now in the Reichsmarine onboard the cruiser Berlin.

Just as John was contemplating leaving, Thomas, his fellow clerk, appeared in the doorway and went straight up to the counter for a beer. John waved him over. "Thank God you're here," John said. "I was afraid to leave and afraid to stay with this loud crowd. I was just thinking of slipping away at any rate."

"You've got a full bottle of wine here," Thomas said. "You can't leave yet. Now that would be odd!" So they sat and enjoyed it together. The large clubroom was full now to the brim with people from all walks of life.

Excitedly, Thomas asked John, "That's Hermann Goering over there, isn't it?"

"Yes," replied John, "and Captain Wilhelm Canaris is over there also."

"Really," answered Thomas with great interest and sitting up a little straighter. "You know I've heard Canaris is a well-known German spy," he whispered. "At the British foreign office that is," he whispered even quieter. "They call him 'K.'"

"Really," John replied, looking at Thomas with interest and then they both looked over at Wilhelm Canaris. He exuded sophistication, just standing there with his straight back and solid, unflinching face to match.

"No shortage of confidence there," John said. They both nodded.

"Haysley will want to hear about this little gathering."

*
**

One of the highlights in the average Nationalist's life was the, "The Party Rally." This was held in the huge Sports Palais on Potsdammer Strasse and was a function the people looked forward to. Here in all his glory, Herr Hitler would proclaim to his people, that Germany, their wonderful Germany with its wonderful people, would never kneel to any other nation in the world. He would state they were a growing nation and needed more living room. He would shout, "We Germans need more land and freedom, our frontier is the whole world!"

Foreigners and Jewish people were not admitted, but all one really needed was a German passport to gain admittance. Strange as it may seem, many people with British passports were considered German nationals, so there were ways and means that admission was possible. Many people at this time as well possessed two passports.

In point of fact, John had a German passport and a German Diplomatic AUS WEIZ, which could get him anywhere or almost anything. On two occasions, he was able to gain admission to these massive meetings or Party Rallys and report back.

The politics in Germany were really heating up now. Adolf Hitler had secretly threatened President Von Hindenburg with a public scandal over funds gone awry, unless he consented to make him Chancellor. There was a great debate amongst the German people, before the old president was forced to appoint Adolf Hitler as chancellor in January of 1933, and then shortly after, there was the notorious AHNENTAFEL, which was an Ancestry Register that required racial purity back to January 1800.

There was also the Civil Service Law, which was promulgated April 7, 1933. This required every civil servant of the Third Reich to establish his or her ancestry. This was strictly observed and made life very difficult for Jewish people or anyone who had a Jewish parent or Jewish grandparent.

Many Berliners felt threatened by the new laws, as was the case with a young German couple John would stop and talk to occasionally on his way home. They were average middle class people and had a nice little house and a garden with beautiful plants. They began to covertly dig underneath their garden until they had a kind of a cellar. When John asked them or anyone asked them what they were doing, they told them that they were going to install water pipes for their garden, but John could tell that this wasn't what they had done because when it came summertime and water was scarce, their plants and flowers would droop. When John looked more closely, he found hidden in the bushes, a pipe, and he knew that beneath that pipe was an air raid shelter or a hiding spot. A lot of people were doing that, especially in the suburbs. They all did the work themselves and very secretively.

Some of the things that Herr Hitler was allowed to do amazed John. It was well known that Adolf Hitler hated the Reichstag, the House of Parliament, and the Chancellery buildings. It was only a few weeks after his glorified and drawn-out procession through the Brandenburg Gate, heralding his appointment as chancellor, that he once more said, "Burn them down," and his gang did cause the Reichstag to be destroyed by fire.

In the news, the Nazis were claiming that the fire was started by a Dutch boy who was playing with matches, another innocent victim. Pictures were taken of lots of firemen at the site with their hoses. It was broadcast to the world that the firefighters were not able to put out the fire, because it had such a hold on the building already, but observers on the spot knew differently.

John was one of those observers, standing a fair distance away at the time between Unter den Linden, a very famous street in Berlin, and the Brandenburg Gate. A number of people had gathered but were staying out of the way of the firemen who were rushing to the scene, where the buildings were blazing fiercely. John was near enough to the fire to see the firefighters, and there were a lot of men all around with their hoses, but they were of no use. They had no water supply. This point was never revealed to the German people.

While John was standing there watching this travesty, he was fortunate to have his camera and took quite a few pictures of it. No one stopped him or bothered, but he was careful about it. He watched for hours, smoking his pipe to calm his emotions, all the while shaking his head in dismay at the loss of a beautiful and historic building.

John rushed into Captain Haysley's office the next morning, yelling "They burned that Reichstag and then they burned down the president's building. They burned them both down, just because Hitler ranted on about how he hated them."

He calmed down a lot when he saw the shocked look that he had created on his superior's face, "What's this?" Captain Haysley said.

John hurriedly went on, like he was on fire himself, "It was bizarre, there were people standing around looking at what was going on, and the Germans were quite happy. They seemed quite content with what was going on, even though it will cost them a lot of money."

Captain Haysley stood up and headed for the sherry barrel, "It seems they are starting to love their victorious Führer now; you'd better watch out," Haysley replied.

The ultimate scheme that Hitler was planning was known immediately following the fire, when he forced an emergency decree to be signed authorizing him to arrest and execute "any suspicious person."

Thousands of his political opponents and non-supporters were arrested and imprisoned. In March of 1933, the first Nazi concentration camp was secretly started near Dachau to accommodate these Germans, and it was kept very quiet. Hitler was still talking of great prosperity for Germany and was distracting the people with positive propaganda, such as the planned 1936 Olympics in Berlin. The vast majority of people were confused and conflicted but soon began to come to grips with the new racist, Nazi policies.

*
**

Two months later, on May 10, 1933, Hitler ordered that all the books which he disliked, or decreed seditious or licentious be destroyed. Young Nazi gangs raided the Berlin Library and carted away truckloads of famous literary works to be burned in the streets. Later, in July of that year, Hitler outlawed the Socialist Party and prohibited the creation of any new political parties in Germany, making the Nazis the one and only political party in Germany.

One thing John noticed about all of the German officers that he met was that they all seemed to hate the Jewish people. With one exception, and that was Field Marshall Erwin Rommel. Perhaps he and John had more communication with each other over the coming years, but he never once said that he disliked the Jewish people, not to John. In fact, he thought at times that Erwin Rommel sympathized with the Jewish and their ideas. He may have been wrong. To John, he was a wise and humble man. When Erwin Rommel was not in uniform and was not speaking, John thought he could be taken for an English gentleman and that is praise indeed, for a German.

It was one morning while walking to work that John actually met Herr Rommel for the first time. As mentioned before, on his way past the government offices on Bendler Strasse, he would often meet many of the German officers going to their place of work. He'd say "Hello," and they'd just say "Hi, Hi," and nod at him, sometimes with a wave of the hand, but not the Nazi salute by anyone at this time in the early 30's. They didn't know who John was, and they would just see him out of the corner of their eye, and look at him as if he was insignificant.

On this occasion, just as they approached each other, Herr Rommel, slipped and fell on his knee, dropping his short stick on the ground. They used to have these little canes in those days, little short canes with round tips on the end of them. It rolled forward and stopped at John's feet, and so he bent down and picked it up, handing it to Herr Rommel, who was slightly embarrassed and politely said, "Danke schön."

Later in the German Press Club, John met the dashing Herr Rommel again, and they had a short chat. John was standing at the bar, when he ordered a Pimm's in English, a very popular drink then. Rommel turned and smiled at him saying, "Ah, I remember you." Later he picked up John's tab saying, "My friend wants to see you, because he's got an English radio set that won't work." John did go and see Rommel's friend but at a later date, but that was the first day he met him.

John didn't run into Rommel in the Press Club very often but would meet him in other places sometimes. He noticed that in uniform Rommel was just another German. It was very difficult to understand the German way of thinking, "One minute a gentleman and a minute later a Hun." When John would see Rommel coming down the street in full uniform, he'd walk right straight by him as if he'd never met him, and other days when he was on the street, wearing civilian clothes, you would think he was an English squire. Erwin Rommel was just like that.

Chapter 17

ILSE LIEBERT

Every time John returned from lunch, he reported to Captain Haysley. It was routine by now to have a small glass of sherry with their discussions. "I met Field Marshall Rommel today," John said, with a look of accomplishment on his face. The captain looked at him sternly.

"Well, what did you think?" he asked curiously, nonetheless.

"He's shorter than me and he's pretty stubborn," John remarked casually taking a sip.

Captain Haysley laughed out loud banging his glass down, a stream of deep burgundy droplets ricocheted out of his glass splaying across his desk. "Try and find out something useful next time, won't you," he remarked with a grin. "Your lunch time can always be extended if you are talking to someone important," he encouraged, and so John took full advantage of that.

In the front office, however, it was a different story.

Miss Avery was still running a tight ship and it was getting busier all the time. She wasn't happy that John spent so much time away from the office and was always trying to find jobs for him whenever he returned. From time to time, they had a little trouble with their typewriters, and one day she asked him, "Can you fix them?"

John said, "Sure, I can fix them," and he did. Quite a few were acting up, with pulled ribbons or bent keys. John knew typewriters inside and out from his time in England when he had worked as a typewriter mechanic in his spare time. The girls were all friendly with him again, and he was enjoying the moment when Miss Avery showed up. "I want you to do this, too!" she said, waving something in the air.

The girls' eyes were focused now on the both of them, and Miss Avery just glanced around at the girls with her "stern look" and they all went right back to their jobs. John walked casually away, saying over his shoulder, "I've got a lot of passports to check and places to be." He stopped then and looked at her, "You've got your job to do and I've got mine." She didn't like it of course and turned to stomp quickly in the other direction.

John and Miss Avery had a number of run-ins after that. She was from a very upper crust background and had grown up in Vermonsy in the east end of London. She was very proud of that fact and, when she used to phone home, she would become even more top hat and that aura of snootiness would linger on her for a while. The office staff at the consulate was constantly increasing in numbers as the passport applications multiplied.

One of the new young secretaries brought in was Miss King, and she instantly began to get friendly with John. Her flirtatious behaviour was very obvious. None of the other girls in the office were ever as kind to him as she was. It was never anything serious however, as Miss Avery would not have allowed it. Still, John couldn't help but dream about her on occasion, as she really was a sight for sore eyes. Miss King was very beautiful, a petite girl with bobbed blonde hair, who spoke perfect German. She was of Norwegian nationality and had an energy and liveliness about her that was contagious. Everyone liked her and she was very good at her job, which was appreciated. Her duty was to check and type every application for a visa, and after she had received it, she would pass it on to John or any other clerk who was on duty. They would then countercheck this, verifying all the visa applications. In particular, for persons who "Did Not Intend" to return to Germany. This also applied to all German nationals, irrespective of rank or position. Miss King was exceptionally nice to John, and they used to do little favours for each other in the office.

"Are you busy, John," Miss King asked, at the same time knocking on his open door and then barging right in. "How are you today?"

"Fine, and yourself," he said, smiling back.

"Good thanks. Hey, I heard there's another party tonight upstairs. Are you going?" she asked bluntly.

"No, I never get invited," John said in a huff. "And you?"

"No, me neither; I am too new, they tell me, but I think it's because I'm not from Cambridge, and I'm not part of their little club." She smirked at John and shook her hanging head. "I was wondering if you would fix my stapler; it's jammed," she said, with her eyebrows raised high and her sweet round mouth begging please, without actually saying it. "And I'll get you a cup of coffee, or would you like tea?"

"Yes, tea would be nice," John muttered, picking up her stapler and instinctively without even looking, he knew that Miss King was undoing her top button right at the neck, which had looked uncomfortably tight. When Miss King returned, she quietly closed the door behind her, and John instantly stopped what he was doing. He thought she might have a cup for herself and wanted to talk, but she just put the one cup down. "Thank you," he said curiously. "What are you up to?" Miss King jumped up a little to sit on the desk, her skirt lifted up to a dangerous point for on-lookers with the top of her stocking showing a hint of lace against her skin. John instinctively reached for it and stopped himself, looking at her — with caution on a thread.

"You're very naughty, aren't you," he said cheerfully.

"Not really," she replied innocently. "I just don't like the German boys. I'm scared to go out sometimes."

"That's probably for the better anyway," John said, as he reached around both sides of her hips and with one arm under her legs, gently lifted her off the desk with ease. "I wish we were somewhere else right now," he said, giving her a little kiss on the cheek, "but I have to work now."

John was very worried about losing his job. The no sex rule, even within the consulate, was taken very seriously. It was completely frowned upon and would not have been tolerated. One of them would have been sent back to England, if they had been caught.

***

The magnificent party hall upstairs was designed almost like an oversized flat and was fully equipped with all the amenities to make it really comfortable for entertaining. There was a large dance floor in the middle made of polished pink granite, with little groupings all around of soft plush, gold-coloured lounge chairs surrounding their individual little tables. John became so curious about the parties upstairs that it drove him to stay on sometimes in the evening to see what trouble he could get into. Alfred was always there, and they quite often sat together having a drink and a smoke while watching the people come and go through the upper window. One night he saw Captain Canaris and his wife attend and on the same evening he recognized Richard Tauber, the well-known opera singer whom he had met on the train and who was now singing more in England than he was at home. John was really jealous and even tried to get in once to see him, but even in his best suit, they treated him like poison and shooed him away. He knew there probably was a good reason they wouldn't let him in. Sometimes the weekend parties got quite rough and rowdy. It was obvious they had a good time, as witnessed by their condition the following day.

On occasion John was sent to pick up supplies for the consulate, and so he went to Potsdamer Platz, a fabulous shopping area in the heart of Berlin. It was one of the biggest thoroughfares, full of shops large and small, and Berliners went there regularly. Potsdamer Platz had quite a few small English shops that John would always frequent. He used to smoke a pipe and a cigar in those days. Cigars were cheap in Germany, and you could buy 50 or 60 cigars in a bundle for two marks. Of course, getting English tobacco was quite a problem, and John used to normally buy it at one particular store where there was a special chap whom he got to know a little.

Potsdamer Platz was always exciting, a very pleasant place with its big department stores. Lever Brothers had a shop there selling Sunlight soap and on the outside was a enormous painted sign that read, "Believe in Sunlight."

Many of the roads converged to the middle, like the spokes on a wheel, with a policeman standing there to guide the traffic. They had no signal lights in those days, and John used to make a practice of walking straight in front of where the trolleys had their stop; he knew exactly where it was, and the policeman would have to stop all the traffic so he could go through. John thought that was quite the fun thing to do.

The buses roaring through the Platz were also worth noting. They were great big buses, so broad that if you didn't look out, they'd knock you over when they turned a corner and you were on the sidewalk. The buses in those days were all wooden buses, with wooden seats – not very comfortable.

On his way home, John would quite often stop in at the Adlon, the world famous Hotel Adlon, that is – where it was common to see someone famous entering the huge building or walking down the spectacular marble staircase into the grand lobby with its extravagant arched ceilings held up by statuesque pillars. The luxury and celebrity status made the Adlon Hotel a popular spot for journalists as well, which had been another of John's previous occupations before attaining his engineering degree, so he felt right at home in the lobby, blending in quite well. He particularly enjoyed the American Bar in the hotel, where he could smoke his cigar and drink his beer in peace while reading the newspaper. As John sat there one day, he could see Joseph Goebbels, the newly-appointed Nazi Propaganda Minister, also sitting in the room, in a dark corner right next to his table. Just like John, he was smoking, drinking, and reading his papers. John easily recognized him from the newspapers and the rallies, with his unusual bulbous-shaped head and the curiously brilliant look about his face. Joseph Goebbels had made a big splash as of late, particularly with the burning of the books – one of his first official acts in which the newspapers had actually made it sound like it was the right thing to do.

As Goebbels stood up to leave, John looked up and could see him putting on his coat and his famous hat. His favourite little dog was also with him and was pulling on the lead, undoubtedly the reason for his quick departure. As he went by, John scrambled to his feet as if surprised to see him there and quickly introduced himself. "Dr. Goebbels, it's such a pleasure to meet you," John said.

"Well, thank you," Joseph Goebbels said very politely, a little taken back. "And who are you?"

"Oh, sorry, I'm John Harrington. I am honoured to meet you," he said, rather flustered, not knowing what he was doing and just hoping to make a good impression so that he might get some information from him one day. He was going to say that he was a reporter or journalist before he blurted out, "I work at the British Consulate." John realized instantly that Goebbels might think he meant the British Embassy, which was actually right next door, and then it would have made sense to see him there. But that was all right with John, as he was not prepared to talk with this important and corrupt man that day, but was just playing it by ear.

"Oh," Goebbels said, nodding and smiling, a little crooked slash out of his large, normally emotionless mouth. "It is nice to meet you. Do I detect a German accent?" Goebbels asked curiously. "Are you from here?"

"No, but that's amazing," John said, and meaning it. "You have a very good ear; my mother was German." Goebbels lifted his eyebrows and waited for more. "And her family was from Berlin," John continued.

"Well, isn't that interesting," Joseph Goebbels said in perfect English, which caught John's attention. "Well, good day to you," he then added with a nod of his head while his little dog was pulling him towards the door.

John's language skills got him in and around a lot of places, and they opened many doors for him, such as this. He certainly didn't tell Joseph Goebbels any of the details – that his mom was a drinker, a chubby woman who used to send him to the off-licence with a jug to have it filled with beer. Now here he was, 25 years later, in beautiful Berlin, and a walk in the spectacular Rose Gardens on a Sunday afternoon could never go amiss.

Pre-war Germany in general was a very beautiful country. The rose gardens in every city were well cared for, so much so, that it was assumed that one would not smoke while in the gardens, and it was considered almost a crime to attempt to pick a leaf or a flower. The gardens were very well tended, not a loose leaf or petal was to be seen, truly German style. All the cities were proud of their rose gardens. Another sight was the Sieg Allee, Victory Lane. On each side of Victory Lane were stone benches, each one adorned with a different stone figure of a Greek goddess or god. It was a long pathway and very impressive. Here the elite of Berlin and other cities met. Husbands and wives would stroll along the paths wearing the season's new fashions and with the officers in full uniform. On the roadway could also be seen cavalry officers brilliantly attired, riding their steeds. No other traffic was allowed.

Early one morning at the consulate, John heard a little tap on his door, and he looked up to see the prettiest woman he had ever seen. The way her shoulder-length, blonde hair framed her perfectly innocent face took John's breath away. Her tall thin body and her incredibly long legs ended at the sexiest of high heel shoes, and her burgundy dress suit was stunning, the way it fit every curve and was adorned with a white fur half-jacket and gloves that were obviously expensive. John just stared at her until she began to squirm a little, "Hallo," she said.

John jumped up clumsily and semi-bowed to her, as he introduced himself as if she were a princess and then invited her into his office, motioning for her to sit in one of the comfortable leather chairs. "How may I help you," he stammered out, as if his tongue had suddenly swollen twice its size.

"I am Dr. Ilse Liebert," she smiled at John to see if there was any reaction, but there wasn't. "I have a daughter living in South Africa, whom I urgently need to go see," she said. "I have applied for a visa to visit her," she stated, gazing at John with the deepest, most seductive eyes he had ever seen. "But I have not heard back yet, and it has been almost a month."

John was overwhelmed by her beauty and found himself greatly distracted. He was admiring the small burgundy and white cap that matched her exquisite outfit, when suddenly he realized what she had said and, with a concerned look on his face, he replied, "To travel to South Africa is a very complicated matter." He went on to explain, "You see, I can only give you a visa to England; I can't get you the rest of the way," he said routinely, as he had many times before. "But there might be a way," he said in a hurry. With a comforting smile, he continued, "Leave it with me, and I'll see what I can do."

"Thank you so much," she said with a look of satisfaction on her face, as if she was used to getting her way. As Dr. Liebert was leaving, she turned back to look at John, "My father and I are having a dinner party tonight. Would you like to join us?" she asked him, with a little glimmer of genuine intrigue in her eye that was impossible to refuse.

"I don't think I…" he said hesitating as if he was stung by cupid's arrow itself. "Oh, well, yes, I will come, thank you, I would be honoured," he said with sudden enthusiasm.

"Seven o'clock then, I'll hope to see you," Dr. Ilse Liebert said, as she wrote her address down.

In a bit of a daze John whispered back, "That would be delightful."

Dr. Liebert seemed to be a "Lady of Means," which of course meant she might be Jewish. It turned out she was a doctor of literature. John never discovered just what kind of a doctor that was or what she did for a living, if anything. Around this time, doctors of all kinds were "ten a penny." After she left, John did a quick check to see the status of her application, and everything looked fine. There should have been no reason that she was refused. It was not the British Government that had turned down the visa and so he knew he would have to look a little deeper.

He discovered her family was quite well-off, and well spoken of, in Berlin. They owned many luxury apartment buildings and had numerous shares in local factories. John went to the party that night, wondering the whole while what he was going to tell Captain Haysley. It was just a short walk, very nearby on Kaiser Allee. This was a lovely district where the wealthy Jewish people lived and also many high officials of the German government. Most of the families in this very nice neighborhood had their own swimming pools and decorative yards with large garages. The majority of the rich Jewish people in Berlin lived in this district.

As he entered the front door, John was greeted by the beautiful Dr. Liebert. "John, you made it, how fabulous," she said taking his coat and giving it to the butler with a smile. She grasped one of his hands and cupped it into both of hers, gently blowing on it, as if to warm it up. "Come on in and let me introduce you. This is my father, Eric Liebert."

"Herr Liebert," John said shaking his hand.

"And this is my little brother Herwig," she said, introducing him to a very tall lanky teenager.

"Hello, Herwig, it's nice to meet you," John quickly said as Ilse was pulling him away.

"John, this is our neighbour, Herr Wolfgang Berhandt and his wife Maddie, and their three children are here somewhere, too," she said looking around with no success. They shook hands and together they all peered out of the window to see two girls and a little boy playing with the Lieberts' miniature schnauzer Schotzie. Quite a young puppy still, her grey and white fluffy fur had not yet been trimmed and her back end was happily swaying back and forth before she flipped over onto her back, in hopes of a tummy rub, exposing a spotted fuzzy stomach.

"Isn't that cute," Maddie commented, almost tearing up and looking around for a similar response from the others that never came.

"Can I get you a drink, John," Ilse's father asked him. "Do you have a preference?" He motioned towards the bar, with a complicit smile and one eyebrow raised. John hadn't noticed it yet, but Herr Liebert's bar was enormous, with three rows of glass shelves displaying a fabulous selection of bottles and with a giant decorative mirror behind them all making it look twice as big.

"Well, isn't this just the bee's knees," John said happily walking over towards the bar with Ilse's father. "You have everything here!"

Herr Liebert was quite proud of that. "It's hard to get all these liquors right now, no? But I have special connections," he said, with a little grin. "There I have bottles of rum from the Caribbean, many different kinds, and here we have brandy," he exclaimed, while swirling the brandy around his glass. "That's my favourite; I have four different kinds from France and Belgium."

"That is very impressive," John said, with a sheepish grin, "Have you got beer?"

"Have we got beer? Of course, we have it all," he said, as he handed John a beautifully wrapped cigar, "Zigarre?" It was a real treat to be at such a first class party.

There seemed to be no shortages here in the Kaiser Allee, and it turned out that many of the residents were now having these lavish house parties and socializing in their own neighbourhoods, especially the wealthy Jewish people. One of their guests was studying to be a lawyer and another guest was a banker, but the most interesting of them all, John thought, was Herr Berhandt, who turned out to be a draughtsman. He was unlike John in many ways, the most obvious being the way his wrinkled ill-fitting clothes sat on his extremely thin body, and it was also obvious even behind his distractingly crooked glasses that he was unshaven. That was something John would never do, appear unkempt at a party, yet they got along marvellously.

"Where do you work out of," John asked him nonchalantly later in the evening.

"I work on Bendler Strasse in the German War Office, and yourself?" he asked.

John looked surprised and said, "I work right near there, at the British Consulate on Tiergarten Strasse."

"Oh, you are British, how wonderful. I wish we had your government," he said very seriously. "It is so horrible here, this damn Hitler and his national socialists, they'll be shooting us next, it's terrible."

"It is horrible," John shook his head in agreement and took a sip of beer out of his delicate long-stemmed glass. "We'd like to have him out of there, too, and his thugs, but there's not much we can do."

"Well, if I can ever be of help, you just let me know," Berhandt said. "I mean it too; I worry a lot about this Hitler and how safe my children are going to be here."

"Well, thank you," John replied, raising his glass to him. "You never know when I might need a good draughtsman."

Soon everyone had left the party except Ilse and John, and her brother Herwig, who now had an undone tie dangling around his neck and a big red kiss mark on his cheek.

"Well, I guess I should be off as well," John said as he got up.

"Are you sure you won't stay for just one little nightcap," Ilse asked desperately. Herwig took the hint and said, "Well, I'm off to bed now. You two be good," and laughing he added, "Good night, John, it was nice to meet you."

Ilse was finally ready to relax, and it was the first time all night as John had been watching her closely. "You have been a wonderful hostess, and you have such a beautiful home," he said, shaking his head in disbelief. "And, what a wonderful meal, the best I have had in ages."

"Thank you," she said modestly and handed him a small glass of brandy filled nearly to the rim. Her hand touched his as they met the glass together, and a little spark of electricity almost made her drop it, but John's quick reflexes jumped in. They sat and talked for a few hours and got along very well together. Ilse was not only gorgeous but also very interesting.

"Were you born here?" John asked her.

"Oh yes," she said, "I was born and raised here in Berlin, and I don't really even like to travel. I have everything I need here; I love my Berlin."

"But what about your daughter in Africa," John asked.

"She has gone to school there and lives with her father, but we're not married."

"Oh," John said and thought to leave it at that for now. At this time of the evening, John found himself completely overwhelmed with her beauty and was having a hard time containing himself. "I have to go now," he said, rising from the couch rather awkwardly, the brandy starting to go to his head.

"I have a flat we could go to," Ilse suggested eagerly. "I have a car too. We could be there in seconds."

John replied reluctantly, "No, I am so sorry; I would really love to, but I just cannot tonight.

Ilse knew when to stop pushing and silently helped him find his coat and put it on. "Do you like the cinema? Would you like to go to a cinema with me, John, next week?" She paused hopefully, waiting for an answer. "Come with me Johnny, please," she said holding his arm. "There's a picture playing in Cheshire."

John raised her hand and kissed it, "Yes, I would be honoured to take you to the cinema next week, but for now, it must be good evening." It was emotionally painful when John separated their hands with a tug, as if magnets had stuck them together.

Captain Haysley called John into his office early the next morning. "I hear you were partying with some Jewish people last night."

"Yes, I was, but how did…?" John replied, before Captain Haysley cut him off laughing.

"Thomas told me," he said laughing even louder. "There are no secrets in here. So, how did it go? Did you learn anything interesting," Captain Haysley asked, pointing over to the wall, "Coffee!"

John looked over and saw a brand new coffee steamer on another new shelf, with a few cups and a little bowl of sugar. "That's incredible," he said, jumping out of his seat and looking it over.

"Well," Haysley said, "how did it go?"

"Oh, it was really nice," John said, "They were really nice people, very polite, perfectly normal, no need to worry there. I did meet an interesting man, Wolfgang Berhandt, a draughtsman for the war office. I think he might be useful."

"Check him out," Haysley replied, savouring another sip of his precious coffee. "I heard this girl of yours is quite the looker."

"She's not my girl, I am just being friendly with her," John began to explain.

"It's okay, it's okay, relax. I just want you to be careful — watch out you don't get yourself in real trouble."

John looked at him inquisitively, "I did think at one point what a fine contact she would have made for us. You know she speaks many languages – French, Dutch, Russian, Ukrainian, Afrikaner, English ..." he optimistically said, but already realizing it could never be.

"No, no," Captain Haysley replied, "she is a wealthy Jewish person, and they are under too much pressure right now; it would be too obvious."

"Well, do you think we can get her a passport to leave Germany for a visit in South Africa?"

"I'm not sure," Haysley replied while nodding his head, "But, yes, of course, we'll see what we can do about that, I am sure it is possible."

The following week John was eager to go to the cinema, and as he lifted the unusually heavy, solid brass lion's head door knocker at Ilse Liebert's home, it slipped out of his hand with a loud clang against the gigantic arched door. Ilse opened it and quickly grabbed him by the tie and pulled him in. It was obvious then that she did not want just a friend but a sleeping partner. That was all it took and there were no words; nothing could have stopped the animal magnetism they shared as she wrapped her long legs around him.

They went to a lot of movies after that and quite often they were just a little late. In those days, to visit the cinemas was an education in itself. Ilse just loved to go and would normally drive them in her automobile, a Maybach-Zeppelin. It was a huge, opulent machine, seagreen with black fenders and a roll-down roof. Maybechs were very popular at the time, for those who could afford them.

One picture they saw that John really enjoyed was called The Scarlet Pimpernel, about a spy. Also there were the controversial but very well-attended movies such as The Ringer by Edgar Wallace and Die Hexe, (The Witch). The cinema was very popular in the thirties, and it was always a packed house. Ilse and John used to chuckle and be amazed at the comments that people would make throughout the film. They would yell and scream or boo or cheer; it was really incredible.

On the way out one day someone yelled at John, "She's a Jewess. What are you doing with her?"

John was shocked, and it really hurt Ilse's feelings, even though it was true.

"Why should that matter so much?" she said through her tears. "How do they even know, John," she cried out, as she started up her Maybach.

"It's your wealth," John replied, as he looked at her sympathetically. He knew it was not her physical appearance that made them think she was Jewish, because she actually looked quite Aryan, a real blonde bombshell, but it was her clothing and her furs that gave her away.

Sinister thoughts were going through John's mind now, and he knew they would have to be more careful from now on, just as Captain Haysley had warned. They would always have to be looking over their shoulders, watching out for the Brownshirts.

Ilse Liebert still wanted a visa to visit her daughter in South Africa and was missing her terribly, and John was still trying to get it for her, but he couldn't at first. One could not get a visa from Germany direct to South Africa. For one reason, the German government had to have full information about how much money a person was taking out of Germany. The passport office in Berlin could only issue a transit visa to England for the person. One would then have to obtain a visa from the British government to go on to South Africa. Rather complicated, but not impossible. However, Ilse had Jewish parents, and so she was not able to obtain a German passport at this time, primarily because of their wealth. They would not issue her a passport unless she gave them basically everything she owned, outright. She would not even consider doing that, and so John kept trying to see what he could do for her.

On the weekends, if John wasn't going out with the other fellows from the office, he would go and see Ilse. They'd drink bottles of liquor from her dad's bar, bottles of brandy and bottles of rum. They used to sit and drink until the early hours, and then John would get up and say, "No, I've got to go."

She lived quite nearby, just behind John's place, and he used to enjoy walking, but every time she'd say to him, "Stop the night," John would always droop his head, saying, "No."

"I'll give you my key," she'd persist.

"No," he would always have to say as he kissed her goodnight. She tried her best to keep him there overnight, but no, he just couldn't risk it. All he could think of was Captain Haysley saying, "You shouldn't get too close."

Chapter 18

BERLIN 1933
THE ENIGMA MACHINE

Upon reporting to Captain Haysley after the weekend, John's train of thought was sent off in another direction when Haysley asked, "Your land-lady is Mrs. Hammersmitz, is she not?"

"Yes, Anna Hammersmitz," John replied hesitantly, with a confused look on his face. "She is working as a night cleaner in the War Office building," Haysley was reading aloud from a report. John nodded yes, still confused and now becoming worried for Anna's safety. He had grown quite fond of her; she was such a nice old lady and the Hammersmitzs treated him like a son.

"We are trying to find out about this particular machine they have in there right now," he said, looking up at John. "The Enigma Machine, they call it; have you heard of it?"

"Oh, yes," John answered quickly. "I've read all about the cipher machines."

Haysley's eyes were piercing right through John's inner fear for Anna, as he spoke, "The men are being briefed on it this afternoon, and I want you to attend," he stated. "That's an order. Find out anything you can about it; apparently it's a new version again, so get pictures if you can – heck, get a machine if you can." Haysley sat back and struggled to relight his cigar butt, which had shrunk down to only an inch or so. "This is top priority; I want this to be your main job until we get some results. Everything else is to come second, got that," Haysley said, getting louder with each word. "These orders come straight from the top!"

"Yes, sir," John answered, already contemplating his next move. "We are having a briefing this afternoon at one o'clock, and I want you and all the other clerks and agents to be there. Perhaps together we can find a way to get our hands on one of these decoding machines."

As the agents gathered, the discussion had already begun and many ideas were being explored. One of the new men, Robert, was informing them of what he knew, "It was the German manufacturers who have named it 'Enigma.' It's a secret writing machine that scrambles the words of a message, so that only those informed of the codes can understand it. It looks like an old-fashioned typewriter with an awkward attachment underneath, where the drums roll around to change the letters."

Robert continued with his report, "This new enigma machine is a really good model. They had them here in Germany before this, and they were common in the United States too, but now they are all out of date. All we really need to know is the principle of how they work. If somehow we could get one, or at least find out the number of springs and rolls and the number of taps and everything in it, that would be a start."

Thomas continued for him, "There have been quite a few different decoding machines over the years. Our British intelligence had them in the first war, but these are the newest and are far more advanced cipher machines that what we are used to. They have been updating them every few years." He took a deep breath, "And now this latest, the Enigma, has become the most advanced version to be used by the Nazis.

There was an awkward silence.

"I might be able to get into the government offices at night," John said reluctantly. "But I'm not sure yet."

"Well, just see what you can do," Thomas told him. "But keep Haysley in the loop, and let him know how it's going – and for god's sake, be careful man.

"It turns out Phil here is able to get into the cadet school where they are training for communications, but he is not sure if they have an older version or if it's this new model Enigma, so I want all of you to be extra careful," Thomas said again, filling his cheeks with air and unknowingly making a funny face as he let it out. "As for me," Thomas continued to explain. "I am off to Poland to the plant where we think they are assembled and see what I can dig up there. That's all now, good luck, men."

Walking home, John was in turmoil. Should I attempt to do this? What about the dangers to poor Anna? No, I have to, he thought, but only if I can do it safely. As he opened the large main door to the block of suites, he could see that his landlord's door was open as usual, and he could hear Anna and Horst Hammersmitz talking. He didn't even want to talk to them right now, but he knew they were waiting to see him go by their door and so he walked slowly, not looking their way until Anna called out to him. "Hallo, John, how are you tomorrow," she said, very proud of her English. John flashed her a big smile; she always tried to speak a little bit of English and it always made him chuckle inside, at how it was always just a little wrong. Some nights they sat together and he would teach her new words, but her husband Horst thought it was a waste of time and usually turned the radio up louder to drown them out. "Could you help me for a second?" Anna asked John, who stopped in his tracks and then quickly turned back into their flat.

"What is it," John asked, now directly in front of her. "Would you mind terribly to move this table for me," she said with longing eyes, "I hurt my back at work last night moving this huge cabinet and now I am in so much pain." John moved the table with ease and remarked, "Anna, why do you not take some time off? Good grief, you must rest after an injury like that."

"Oh no, I'm okay," she said, with a big sigh. "I'll be fine. They took my helper away and now there is just me. He was Jewish, you see, and they didn't want him working there. Now I have no helper." She shuffled around, "Well, I don't really need one except for the heavy moving; he was good at that." John could not believe his ears; what a good opportunity this could be.

"I could help you move things," he said.

"Oh no, you are too busy. I couldn't put you out like that."

"I don't mind," said John, "I'm a night owl anyway, and besides I have a few holidays right now." He shook his head. "No, no, I cannot bear to think of you moving things on your own, and with a sore back. At least I can come and help you do that, until you can get someone else."

So, that very night, John went to work with Anna and exactly four more times after that until he felt he could no longer risk it. The sentinel or guard on duty never once questioned Anna about her companion in the dirty overalls. Once he was in, it was easy to move around the building, first helping Anna shift furniture and then fetching coffee in the lunchroom, which gave him an excuse to sneak away. John was able to take pictures of the Enigma machine and count all the parts and make drawings as best he could, and there were a few other interesting things he saw there in the war office that he was able to report on. John knew that, if he'd have been caught, he'd have been shot and that could easily have happened.

On his last visit, he saw an office with the name W. Berhandt on the door, and he wondered if this could be Ilse's neighbour whom he had met at her house, the skinny man with the crooked glasses. If so, this could be his way out. He feared for Anna's safety and decided it was far too dangerous to continue this charade, even though she didn't know it. John asked Ilse outright one night, "How would I meet up with Herr Berhandt again?"

"Oh, he usually stays home in the evenings, but sometimes he goes to the Carlton English Club on Martin Luther Strasse," she replied, "Do you want to go there tonight?"

"Very well," John answered, even though the Carlton Club was not really one of his favourite haunts, but to follow a lead it was well worth it and, to his joy, he was able to have a successful conversation with Berhandt.

Herr Berhandt now had a big wad of glue on one corner of his crooked glasses and, even with his slightly receding hairline, you could see he was still quite a young man, who obviously loved to drink and smoke, but only when his lovely wife Maddie was not watching. Normally a quiet man, he would get louder as the night drew on. Yet even then, he was still brilliant in many respects, as well as being an easygoing and eager to please sort of fellow.

When John asked him about the Enigma machine, he was more than happy to get drafts for him. He used to personally make up really nice plans of the Enigma especially for John, and then John would have them sent back to England through the diplomatic bag, and that's how it was done.

Chapter 19
THE NEIGHBOURS

John was so thankful that Anna and Horst were no longer in any danger, not from his actions at any rate. He was extremely careful about the espionage and would have been horrified if anything had happened to them. They had no children at home, but they had two sons training for the military. One of them, Hans, was in training for the German Air Force and they were so proud of him. They were true Nazis in every sense of the word.

Captain Haysley was very happy with John's results on the Enigma. "Good job, man," he stated, while pouring two little glasses of sherry to toast him. "Let's hope our good fortune and your wiliness continue."

"I have other news too," John said, excitedly. "I saw Herr Goering at the Carlton Club last night and, when I asked the waiter, he told me that was his favourite place and he goes there all the time."

"Well, isn't that interesting," Haysley smiled even more. "Good, John, very good." Captain Haysley took a big swig of his sherry and braced himself on the floor. "We may very well be in need of your guile sooner than we thought," he said looking up. "I read today that Hitler withdrew from the Versailles disarmament pact. You see, we were right and Churchill is right, this guy Hitler wants a war.

"Your lady friend is lucky her money is tied up in buildings and shares. If it was cash in the bank, she might be in big trouble. We have just found out that one of the wealthiest bankers right here in Berlin was secretly sent to a concentration camp. The charge was listed as offending a German National girl."

John continued to be cautious, and a few weeks later his landlord Horst Hammersmitz in the suite below him asked "Would you like to go the Russian nightclub with Jacoby and myself on Friday?"

"Yes, I would love to," John rapidly replied, as if the opportunity would fade if he didn't. He was always anxious to get out and about, to see more of the sights that Berlin had to offer, and the Russian club was amazing. "What time shall we leave?" John asked, in anticipation.

"Mr. Jacoby likes to leave at 5:45 sharp. Be at the front door, and he will drive us," Hammersmitz replied.

Everything was changing now in the beautiful city of Berlin. John had to be considerably more vigilant everywhere he went. Rules were not to be broken, but it was their own lives at stake if they were. Nobody really knew what to expect or how to react.

Herr Jacoby and his wife, who lived in the suite above John, had a business as dealers in new and secondhand furniture at a store on Budapest Strasse. It soon became a custom of John's whenever possible to go out with Mr. Hammersmitz and Mr. Jacoby on Friday evenings. Their wives never joined them. They went to various nightclubs, but the Russian club was their favourite. It was just out of this world, a very tightly knit club, yet it was friendly. They would give John the evil eye when he entered, until Mr. Jacoby would routinely introduce him saying, "This is Johnny." Then it became entirely different and the owner would lean in for a big hug, shouting "Johnny, Johnny, how are you keeping now?"

As a member, as soon as you entered the club, you were handed a bottle of vodka and you were expected to drink it, and you were always invited to join the band and sing, which John enjoyed a lot. The band consisted of both male and female players, and were they players! It was always a fun evening, with anything you wanted to eat or drink. And everything was first class. They often did not know what time they arrived back at their apartments, but they would get home contented with the world and everything in general. This night was no different, and they returned as usual feeling no pain and retired for the night or day as it were.

Early the next morning, John was awakened by a policeman at his door. He stood there in his housecoat while the young officer in his new black uniform asked him, "Sir, do you know the tenants above and below you?"

John said, "Yes, as friendly tenants, but why?"

"Well," the policeman said, and these are the exact words translated. "They could not have been very friendly because Hammersmitz went upstairs and removed Jacoby's head!"

John was dumbfounded and didn't know what to say, and so he said nothing. The policeman said, "Sir, do not worry, it will be taken care of; he was only a Jew."

The next day the Jacobys' suite of rooms was empty, and that was that.

Apparently Horst had just found out that Jacoby was Jewish and had been told by the party what he had to do. The Nazis didn't like Jacoby for some reason, but John thought he was a really nice fellow. It seemed to John there was a trait in the makeup of some German people. One moment they were your friend and later, well, just ruthless. One had to see these things as they happened to believe that they really did happen. John was changed deeply after Jacoby was murdered, as if the war had now begun in earnest. He never went to that Russian club again and he never forgave Horst, or spoke to him ever again.

Jacoby's murder was a horrible shock for John, and he was shaking a little as he sat with Captain Haysley the next day, who was also worried as to what he should do about it. "He was killed; they cut his head off," John said in anguish. "He was my friend. I used to go into Jacoby's warehouses on Budapesta Strasse when I first got here, just to look around. They had a big factory and store where they would sell the furniture, but that's all they did. There was nothing clandestine. Jacoby's father was always there and he was just the same as him." John finally took a breath, winding down, "Just like him, a proper little Jew he was." John wiped a tear from his face without letting the Captain see him, "His wife was German, too, but she wasn't Jewish and she had a son from that marriage, and now, they have all disappeared."

That evening John was still upset and did not want to go home; he just could not believe that Horst would do that to Jacoby, their drinking buddy, but he also knew that Hitler's men could be very persuasive. The British consulate building in Berlin was bustling with delivery trucks and new staff arriving steadily. Captain Haysley was the one centre of stability that John could always rely on. "What do you have on for today, John,"

171

he would ask calmly, while looking over at the new stack of papers on his desk.

"I have a large pile of applications on my desk, too," John said, hoping it was enough to distract the Captain from his pile of unknown paperwork. "And I have a few interviews I was planning on conducting today; I was hoping that Frank could drive me."

"No, Frank is busy today, maybe just stay around here for the day, see who's over at the Press Club later," he said, smiling with the smallest of winks.

"Right," John said as he whirled around on his heels and departed.

The summer's heat was intense this year, but as usual the Press Club was cool and comfortable inside. "Pilsner," John ordered in perfect Berlin German. "Oh, you better make it two. It's darn hot out there." John went to his usual table with his newspaper under his arm and two beers in his hands. There were a few German officers at one table and two very stiff-looking German clerks at another. No one paid much attention to John nowadays; he blended in as a familiar face. His first empty glass, still frosty, hit the table just as Erwin Rommel came in the door. The sweat was running down the side of his cheek as he stopped to regain focus from the bright light outside. As he began walking again, he spotted John and nodded hello. "Ein Bier hier," he said, raising his arm in the air like a school child trying to get attention and then he came over to John's table. "Hello again," he said very politely. "Thank you for helping my friend with his radio. He told me he had offered to pay for it, but you refused."

"It was nothing, just a loose wire," John said. "Please have a seat."

Erwin Rommel sat down and his beer arrived promptly. "It's a good day for a cold beer," John said with a smile and a big sip of his almost empty beer. "I'll have another one Teddy, danke."

"Maybe I'll have another one, too," Rommel said. "It is very dry out there." He looked towards John with a smile, and obviously felt that he had to explain himself. "We have a villa just near here in the Tiergarten, and we are on holiday this week, so I thought I would just walk over here for a quick change and to get away from the heat."

"That must be really nice having a villa here," John said dreamily. "It's so beautiful with all the lush trees and the wonderful birds and animals."

Erwin Rommel nodded. "Yes, it is very nice in the park and my wife loves the flora in the Tiergarten. We walk quite a lot there."

Both men sat in comfortable silence, contemplating the Tiergarten, which, at that time in 1934, was quite a big place – a really lovely park with very old trees and vegetation, some of the oaks known to be 400 years old. There were still many acres of wilderness there, right in the city, and a large part of it had been developed into a magnificent area for recreation and for enjoying nature. The British consulate and German Press Club were located right at the very south edge of the Tiergarten near the middle.

Rommel waved a little circle in the air, indicating to the bartender more drinks. They were both enjoying themselves considerably, knowing they would soon have to leave the cool building behind for the intense heat outside once again. "I see you have an injury. Is that from the war?" Rommel asked curiously.

"Yes, it is," said John frankly. "That's what I got for all my troubles."

"Yes," Rommel said, knowing he had asked enough questions.

"I had nothing like your experiences though," John said with great sincerity and a huge smile. "You're a famous war hero I've heard."

Rommel was taken aback with this praise, and you could see a little blush in his cheeks, the smallest hint of how much he really loved the attention, any attention. Indeed as a young German soldier, Erwin Rommel had also been fighting on those same blood-soaked fields of France as John. He had been there for more than two years and was wounded twice before being sent to Italy. There, he received the legendary Pour le Mérite medal for capturing 8,000 Italians in one day. Officially, the citation read "breaching the Kolovrat line, storming Mataiur and capturing Longarone."

Whenever he was in uniform in Berlin, Rommel always wore the impressive blue and gold Maltese Cross medal on a ribbon around his neck. He was very proud of the medal that very few men were honoured to wear.

Today, however, both men were dressed in casual clothes, and Erwin Rommel had taken off his olive green sport jacket that appeared to be made of brushed silk with almost invisible yellow stripes on it.

"That is a marvellous suit," John said and he really meant it. He wanted to touch the material but thought better of it.

"Thank you," Rommel said very gently, still beaming from the earlier compliment that had made them instant friends. "Yours is very nice too."

"Oh, this is just my work suit, nothing special."

"No, really, this is very nice," Rommel said, reaching over and rubbing the material in John's suit between his fingers with a shy look towards him. "I noticed that you have very smart attire; I appreciate that in a man. A sloppy appearance shows a sloppy kind of man. That's what I think at any rate."

"Yes, yes, I agree," John said.

Just then the door crashed open and in walked a group of men, all dressed in uniforms of different colours and all talking at the same time. Instantly, it was quiet as they had stopped in their tracks while trying to refocus to the new light and trying not to bump into each other. Within seconds they were on the move again, and John noticed one of the men was Wilhelm Canaris, or "K."

How could he ever forget a peculiar nickname like "K.?" And Wilhelm Canaris was a notable figure to look at, in any case. Sometimes, John thought, that K. resembled himself with his high cheekbones and similar hair, except, of course, that John was considerably taller and had no sign of grey in his hair yet. Oddly enough, that similarity in appearance gave the two men a slight bond, a curious interest in each other.

Rommel and John both felt the eyes on them now, from the young new lieutenants and sergeants who had entered with Canaris. John looked into Rommel's eyes, as much as to say, perhaps we should go – but before he could actually speak, Rommel beat him to it.

"When I am in uniform, I am a soldier and my duty is to fight for my country, but when I am a civilian, I must serve humanity," he said with a loud flourish, as if the spotlight of the movie cameras had just focused in on him.

"Well, then, we shall have another," John said, sitting up a little straighter with a grin and moving his newspaper further off to the side, as much as to say work is done for the day. "This is my turn to order a round," and he twirled his hand above his head indicating two drinks to the bartender. They instantly arrived and soon it was the two of them watching the new officers, who were relaxing and taking their hats off to cool down, rubbing their hands over their heads to cool their scalps.

Canaris did not have a hat or uniform on, but was dressed in civilian clothes and looked considerably cooler than the others. He had positioned himself in such a way, with his back to the wall, so that he could always keep one eye on the complete crowd, Rommel in particular it seemed, or at least that's what John thought.

Rommel looked directly at John and very seriously said, "When you are not talking, just listen, because when you are listening, you are also thinking." With a stern nod of the head, he continued, "Speech can hurt you; but with thinking and listening, no one can hurt you."

John truly enjoyed talking with Herr Rommel; he was the man who gave him a different slant on the German people. The Prussian side, a rough and tough group, intelligent and determined, yet with a gentleness that was undeniable. As a youth, Rommel had a young fox as a pet that he used to play with, and he had a couple of dogs too. His youthful friends nicknamed him "The Fox." That may be why, later while commanding in the Sahara Desert he became known as "The Desert Fox."

When Herr Rommel was in Berlin, he wasn't much of a socialite, but he did take pleasure in going to the Kaiser Wilhelm Church. He was very religious, but of no particular denomination. The Kaiser Wilhelm Church was a big church that dominated a square in the centre of town. Inside, there was a spectacular mosaic wall, with a depiction of Queen Victoria amongst other guests, attending the coronation of Kaiser Wilhelm I. This might have been one of the reasons that this church was often called "the English church" among the locals. The minister at the Kaiser Wilhelm Church was called Jacob Strauss, and looked very tall and powerful in his white robes. He was a friendly man, getting on in age and known for sometimes just prattling on. John was sure that Pastor Strauss was Jewish, though he never bothered to check it out. Mr. Strauss, Herr Rommel, and John would often discuss the topics of the day, but one had to be careful what one said, even in the early thirties.

John heard a lot of English on the streets of Berlin. About forty worked at the British Embassy located on Wilhelm Strasse and then in the consulate there were at least forty more. There were also various British and American industries located in Berlin. The Lever Brothers, (the Sunlight Soap people), had a big factory and a lot of English speaking staff. The company that made Persil, the laundry detergent, was located in Berlin as well. The makers of Goldflake and Players cigarettes had factories there and the cigarettes made there were stamped In Deutschland Hagenstuff, or "Made in Germany."

Many people spoke English in Berlin and not just English people. There were still many tourists in Berlin before the war, and John would go into the store to buy cigarettes and tobacco, and he was able to pass the time of day in English with the shopkeepers; it was a real treat shopping at the Potsdamer Platz in those days. The British Consulate office saw its share of English people, of course, and it was always full of interesting people coming and going. Eventually John got to know most of the staff there. Atkinson still kept him supplied with gifts and gadgets, and Captain Haysley still summoned John up daily for their regular update and beverage, usually sherry.

When John arrived in Haysley's office one day, the captain was sitting in his office reading a single sheet of paper held in one hand and carefully balancing a cup of coffee in his other, all the while with his feet up on the desk. "An order has just come down from Captain Foley's office that we are to not be as stringent with the passport applications of Jewish people," he said, looking at John blankly then continued, "Unless they are unusually questionable or suspicious."

"What exactly does that mean," John asked, curiously. "I mean, I let all the Jewish people through already, as long as they are not in the Black Book."

"I think he must mean these questionable ones I have here," Haysley said, shaking his head and patting a pile of papers, almost covering his desk by now.

"Is there anything I can do to help you," John asked sympathetically.

"Don't worry, John, I'll check into this," Captain Haysley said in a low voice. "I think he just wants to make sure we are doing all we can for those poor Jewish people."

Captain Haysley lifted his feet off the desk, spilling a little coffee out of his cup. "So, how was your weekend? Did you meet anyone or see anyone special?" he asked with interest.

"Actually …" John said, as he paced back and forth in front of the coffee maker, longingly looking between it and the Captain.

"Oh, go ahead," Captain Haysley said impatiently.

"I ran into Herr Rommel last Friday at the Press Club, but you were not here when I got back," John said as he fumbled to steam himself a tiny cup of coffee. "I rather like the fellow," John said truthfully. "He seems to be a very delightful person, and we had a good talk this time and shared a few beers."

"Really?" Captain Haysley answered in surprise.

"Yeah," John got all excited suddenly, almost spilling his little coffee. "And Captain Canaris came in with a group of officers while we were sitting there," he said cautiously, "and I got the feeling that Rommel was a little afraid of him, but it was probably just the uniform that did it." Smiling back at the receptive look on Captain Haysley's face, John said, "He's an exceptional listener, Rommel, and a quiet speaker." John took a sip of his coffee, "He seems to be a very private sort of man, and I don't think he'll be sharing any military secrets with me soon, though." John burst into a little chuckle, but the Captain didn't find it very funny. "Yea, I like his company and I think he might like me too. I ran into him again at the English church on Sunday. Can you imagine that?"

"You had better watch yourself," Captain Haysley stood up and wandered around the room, thinking. "Be very careful what you do there, because this is tricky work."

John drained his little cup and jumped up from his chair, "If I do wrong, you just tell me."

Captain Haysley stopped in his tracks and, suddenly almost breathless, he said, "If you do wrong, you won't live long enough for me to tell you."

On the way back to his office, John spotted Miss Avery. She put her nose in the air indicating she didn't want to talk to him. She knew he had been over in the press club and was still mad at him from the day before, when John had specifically gone to visit some people after she had already recommended them. John did that quite often, made his own inquiry. For example, if it was someone that he thought was not where they should be, he would investigate and quite often would be seen leaving the consulate as just an average looking person, or occasionally he could be spotted in overalls slipping out the back door. That was the idea of his disguise — that he could go places where others in the office couldn't go. In this way, he was able to investigate the credibility of many people. Normally he wore a very smart suit around the consulate or at the press club, but that certainly wasn't considered "dressed up" compared to the "stuffy" people in the office with their high collars and their ties and their ribbons.

Officially, the Black Book now had its own room, complete with two men in charge of just that list and its particulars. John would bring his questionable applications to them, and then would occasionally stay to visit with them while they looked them over. He was always looking for an excuse to get outside and meet new people.

Once or twice while he was there, he ran into the adorable and tiny Miss King with her blonde, bobbed hair, who was always trying to do favors for others and these men were no exception.

Can I get you hardworking boys a cup of tea?" She spoke so sweetly that all the men would say yes, even if they didn't want one, just because they wanted to see her come back again.

"Cute little thing, isn't she?" one of men said longingly, and they all nodded in unison, a little mesmerized as they watched the way her high heels made her shapely hips sway back and forth with each step as she left.

Later that evening, John was relaxing in his flat and listening to the radio, when Ilse Liebert called him on the telephone, "Hello, Johnny, would you come with me to the cinema tonight?" she asked hopefully. "There's a flick that everyone is talking about. Please, Johnny, pleeease, I am so lonely."

He was a little tired but that had never stopped him before. "Sure, Ilse, I would love to go with you; I'll be right over." Later that evening they talked and drank until late into the night as they often did. When Ilse's father and brother Herwig were away, she knew she could get him drunk, but John knew just how far he could go without getting caught.

She said to him, "Johnny, I may get you drunk and you will fall asleep, and then I am going to put you to bed, yeah."

Truthfully, he would have loved nothing more than to stay with her overnight, to spend the night and wake up there in the morning, but if the captain were to find out, well, he knew what would happen. Orders were orders. He had to be very careful all the time, because he just never knew who was watching or when.

As he was leaving and standing just inside the door, he gave Ilse a long kiss goodbye and caressed her beautiful slim body from the buttocks up with both hands. They both yearned for more, but it was too late in the evening and John had barely enough control left. As he cupped her perfect face in his hands, she whispered softly in his ear, "Will you come to a party this Saturday? My father is having some business friends and said that Herwig and I could have our friends, too, and make it a real party."

"Of course, I would love to come. What time?" John replied stepping back to think about it, as if the burden of leaving had just been relieved.

"I'll call you on Saturday," Ilse said with a little mysterious twist in her voice.

Chapter 20
CONNECTIONS

Saturday would just not come fast enough this week and John could hardly keep himself at work. The parties over at Herr Liebert's were always exceptional, with great food and conversation.

John had just finished brushing his hair down, the curly ends needing a bit of hair cream as usual to keep them from curling up and exposing the scar on his forehead. He was checking one last time in the mirror when the phone rang. It was Ilse, "Are you ready, Johnny? I'll be right over," she said before waiting for his answer.

"I can just walk over," John said slightly confused.

"Oh, no," she said. "I have something I want to show you first. Besides, it is too busy here with the caterers and Herwig's girlfriend is driving me crazy. I need to get out for awhile."

"Okay, I'll be at the front door," John said bluntly, not liking surprises for the most part.

When she arrived, the car squealed to a stop, and Ilse waited impatiently for John to get in. For the first time he felt uncomfortable with her, a little bit of a kept man sort of feeling, even though that was not the case. Suddenly, he felt a little sorry for himself and hard done by, that he was no longer able to drive his own vehicle. It made his leg ache some, as he crouched down to get in the car.

Ilse leaned over to kiss him, but her lips landed on his cheek as he was still manoeuvring himself in. He smiled back at her with a curious look she had not seen before. "What is it, John, is there something wrong?" she asked very politely.

"Nothing, my dearest Ilse," John replied, "I just worry about you sometimes, with all that is going on here nowadays."

"Oh, don't be worried about me," Ilse said with a huge smile. "I can take care of myself."

"Just where are we going?" John asked firmly.

"I have just bought a new group of suites on Uhlans Strasse, and I wanted to show them to you before the party to get your opinion."

As Ilse pulled in front, John could see the finishing touches had literally just been completed on the incredible new art deco building with many floors of beautiful modern suites, and as they entered number 408 – one of the penthouse suites – John was taken aback with the elaborateness of the interior with its pillars and marble floors. The suite itself had already been furnished with a velvety blue settee and lounge chair. Ilse took him by the hand and led him to the middle of the room. "Well, what do you think?"

"It's very nice," John said, knowing that was a great understatement. "Who are you renting them out to? They're very lucky people." Ilse smiled and nodded in return. "It will make you a pretty penny on the rent, I would assume," John said, wandering off a little to explore more, but Ilse would not let him go.

"I thought maybe you would like this one, John," she said and held up her hand with the key in it. "I want you to have it while you are here in Berlin. I don't need the money and it could be our little getaway."

John was stunned at her generous offer, but closed her hand gently with the key tucked inside. "Ilse, Ilse, I cannot live here. I would lose my job at the consulate, if they knew we were sleeping together, and I could never make you leave here." He shook his head, knowing it was not even a question to consider.

Ilse was looking very disappointed, "I will stay here on my own then; I have decided," she said firmly. "I have to get out of that house. My father is driving me crazy and won't even let me bring my friends over."

"But what about tonight?" John asked.

"The party? Oh, that's an exception, John. I need more fun — I don't like to be so bored," Ilse said, as a little tear ran down her cheek. John took her in his arms and held her tight. They both felt comforted again, as if that was where they had always belonged. They worked their way over to the new chesterfield and cuddled in the most intimate way. This would have to do for now, and both of them knew that even this could not last forever.

The party was in full swing when they returned to her home on Kaiser Allee. They entered quietly, and Ilse disappeared into the little greeting parlour off to the right with John's packages in her arms – a large bag of white sugar and a bottle of French brandy. She was placing them on the side table when her father spotted John in the hallway and rushed over.

"There you are," he said sternly, looking at Ilse and the new gifts she was placing there. "Thank you John, that is not necessary."

"Very welcome," John said meekly, sensing how upset her father was with Ilse for being late.

"You were supposed to greet our guests tonight, were you not?" A little vein on his neck was beating in silent anger. "Where were you?"

"I took John over to see our new apartment," she replied with a smile.

Herr Liebert relaxed, "Oh yes. What do you think, John, aren't they fabulous?" He was ready to celebrate once more, his anger quickly forgotten.

John's expression said it all before his mouth could. "Unbelievable," he said, "extraordinary architecture."

"Would you like to stay in one?" Herr Liebert asked, "They're not spoken for yet."

"Thank you very much, but no. I am very close to work where I am now, and I am quite happy there. Thank you again though."

"Very well, as you wish," Herr Liebert said turning to his daughter. "Ilse, get this young man a drink and I will introduce him around." Herr Liebert motioned with his shoulder for John to follow him, almost spilling his drink at the same time. "I am so glad you made it; some of my guests like the British. Well, all foreigners for that matter. You are British, aren't you, John?"

"Well, I was raised in Australia," John was saying, when Herr Liebert raised his glass in the air and loudly stated: "Everyone, this is John Harrington. He's working here at the British consulate and we have become good friends so make him feel at home. Come, John, and meet Herr Wolfgang Berhandt.

"Yes, hello, we have already met," John said with a smile, "and how have you been?"

"Well, as good as can be expected," Berhandt said, crinkling up his forehead as if in pain. "It's starting to feel like we should leave here and go somewhere where we won't be persecuted, but I don't even know where that would be anymore, and this is my home. I was born here. I would like to stay here." Berhandt appeared thinner than before; the stress was starting to show. "I still have my job for now, but I don't think I will have it for much longer. Already I feel the eyes looking at me and questioning me as to my usefulness just because I am Jewish." His soft voice was growing louder. "Fortunately, I am a great architect so they need me," Berhandt said, before letting out a long laugh, embarrassing to all of those around him. Some of the small crowd stopped to look at him momentarily but were soon absorbed in their own conversations.

Herr Berhandt leaned over and whispered, "You don't think you could get me some of that sugar like you brought here tonight, could you? My wife is a wonderful baker and my two daughters have a birthday coming up."

John instantly replied, "Of course, I will, yes. How can I ever thank you for those wonderful Enigma blueprints you drew up?"

"Oh, I am so glad they were of use to you. They won't let me anywhere near that area any more and there are guards everywhere. Now they have three of us together in this huge room, with all of the maps and plans of the city and all of the underground tunnels and facilities laid out. We have been given a direct order from Himmler himself to make drawings and plans for underground bunkers." Berhandt looked at John very seriously and rubbing his forehead said, "One bunker for each of the different top officials, so that no one will ever know which one Hitler is really in. We are to come up with at least 20 different choices, they said, for his highness to choose his favourites from." Herr Berhandt had a look of disgust on his mouth, like he was going to throw up, but instead he gave an outrageous Nazi salute, swirling his hand in the air, every finger showing a form of disrespect.

"Yow," John said, realizing the implications of such plans.

He was deep in thought when Ilse grabbed him by the arm and pulled on it. "I am taking John away for awhile," she said quietly. The two men nodded at each other.

"Later," Herr Berhandt whispered.

"John, I want you to meet Freddie and Lili Solinger," Ilse said, as she stopped at a handsomely dressed couple. As soon as they turned to face him, John recognized the wonderfully elegant couple from a year previous, when they had briefly met at the Russian nightclub. They stared at each other for a moment, trying to place one another's faces, until Ilse blurted out, "This is Johnnie, my British boyfriend."

John was a little upset by that comment and gave her a discreetly innocent look that made everyone laugh.

The others were instantly curious. "I think we have met before," Freddie said, reaching up to shake John's outstretched hand.

"Yes, very briefly once at Sinyaya Ptitsa, the Russian nightclub," John said. He did not want to remember who had actually introduced them, his neighbour Jacoby who had been beheaded not very long ago. John took the elegant hand that was offered by Lili Solinger and kissed it with a big smile; she was so beautiful with her long brown hair flowing around her shoulders.

"Yes, I think I remember you work for the British Embassy, ja?" Freddie remarked.

"Yes, the consulate actually, I am a passport clerk there, nothing special."

"You are special to me," Ilse Liebert quickly remarked.

Lili appeared quite upset about something and Freddie gave her a reassuring hug with one arm and just then, raised the other arm saying, "Oh, here is my brother Karl. Have you two met before, John? Karl, Karl, come over here."

Karl Solinger entered the room with a presence, a handsome rugged man with defined features similar to his younger brother Freddie. There was a distinct family resemblance. Karl had a serious look about him, as if he was very uncomfortable in a crowd, even with his neighbours and the people he knew. Freddie introduced them.

"Hallo," John said. "It's very nice to meet you."

"I've seen you before at the club," Karl said, a little surprised. "You know Ilse Liebert?"

"Yes, we have known each other for some time now," John answered, suddenly realizing this man also cared deeply for her. "We met at the consulate when she applied for a visa to visit her daughter in Africa."

"Oh, I see," Karl said.

John thought a ping of jealously was rearing its green envious voice. Following in behind Karl was a delicate man with fine bone structure, who was wearing an informal tuxedo from which he bulged just a little. He quietly manoeuvred in close by Karl's side, and Karl uncomfortably moved over to allow him space. "John, this is Dr. Burns," Freddie introduced them, while his wife Lili finally smiled. Ilse Liebert tugged on Karl's sleeve, and they wandered off together towards the kitchen. Both John and Dr. Burns looked with curiosity and longing after their dates who were leaving the room.

"Hello," John said to Dr. Burns, nodding politely.

Freddie winked at John, "Dr. Burns is a very good friend of Karl's."

Lili slugged her husband in the arm instinctively and, along with the shocked look she gave him for his brazen words, that explained a lot to John.

"Dr. Burns is an Englishman, too," Freddie continued. "So you will have a lot to talk about."

John was quite surprised to hear that and questioned Dr. Burns, "Oh, where are you from originally?"

"London," he said, with a very unconvincing British accent that made John realize he was not really from there, but was lying to them for one reason or another. He was just a young fellow and John thought it might have been part of his disguise, a way to hide his sexual preferences. Freddie kept talking, just to interrupt the awkward silence that was approaching, "Dr. Burns is a British agent for a German photographic firm, Kranich of Berlin, and travels frequently."

"Really," John said eagerly, his eyebrows lifting way up. "My father owned a photographic business in Sydney, Australia, when I was a young boy, and he used to travel quite a bit also. What do you do in Britain for them?" John asked curiously.

Dr. Burns explained, "We are importing, from London, a special kind of carbon tissue used in the manufacture of bank notes, postage stamps, and for other commercial use." He hesitated, "We are primarily making postage stamps."

"Yes, this is just what my father did; it's a process well known in Great Britain," John said with great enthusiasm. "Where do you have to get this tissue from now?"

Dr. Burns said, "I get it from this place in England called Ealing."

"Oh, really," John stated, looking toward Ilse and Karl who had rejoined their circle, but now he was more interested in what Dr. Burns had to say. John continued, "They print stamps photographically, you know, even to this day."

"Yes," Dr. Burns said as he smiled at John's expertise, "and we cannot make this tissue in Germany, and so we have to bring it in."

"I know all about that," John beamed excitedly and then he leaned over and shyly asked the delicate Dr. Burns. "Do you think perhaps I could see some of the processes you describe," never thinking in a million years that he would say yes.

Instantly, Dr. Burns said, "Sure, of course. We will do it one day."

Just then Herr Liebert appeared in the doorway leading to the majestic dining room. "Dinner is served," he said with a flourish, and then disappeared again.

Ilse looped her arm in Johns and said, "This way, follow me."

As the fabulous dinner was served, Herr Liebert was sitting at the head of the table with his daughter Ilse on his right and his son Herwig at the other end. "How is that new factory going, Freddie?" he asked.

"We have it all up and running now," Freddie proudly replied. "There are a few new machines we are having trouble with, but generally, we have never been busier."

Herr Liebert looked at John explaining, "Freddie and Karl Solinger have a new contract with the German government to manufacture all the uniforms for the army, navy, and the air force." He took a bite, "Can you imagine that. They own..." he said with a pause, "how many factories do you own?" he asked, but then answered himself before either Solinger brother could get a word in. "They own at least seven big factories, and they employ about 500 men. It is quite a good contract, don't you think?"

"Very good," John said. "I have noticed there are many new uniforms everywhere these days."

Karl, the outspoken and larger framed Solinger brother, interrupted John while angrily looking at his brother Freddie and saying, "But we do not manufacture the civilian uniforms anymore or other government departments, everything is Nazi."

"We don't need to any more, with this contract," his brother Freddie quickly said.

Karl shook his head, "I don't trust this Hitler's army. We are of Jewish extraction, you know," he said bitingly. "They will know that too; they are not stupid."

"We are safe though," Freddie argued. "As long as they need uniforms for the army we will be needed, it's a win, win."

Freddie's wife Lili spoke up now, the most vocal she had been all night, and as the words rolled off her beautiful lips, the whole room was mesmerized. "You are both right, don't you agree, Herr Liebert." She looked right at him. "The Hitler army is very dangerous to us now as Jews, and I know first hand because I have just found out today that my uncle has been killed because of his opposition to the new policies."

There were a few gasps, and "so sorry" echoed around the table. Karl, so boisterous only moments before, quietly said, "My God Lili, I did not know!"

Lili delicately put a hanky to her nose. "But if we support the government and assist their cause, I mean, would it not make sense that the more uniforms we make, the safer we are? Wouldn't it," she looked questioningly at the most senior man there.

Herr Liebert shook his head and spoke loud and clearly, "I don't think the Nazis can be trusted at any rate or at any cost whatsoever." There was silence and he lifted his glass in a toast. "We shall not dwell on that tonight; tomorrow will be earlier enough as it is. Lili, with the greatest respects to your dear uncle," he looked at her mournfully, "now it is time for cake and a brandy, and we shall toast to more peaceful times again." Everyone toasted "To Peace," and with that the topic ended.

The soft notes and familiar rhythm of the "Destiny Waltz" began drifting in from the next room, and John got a shiver throughout his whole body. He sat up bravely and casually wiped a tear from his eye; no one noticed. Little did any of them truly realize just how dramatically their worlds would be changing after this very night.

Chapter 21

NEW FRIENDS

The night of the party at the Lieberts' was June 30, 1934, the night in which Adolf Hitler had ordered the death of hundreds of men, including Ernst Roehm, a long time compatriot of his and leader of the SA. Any adversary still left standing in Hitler's way or hindering his goal of achieving full control over all the armies and police throughout Germany was to be annihilated that evening. It was a night that would live on in history books forever as "The Night of the Long Knives."

The coup on the evening of June 30 had been a well-choreographed scene of murder and mayhem for anyone who stood in opposition to Adolf Hitler, the man to whom the young soldiers were now personally pledging allegiance. And it was Heinrich Himmler's finest hour, when he personally took control and united all of the police forces in Germany under his direction after a night of bloody massacres and quiet shootings all across Germany.

The next day, Himmler could be seen marching with his new police behind him. He was a smallish man, with a constant look of sarcasm on his face behind his peculiar round pince-nez. As the night wore on at the Liebert's house party, John found himself telling Karl Solinger a story about the civilian uniforms. "It has been the custom in the past for people such as myself, living in blocks of apartments, to place our garbage on the sidewalk in front of the block, and on a certain day of the week this would be picked up by two men with a garbage truck. Now, the German government under the Hitler regime has changed all that. "Instead of two men with a truck coming to pick it up, the federal government, not the city, sends two men in uniform. As you know this is important as the uniforms give the men status; they are very official. The two men would then proceed to pick out all metal pieces and bits of tin, and no doubt take them to a foundry where they are to be melted down for making ammunitions and so on."

Karl looked at him with curiosity wondering where he was going with this story. John was getting a little sidetracked, far more talkative than usual. "You may have noticed," he said, "that lately there are no more metal railings of any kind to be seen in Berlin." Literally the only iron railings to be left in Berlin were those in front of the British Consulate on Tiergarten Strasse and the Charlotte Castle and a few churches were also not touched, to prevent pilfering. "I suppose the same thing is happening in other cities." John continued after a sip of brandy, "Following these men are two more men in uniforms with a truck and they proceed to sort out all of the burnable material, to load it up and take it to a furnace. They told me this is used to heat the offices of the government. This is not the end of the garbage collection: two more men come to gather up what remains and take it to the incinerator, and it still does not end there. Two more men come along, also in uniforms, and complete with hose and truck; they proceed to wash the sidewalk clean. Thus we see that the unemployment situation here will be partly solved."

"Yes, isn't that something," Freddie interjected with a laugh. "And there are all these new roads and road workers everywhere lately, have you noticed? What a bother." He looked to John for sympathy. "At least my new Mercedes 170 will not get all scratched up with the new roads."

"That piece of trash," his brother Karl said. "You should see mine, John." John wanted to know much more about their Mercedes, but Ilse yawned a little and suddenly the guests were leaving.

What a wonderful time we have had," Lili said as she gave Ilse a huge hug.

"Please come over to our place soon."

Herr Berhandt cornered John and asked him, "Were you serious about the sugar? Can you get me some, too?"

"Yes, I can," said John. "Could you get me some of those bunker plans?"

Herr Berhandt answered eagerly, "Yes, yes, I will. Where can we meet?" He paused, "I know, how about Tuesday at the Carlton Club? I usually go there after work once a week anyway so my wife will not be suspicious."

"Yes, that would be fine," John agreed.

"Oh, she will be so surprised; the sugar will be a present for her at the same time as it will be for my daughters," Berhandt happily remarked.

"Shall we meet for supper at six?" John said eagerly, and they both agreed.

John was the last guest to leave the Lieberts and was on his way out the door when Ilse held him back. Her brother and father had both gone up to bed, and they were alone once more. "One more little night cap, please, John. The night is still so young," she pleaded. "Well, okay, go on then," he said with a huge smile. "This has been a wonderful evening, you have such wonderful friends."

"Well, thank you," Ilse said as she passed the glass to John. "I have had quite enough of politics for one night though," she whispered, running her fingers gently through his hair and a few barely greased curls popped up. "Why don't we talk about the movies, or better, why don't you tell me more about you, John? I know so little about you; I have so many questions?"

John paused to think for a second and excitedly perked up, "Did I ever tell you about when I left Australia as a boy?"

"No, you didn't," Ilse sighed contentedly and relaxed, easing down onto the chaise lounge, as if it had been moulded after the contours of her body, knowing that John would tell her a story now. She loved his stories.

"I was only nine years old when my parents agreed to send me off to school in England, you know," John said, looking at Ilse and pulling another chair next to hers, just to be close enough to touch her. "My father was living in Sydney, Australia, at the time, and my mother and the rest of the family were living in Fremantle, Australia, hundreds of miles apart, and they rarely saw each other."

"Ah," Ilse said with sad eyes.

John knew he was drawing the story out, but it was still very early in the evening for them, and Ilse looked so sexy and relaxed on the lounge chair that he just wanted it to last all night. He got up to get another drink from the stocked bar. "Can I get you anything, gorgeous," he said, as he began to pour himself a beer.

"Yes, I would love a glass of white wine," she replied. "Go on now, you are leaving Australia for England?"

"Oh, yes," John continued. "The voyage to England was quite an experience, and I wondered what might be in store for me. I don't recall very much about the ports of call, because my head was so full of what was going on around me, meeting people of different nationalities and seeing some place different every day. So many things that I had only heard or read about.

"First, we landed at some island in the Indian Ocean. I was never seasick," John stated proudly, "despite the fact that it became very rough crossing the Indian Ocean. One port of call that I do remember was the Port of Colombo, on the Island of Ceylon. Here one was greeted with the smell of spices permeating the air. At that time, Ceylon – now Sri Lanka – was famous the world over for its tea. That was a lovely place, so different, so new.

"The people were dressed in all kinds of clothing. In Australia, everybody was rough and ready. Here, the merchants were dressed to the nines with funny tall hats, and the docks were filled with Chinese in their particular outfits. There were pomegranates and all kinds of spices and those little things that you grind up, nutmegs. The docks were laden with bags of nutmeg and spices of that sort. Tea, at that time, was packed in huge wooden crates and inside it was lined with lead. These crates were piled high on the dock side."

John looked over at Ilse who was captivated by his story. "I was in a world of wonder. I remember wandering around and talking to the people, and they would tell me all sorts of things. Of course, I didn't know any other languages then – I just knew common Australian and they used to laugh at me because I had an odd accent."

Ilse laughed. "How long were you there?"

"We stayed in Ceylon, oh, two days, while they loaded the silks and furs, tea, spices, all that kind of stuff." John took a sip of his beer, picturing it in his mind. "We also stopped at the Cape of Good Hope on the tip of Africa, and there we were immersed in colourful Africa. We stayed there for two or three days also, to stock up with coal and water because the boats in those days were steam, you know. In the engine room, the glistening steel on the big bars that drove the engines was a sight to see. There was a little fellow there called Harry Smith, but we called him Smithy. He was walking along the gangway pouring oil on the bars from time to time. That was his full time job on the ship."

John let out a huge sigh as Ilse reached for her glass of wine, looking so beautiful and relaxed. He picked up her foot and began to gently rub it as he leaned back in his chair. "Then from there I remember going through the Bay of Biscay, just off Spain. The water was just as flat as a floor, absolutely perfect. You could see the bottom of the ocean, it was so clear. It was supposed to be the clearest water in the world. I've seen the Bay of Biscay when the waves were as high as the roof, but this time it was just calm as could be."

John could see that Ilse was nodding off, so he quietly got up and ever so tenderly placed a woollen throw over her, kissing her forehead and whispering, "I will see you soon, my dearest Ilse," before silently slipping away.

As planned, John met up with Herr Berhandt at the Carlton English Club the following Tuesday. He brought with him a large brown bag with corded handles, the typical shopping bag from one of the Potsdamer shops. Herr Berhandt had a manila envelope stuffed full of paper. "Good evening, John, it's good to see you," he said as he sat down across from him in one of the plush chairs.

"Yes, and to you, too, a good evening, Wolfgang," John replied, staring back down at the menu. "To my delight, they have fresh sole as a special tonight. That's one of my absolute favourites."

"Ah, well done then. I am eager for a martini right now," Berhandt replied, waving his arm to attract the waiter. "Were you able to get me some sugar?" he asked curiously.

Yes, of course, I promised I would," John said with a smile, "two bags of sugar, and I also put in two pounds of fresh butter and a box of coffee."

"Danke schön, thank you so much, now we will have a wonderful party," Berhandt replied enthusiastically. "I got as many copies of the bunkers as I could for you, but nothing much yet as to what has actually been approved for building. I just about got caught taking these drawings out," he exclaimed in astonishment.

"What happened?" John asked, prompting the story out of him.

"Yes, usually I can come and go with no problem, but today I was stopped by a guard at the door and he asked for my papers. He was shocked to learn I was Jewish and he held me back until a senior guard came and identified me. Thank God, they never asked to see inside the envelope, and that first guard was eyeing it up, too. I had my excuse ready just in case," Berhandt's eyes widened.

"Well, that's enough of that," John said point blank. "We cannot take any more chances with you from now on, Wolfgang. This is far too risky. I would never forgive myself if something happened to you."

Berhandt tried to refuse, but John would not let him, saying, "No, you have a family to think of, but don't worry, I will still try to get you supplies from time to time. You just let me know what you need."

As the two men sat enjoying their meals, they could not help but notice all the way across on the other side of the room was Hermann Goering, the famous World War I fighter pilot, acting up and showing off loudly in his usual way. He was strutting around, singing, and lecturing to anyone that would listen.

"He is quite the big fat blob, isn't he, John?" Berhandt remarked in shame.

"Well, he sure is quite the bluffer, that's pretty obvious," John answered with a little more respect.

Berhandt leaned forward to whisper to John, even though no one was near them, "He is out in a different nightclub every night, but the bartender told me this is his favourite haunt — of all things, the English Club." He shook his head, "He's a typical low-type Prussian, don't you think? He has such a big mouth. How do they put up with him, I wonder?"

His rank and uniform have gone to his head, I shouldn't wonder," John said.

Berhandt grimaced, "You just watch, in an hour from now, he will be sound asleep, yup."

"Really," John answered surprised.

"Oh yes, he always falls asleep, and they have to almost carry him out," Berhandt shook his head in dismay. "And this is our new government!"

The men sat in silence for a short while and, suddenly, Freddie Solinger rushed by them, not even noticing in his great hurry to talk to the bartender.

On his way back Berhandt flagged him down and he stopped instantly in his tracks, sitting his bottom half down on the chair.

"Guten Abend. What are you two getting up to tonight?" he asked inquisitively.

"We were just having a meal. Would you care to join us," John replied.

"No," he blurted out. "No, thank you really, I must rush. Lili has invited a few people over for dinner and a small party," he said pausing with a deep breath. "Would you like to join us instead?"

Herr Berhandt smiled back, "Alas, no, I must also head home to the wife, but perhaps John would like to go?"

"Well, John?" Freddie asked. "You are more than welcome; I can give you a lift now. That is if you are ready." There was a little confusion showing on Freddie's face; it was obvious that he was still curious why these two men were dining out together and was seemingly coming to a completely wrong conclusion. He looked directly at John, not wanting to repeat himself but anxious to be on the move again. He almost said, "Well" again, but John spoke up.

"I would love to, if you are sure?"

Freddie motioned him up impatiently.

John looked at Berhandt, "I suppose it would be wise to get a lift with Freddie," he said apologetically. "Do you mind?"

"Of course not, go have fun," Berhandt said with a little wave, showing the back of his hand. "I am done now too and shall be off myself."

They said goodbye and outside John got into Freddie's new Mercedes Benz, an MB 170. It was not a flashy car like his brother Karl's, more on the practical side, but he had hired a driver for the evening on Lili's request. With all the special police around, she didn't want any of her guests having to worry about driving or being pulled over for any reason

The Solingers' home was extremely lavish, and the butler came running when Freddie barged through the front door and went straight in. He slowed once he saw who it was, and with great poise he quietly took their hats and canes.

"This is amazing," John said in wonderment as he circled on the spot to capture the vision of the whole room. Just then Lili met them in the doorway, more beautiful than John had ever seen her before, which was no small feat as she was always breath-taking.

She flew towards Freddie and threw herself around him, "Oh, thank God, you are here," she said in one breath. "Did you get the champagne?"

"Yes," Freddie smiled and laughed at her excitement. "Look who else I found," he said intriguingly.

Lili turned and saw John standing there, "John," she said happily as she rushed over and gave him a hug. "What a wonderful surprise! Have you eaten?"

"Yes, I have, danke," he replied, "I hope you don't mind, I have just come for the wonderful company."

"Oh, this is wonderful," she said, tugging on John's arm and announcing out loud as they entered the dining room. "Everyone, this is John Harrington. He's from the British passport office here in Berlin."

There were only six people there, three couples, but they all answered "Hallo," in unison and then had a little chuckle over how it sounded.

It was a wonderful evening, and they were all very friendly towards John. He made out very well, especially with Freddie's wife Lili, who left him almost speechless a few times. She was really something else, he would say later. She and John managed to get along quite well together. Until late in the evening, long after the other guests had left, she would still not let him leave. Her chief delight was trying to feed him rum and pretzels and trying to get him drunker. John was not sure if the Solingers were going to be a useful contact for him or if he was a useful contact for them, or both, which was actually the most likely. Another enigma.

Either way, John was enjoying all the attention, and Freddie didn't even seem to mind. He was obviously all about the money and the contacts, and perhaps he had other women friends too, John thought. "I really must leave now," John finally said. "I cannot thank you enough for such a fabulous evening; I hope we will see more of each other soon."

Lili spoke with a hollow seriousness about her voice that John had not heard all evening, "We don't go out near as much anymore; some people are so rude."

Nothing more needed to be said, and John just shook his head in dismay. "This is a terrible thing, I cannot believe the audacity of the Nazis," he quietly replied.

"Instead, we have a party here every Friday," Lili smiled with an open invitation towards him.

Freddie joined them and put his big arm around her with a little squeeze, and she leaned into his chest as if it was a cushy bed at the end of a long day. "I will walk you out," he said to John and then turning back to Lili. "Then I will tell the driver to go home."

Outside Freddie said to John, "You are welcome to come on Friday, John; we love interesting people like yourself."

"I wouldn't want to be a bother," John stated, in case Freddie was just being polite. "No, really it would be nice, come whenever you want," Freddie laughed. "We might be good for each other."

Chapter 22

PROPAGANDA

The following day, John was feeling a little under the weather, but after his morning walk to the consulate he began to come alive. Captain Haysley was intrigued with his exploits and sat there sipping his coffee and listening intently as John spoke of his interesting night.

"We saw Hermann Goering again, at the club, and later Freddie and Lili Solinger invited me into their home."

"Well, now," Haysley replied curiously, "Mrs. Solinger is quite something, isn't she? Do you get along well with them?"

"Yes, we seem to get along very well, thank you very much," John replied, curious himself now as to the captain's intent. He never really knew how much the captain was involved in those late night parties upstairs in the consulate, where wealthy, connected Germans like the Solingers might even be found.

"Yes, I see," Captain Haysley said, opening his eyes a little wider and looking at the envelope in John's hand.

"Most important of all, here are the bunker plans that Berhandt has given me," John excitedly blurted out while placing the envelope on the table.

Captain Haysley opened the envelope at once and laid all the plans out on his desk. They both studied them for awhile, noticing that there were dozens of different drafts, including some for other cities. "Did he say which ones they are going to use?"

"No," John replied, "there has been no decision on that until the new government buildings are all built. Most of them will have their own bunker to begin with," John added. "Well, that's what Berhandt assumes."

"This is grand stuff John, great work," Haysley remarked with a very happy look on his face. "I wonder what else this lad might attain for us?"

"Oh, I don't think he can do much more now; he is already in fear for his job because he is Jewish, you know?"

"Hmm, yes, very well," Haysley calmly said as he got up to stretch his legs. "I have heard that Wilhelm Canaris is in town again, and perhaps you might see him at the press club one of these days, so keep an eye out, won't you?"

"Yes, of course," John said, as he also rose to his feet. "Is there anything in particular you want to know?"

"No, just the usual, who all his spies are and all that," he laughed. "I've heard that you have a lot of interviews, so get busy now."

John could hardly wait for it to be a respectable hour before going over to the Press Club for an early lunch. That was always his favourite part of the workday. While there, he could truly relax as he smoked his miniature cigar and read the newspaper with a cup of his favourite coffee.

Then, lo and behold, one day soon after that, in walked Wilhelm Canaris, alone. Apparently he had the same thought of relaxing and had come to the same conclusion that the Press Club was the best place to be. He sat across the room, also with a Zigarette and a coffee and newspaper. The two men smiled at each other and carried on with their routines. Before long Wilhelm Canaris came over to John's table and said, "May I join you?"

"Of course," John said, very surprised that his heart was beating quickly.

"I am Captain Wilhelm Canaris," he said, putting out his hand to shake John's.

John instantly returned the gesture. "My pleasure," he said, "John Harrington, the British passport control office."

"Yes, I have seen you around," Canaris said, followed by a jolly laugh, "but I couldn't place just where, besides here, that is."

"Please sit down," John motioned. "I know I saw you talking to Herr Rommel the other week, didn't I?"

John nodded. "Yes, we get along well."

"Isn't that interesting," Canaris said happily, which made the hair go up on the back of John s neck. "He's quite the little Prussian, don't you think?" he added with a huge laugh. John looked at him crossly, not speaking. "Oh, just kidding, I actually quite like the fellow myself.

"You must work for Captain Foley," Canaris suddenly stated as if just putting the connection together.

"Yes, I do," John replied cautiously.

"A wonderful man, really wonderful," Canaris commented and soon the two men were talking up a storm. The age of deception was descending upon Berlin quickly now, and with this man it was no exception. One had to be very careful at all times when speaking. John and Canaris talked many times after that day, and they got to know each other quite well. John was never sure what to say to him, but it got easier. Canaris was interested in John's acquaintances in the theatres when he was younger and loved to hear his stories of the actors and actresses whom he had encountered.

Back at the consulate, Captain Haysley encouraged John to continue talking with him, but as usual to "be very careful."

Around the office in general, Canaris was a common topic of debate. Everyone wondered "just whose side" K was on? They had a slight suspicion that Canaris and Churchill were friends, but they might have been wrong. Deep inside John knew that from the way Canaris talked about Churchill, there was definitely something between them. Overall, he thought Wilhelm Canaris was a quiet and nice man even though he could never be trusted.

Wilhelm Canaris had served in military intelligence as far back as the First World War, where he was an intelligence officer on board the SMS Dresden. The story was told that it was one of the only ships that frustrated the British fleet for an unusually long time due to their tactics of deception. After the war Canaris remained in the navy where he had been promoted to Captain in 1931 and presently he was the commanding officer on the battleship Schlesien. He became active in the secret intelligence unit again and began to meet with the top Nazis in the new government.

In January of 1935, Wilhelm Canaris was given the head position of Germany's Secret Service or military intelligence agency, die Abwehr.

Adolf Hitler was starting to take notice of him now, and soon he was promoted to Rear Admiral and was becoming very well known as "Admiral Canaris."

The teetotaling Adolf Hitler was very busy at this time, introducing new anti-Semitic laws on a regular basis. When President Paul von Hindenburg died in August of 1934, Hitler had become head of state and, with that title, came total power. He was now personally in complete control over all the politics, armies, and the police in all of Germany. He had declared himself Chancellor of the Third Reich, the Führer. Berliners were distraught with the changes in their wonderful city and the new Nationalist government was becoming very unpopular with the general public. No one really knew what to expect next, or what they could say or do anymore without reprisals.

The atrocities now occurring in their fabulous city of Berlin were almost unbelievable and would have been unbelievable if they hadn't been seeing them with their own eyes. Berlin was no longer a delightful place to be. The Jewish artists and performers living there were being forced to join Nazi Unions, and so the entertainers and scientists had stopped flocking in to the city. Now most of those who remained were planning their departures.

Adolf Hitler, meanwhile, was taking pills and drug injections, and was leading a grandiose lifestyle with his new young mistress, Eva Braun, tucked away at home while Wagner played on the phonograph.

As a change of pace, John met a young Canadian girl, a Miss Gerry Fulton from Nova Scotia, who was working in Berlin. One day she came to his office at the consulate to enquire about her passport, and John looked up her record. Miss Avery was now sending many dubious applicants straight back to John's office in the hope that he wouldn't have to leave the consulate and check them out himself. Miss Fulton was a complete eyeful, John thought, as she entered the room wearing a puffed-up dress with large polka dots on it with a little matching usher's cap pinned to the back of her thick curly red hair. Her smile was simply adorable, that of an innocent he thought, as she reached to shake his outstretched hand.

"Hello, I'm Gerry Fulton," she said, in what sounded to him like a peculiar accent, energetically shaking his hand.

"Hello," John replied, motioning towards the chair. "Please have a seat."

"Well, and who are you?" Gerry asked brazenly, not budging from her spot while her enquiring eyes focused on John's.

"Sorry, I'm John Harrington," he answered shyly. "Passport control," he added realizing how redundant that was as soon as he had said it, and so he quickly proceeded. "What can I do for you today, Miss Fulton?"

She plopped herself down on the leather lounge chair and then immediately sat bolt upright again, and in her quirky, Nova Scotian tongue said, "Please call me Gerry."

John instantly liked her. She reminded him of when he was younger with his Australian friends, all of whom had their unusual accents and mannerisms. "I was told to check in here and to be sure my British visa was in order," she stated bluntly. John was a little taken aback and was rapidly reading the card for more information on her.

"I see you are working for the German government," he said, waiting for an answer that never came. "What exactly is it you do for them, Gerry?" he politely inquired.

"They're paying me to teach the German Air Force officers to swim," she happily replied — as if that were perfectly normal. John started jotting down notes, but Gerry wasn't that forthcoming with her information until he asked her about where she was living and whether she liked Berlin.

"I hardly know any English people here," she said, getting up and moving over to the window where she stared out longingly. "Do the girls in the front office ever go out?" she asked John.

"Not that I've ever seen," John replied with childish honesty.

Gerry bounced towards him and leaned over his desk, "I see you are writing in shorthand," she said curiously. "I've always wanted to learn that, but I was too involved in sports." Her voice got quieter as she sat back down again. "Hey, maybe you could teach me," she then blurted out.

John paused for a moment, looking into her cheerful freckled face. "Sure, why not," he said with a tilt of his head. "Why don't you come over to my flat tonight, and we can start right into your shorthand lessons there. Just shorthand though," John added quite innocently.

After she'd left, John went right up to Captain Haysley's office with her file. "You need to see this application," he said, as if he had just caught a mouse and dropped it on the front doorstep. "Miss Fulton is from Nova Scotia, Canada, and is working for the German government … teaching swimming," he added quietly. But he could see that the Captain was not really paying attention to him, or so he thought.

Captain Haysley looked up from his papers and smiled calmly saying, "I presume the reason these officers need to swim is for when they attack England; some are bound to be brought down in the English Channel."

John was a little taken back by his comments and was now speechless.

"That's okay. I'll take care of this one, John," Haysley replied looking up after the long silence. He held his arm out, gesturing for John to give him the file.

"She seems like a really nice girl," John mentioned, not eager to give up the file.

"That's fine," Haysley said grudgingly as he had to lean out of his chair to seize the file out of John's hand. "Just help her out in any way you can; I will take care of her visa. It's all fine," he said with finality.

John breathed a sigh of relief at Captain Haysley's final comments as he left his office. "I am just helping her out," he thought to himself.

John was really curious about this young lady and also about her stories of Canada, so he rushed home after work to tidy up. The caretakers at his block, Horst and Anna Hammersmitz, were still living downstairs and enjoyed sitting with their door open. That evening, Horst was drinking his tea when Gerry arrived, and John came downstairs to let her in. This was John's first visitor in all the years he'd lived there, and Horst almost dropped his cup when she said "Hallo" in her cheery voice.

Whenever Gerry came over after that, the Hammersmitzs closed their door, and John and Gerry had a few good laughs over that. They soon became fast friends and arranged to meet in the late afternoons for their lessons. Nothing ever happened, though they both expected it to. They both found it was just nice having a friend. Gerry soon developed into a helpful contact for John, and they would sometimes discuss the movements of the officers she worked with. She used to say, "I've got a certain group of officers," and then tell John what they were doing and where they were going and any other details she could think of.

They spent a lot of time traveling around the city together, just being tourists. Having Gerry at his side allowed John to go more places and to see more things than he would have normally. She was not only a good alibi for him, but also, as a couple, they seemed to blend into the crowds and remain far more unnoticed than he would have on his own. They had great fun together, and it proved to be very advantageous in the end.

Oddly, however, when John would put his notes together and take his news to Captain Haysley, the captain would usually say to him, "Oh, don't bother with that," but John knew that they were bothering with them.

Miss Avery and her girls were finally starting to warm up to John. He was allowed to talk with them at breaks, although Miss Avery was usually listening in the background. He would tell them stories of where he'd been, at the races or football and other games. Unlike them, he had been encouraged from higher up to socialize, and he really had had to learn the art of listening. Sometimes he would talk about the theatre or the clubs or some of the things that had happened to him as well as his encounters with the various people.

Some of the girls, especially those who spoke fluent German, were a little jealous that John could get out and about like he did, but for the most part they just loved his stories. He used to say, "I just saw so and so," and they would all get excited, crowding around him saying, "Oh, really, tell us more." John really was their eye on Berlin, and there was so much to see that the women knew they were missing.

The German Press Club next door to the consulate still welcomed John in, and he still took full advantage of that and thoroughly enjoyed any time spent there. One unusual day, Herr Rommel was there with a few other officers and he waved John over. "This is a friend of mine from Australia, who works at the British Consulate," he said with an unusually loud flourish.

The men laughed and one replied, "Who is this new friend of yours, Rommie, an Aussie or a Tommy?" They all laughed heartily and welcomed him into their group. John joined them for a short while but soon felt uncomfortable and left. He could not get over the men calling him

"Rommie." He thought that was a little disrespectful, but he had to admit that Rommel did not seem to mind. Apparently, they called him that quite often when they were having fun. John didn't like many of the other officers, but did mix with them occasionally.

Rommel had recently been posted to Potsdam as an instructor in the new school of infantry, and he took great pleasure in teaching the young men. He and his wife Lucie were happily living near the school in Potsdam with their young son Manfred, and John would quite often attend church there to visit with him. Occasionally, John and Gerry would go to Wannsee, a lakeside place quite near Potsdam, where they also ran into Erwin Rommel on occasion. The inhabitants of Wannsee were very antagonistic to the military and the current regime and Rommel often found himself embroiled in controversy. He would get so upset and sometimes he would say to John, "It shouldn't happen ... it shouldn't happen this fighting." Then he would jokingly look at John and say, "If it wasn't for the bloody English, this wouldn't be happening." But he was a nice chap, John always thought.

Of course, Captain Haysley was very suspicious of John's dealings with Rommel. They didn't like it at the consulate that John would socialize and talk with him so much. Haysley warned John on a regular basis, "You bloody well better be careful now. Watch what you say to him. He is a Prussian, you know. They were actually the ones, the culprits who started the last war, not the German people, the Prussians."

The atmosphere in Berlin was definitely changing. All of the Jewish newspapers were outlawed and the persecution of the Jews was becoming more open and obvious, without any voices being raised to support them any more. Herr Hitler had issued a proclamation that all German Nationals were to buy what was called "The People's Newspaper," the Völkisher Beobachter." There was to be one copy for each and every family, all nationals. The reason that all nationals had to buy it was those people who did not buy it would have to be foreigners or Jewish people. It was a way of sorting the wheat from the chaff.

At first, many nationals did not bother to even read the paper, but after a while they would say, "Well, as we have to buy it, we may as well read what is in it." That was the thin edge of the wedge. While just glancing through its pages, one would find some little thing of interest, such as hints on gardening — a popular subject for lots of German people. There were radio notes, puzzles, home economy tips, and articles on sundry other topics. Most of it was factual information, but with a difference. At first, little items of propaganda were inserted. As time went on, a little more propaganda was added and soon the people began to believe the whole story. Many people were depressed at the time and many of them unemployed. Times were hard, and they were encouraged after reading the newspaper that things were improving and that Hitler would make life easier for them. The people needed someone and something to make life bearable for them, and so they would believe that the things they read were true.

Chapter 23
BERLIN 1935 – DANGER LURKS

The hard times of the last few years were slowly improving and Adolf Hitler would make life easier for them, they were told. This is what the people wanted to hear, and they didn't know or care that it was achieved by Hitler and his gang raiding Jewish stores and warehouses. The excuse simply was to provide "His People," as he called them, with a better life. That meant that a lot of Jewish people would be out of work. The majority of the German nationals were all for it.

Some prominent people, Germans and foreigners, estimated that, had Hitler waited for five more years, the Jewish people would have held the future of the German government in their hands. The story was that the Jewish people had too much power and too much money. Once they were in control, it would become a country within a nation, a frightening thought for many people. How many people even wondered why the Nazi government destroyed and raided the Jewish people's factories and stores, and killed the Jewish people? In John's interpretation, one of the main reasons was that Hitler's regime had begun to realize just what the Jewish people had accomplished. Take, as an example, the fact that they owned most of the banks, particularly the Deutsche Bank. They owned and ran most of the big factories, often under assumed names. These factories were, in fact, the life's blood of the German economy, and the only solution according to the Nazi regime was to consume them – to kill the Jewish people who owned them and destroy their warehouses and stores, (after raiding them) and eliminate the Jews completely. Tragedy was now lurking around every corner.

*
**

The British Consulate where John worked was a safe haven for him and also for many Jewish people, who arrived there daily looking for help to leave the country. Everything possible was done to get them out of Germany, as it was the highest directive from Captain Foley himself.

John loved his morning break when he could go outdoors and sit on the bench at the back of the consulate building to smoke a pipe or cigarillo. Quite often, Alfred the caretaker would come over to join him. "Hello, John, staying out of trouble?" he would ask with a laugh, knowing he probably wasn't.

"Yes, yes," would be the usual reply.

Alfred looked at him with a deep understanding in his eyes as he spoke. "They are having another one of their do's upstairs tonight; perhaps you should go home a little early."

"Why won't they invite me to these parties?" John sounded perplexed. "I know most of the people there anyway, from the Press Club next door."

Alfred looked at John in a way that made him realize for the first time that maybe Alfred was more than just a caretaker. "Well, it's probably for that very reason that they won't let you go up," Alfred said. "And that's lucky for the British government of course, isn't it?"

John looked a little confused, and so Alfred explained, "They can get a lot more information out of you this way. You remain incognito and less of a concern."

For the first time, John felt happy that he was not attending the formal party, and he took Alfred's advice and left a little early. Stopping in at the local beer house on his way home, he discovered a few of the fellows from work were there. They called him over. "John, we're on our way over to the Irish pub. We've heard it's still a really fun place to be. Would you like to come with us?"

John thought for a split second; it had been a long time since he was there. "Sure," he said, suddenly beaming. The thought of a smoke-filled room with a few partly naked women and a bottle of their finest Irish whiskey on the table sounded really good at the time.

The second you opened the door you knew you were at the Irish pub. Like the lid coming off a jar, the strong smell of numerous pipe tobaccos drifted out, and the music inside roared loud enough to hold the door open by itself. The pub was packed with loud people with very strong Irish accents, making it hard to tell sometimes what they were even arguing about. It was always a lively time at the Irish pub, with many girls of various ages looking after the tables, quite often giving one-on-one attention to the men. Most of the Irish women serving were wearing similar outfits in various shades of plaid green, each to match their unique color of red hair, like no other green ever could.

The Fräuleins serving them wore dresses fashioned in the eighteenth century "serving wench style," with skirts that were free flowing and open flared for easy fondling, and on the top was one tiny drawstring barely holding a giant bosom in place. "For a little while anyway," the men would jest.

Dancers wore themselves out, and the music never stopped, only slowing down occasionally for a breather, while a beautiful voice would sing a ballad. The room was always crowded, and outrageously loud. When two brownshirts came in the main door of the pub for a look about, it momentarily got quieter until they were booed right back out of the door. John thought it was wonderful that the party just went on.

It was quite normal for a fight to break out somewhere in the large room later in the night and, as John looked over that night to see who was fighting, he spotted Freddie and his brother Karl Solinger sitting in a booth tucked away in the far corner near the back. He went over to talk with them.

"Freddie, hallo. Karl, it's very good to see you again," John said smiling at both of them and nodded his head, a little tipsy.

"Johnny, hello, you must join us," Freddie said motioning towards a seat in their booth. "I am surprised to see you here. What brings you out?"

"The fellows from work talked me into it," John explained, pointing towards the group of clerks who were quite drunk now. One of the young men was wearing only his tie with no shirt underneath it, and another clerk was bothering the other patrons with some sort of provocative dancing on the edge of the dance floor.

"Maybe I will join you for a while," John said, ashamed of his work-mates, but Freddie thought it was hilarious.

"Cheers," he said, laughing and lifting his glass for a clink with John's. They talked for a long time and had a fine evening. Karl was usually leery of a crowd, but after a few drinks he became braver and mentioned they were there for business, and that Dr. Burns hadn't come with him because he didn't like the rough crowds here.

This crowd really did know how to have fun, and the beer was flowing out of the glasses and everywhere, not only in the thirsty mouths anymore. All the tabletops were wet, and there was a little fight at the bar because someone splashed down a beer and it had put out someone else's pipe sitting in the ashtray. They could not help but notice that the fight at the bar had gotten louder and closer to enveloping the whole room when John stood up to leave and Freddie offered him a ride home.

"I have to leave also," Freddie said, "My lovely Lili will wonder where I am."

As they left, John was taken back at the beauty of Karl's automobile – it was a Mercedes 500K sports sedan. He had never seen anything quite as elegant as this cream-coloured masterpiece, with its bulging round fenders resembling huge breasts in the hazy moonlight – so much so that John wanted to touch them with both hands.

"Step back," Karl said rudely as he got in the drivers seat. "You go with Freddie."

Freddie was just getting into the back seat of his chauffeur-driven car, a new black Mercedes coupe, but was waiting for John to join him. You have such nice automobiles," John commented.

"You like that, do you?"

"Yes, indeed. I wish I had such a beautiful transport," John said with great emotion. It was late and he'd drunk a lot.

"Well, you must have one then," Freddie said, laughing and almost sliding off the seat when they hit a bump. "Have one of my cars; we have three, you know, and there are only two of us." He laughed again.

"That is so nice," John replied, "but of course I couldn't."

"Why not?" Freddie replied. "It sounds like the government will own them all soon anyway."

A sobering quietness crept over the car until Freddie broke it off. "Well, you can use them whenever you want," he said.

"Seriously, here is my driver's card and just tell him I sent you. There is one car just sitting there all the time now and that makes me worry a bit because people might notice the extravagance."

"Have you thought of leaving at all or selling out," John asked curiously, hoping to help him out in some small way.

Freddie understood well enough what John was implying, and you could see in his face that he was thankful for his concern.

"No, I won't leave," Freddie said. "I have many connections and important friends here, and the Nazis need me to make their uniforms, so I think I am safe for now." He looked over at John very seriously. "I do have some friends, though, who want to leave Germany, but they are not sure where to go," he said. The driver pulled up to John's block and came to a gentle stop.

"Send them over, man," John said with a grin. "That's what we do over there at the consulate — we get people out of here!"

The following morning John turned on the wireless to hear the morning news. The reporter was announcing another raid on a Jewish home but what caught John's attention was the area it was in. The man quietly spoke with a slight tremor in his voice, "A Jewish home in our most fashionable district, the Kurfürstendamm, was raided last night, and four occupants were jailed for sex crimes against the Aryan race."

"Preparations for the 1936 Olympics are proceeding ahead of schedule, and more news just released, that these Olympic Games will be broadcast around the world from our newest radio station right here in Berlin."

The words seemed to fade away as John hustled around in a daze. "No, no, oh my God. Ilse, are you okay?" he muttered to himself. Lifting the receiver off the phone, his hand shook with the fear that Ilse may have been taken. The phone rang and rang, but no one answered. John put the phone down and left immediately to go over there. Again, there was no one home, but at least he could see that the house was untouched. There were soldiers in the distance, the new black uniformed soldiers with a skull and cross bones on their caps. The Gestapo, John thought, and turned to go home again, best not to be seen. He worried all day, calling Ilse many times, but with no reply and the next day it was the same.

John asked at the office, but they knew nothing. Captain Haysley was finally able to ease his mind saying, "I heard it was another wealthy banker who displeased them."

A whole week passed, and John had learned a few lessons on what kind of questions he could ask at the consulate and what kind of answers he was going to get. He understood a little more of how involved he could become without getting everyone in trouble. Little did he know that Captain Foley was secretly concerned with an intricate system of rescuing Jewish people from the jaws of Nazism; hundreds of people already had gone through and they continued to arrive steadily on a daily basis.

Captain Foley was John's ultimate boss, but they only spoke a few times; still, he thought Foley was a remarkable man and had the greatest respect for him. Captain Foley had his own office and section at the consulate, and John only went there occasionally to see him. His concern for Ilse forced him to visit this time, but Captain Foley had no answers for him — just a warning.

"You should tell your Dr. Liebert to leave Germany now. We will help her." Captain Foley put his pen down and looked John in the eyes. "She should sell all her interests and get out now," he said crisply, and then quietly added, "while the going is still good."

⁂

Under certain conditions on the black market, one could obtain German marks at the rate of twelve or more for a pound sterling. In later years, this went up to thirty marks for one pound. In even later years, one could buy German marks for as much as fifty marks for one-pound sterling. The Americans with their dollars found this very profitable.

It was a well-known fact that members of the staff of many of the embassies and consulates took advantage of the practice of buying German marks on the black market. They all did what they could.

The reason for this was simple, and this is how it worked. In the years 1935-1939, a Jewish person leaving Germany had to have a valid German visa as well as a visa of the country where they wished to go to. The German government would take from them ninety-six per cent of their total assets, meaning goods, property, and money, leaving them with only four per cent of their total assets.

To get their wealth or part of it out of Germany, the Jewish people would have to sell their goods and possessions for what they could get for them. Then sell the marks to one of the staff of an embassy or consulate of England, America, Ireland or wherever they were going. If there was a time limit for when they had to be out of the country, they would be compelled to dispose of their assets through the black market to get the best price. Otherwise, if they were still in the country when the time limit expired, they would be likely to be sent to prison camp, or to work in an industry, or they just might disappear.

The buyer of these marks would then give the Jewish people a cheque payable in the country where they would be going to live, so that when they arrived they would have money in a bank in that country waiting for them. It was a small way in which the Jewish people were cheating the German government system. It should be noted here, that both parties to the transaction were breaking the law of the German government, thus being liable to be sent to prison camp or even to be executed. A sombre thought.

John had to confess that he too did this. Not so much for the money or property – it was a consideration, of course – but primarily for humane purposes, to help out those fleeing the country and because if he did not buy the marks someone else would have to.

John telephoned Ilse once more, and her father answered. "Hallo."

"Herr Liebert, is that you," John asked almost frantically.

"Yes, who is this?"

"This is John, have you seen Ilse? Is she all right?"

"Yes, of course," Herr Liebert answered, "Oh, you were worried about the raid down the street. No, no, do not worry. We have been to Frankfurt on a small business holiday. I guess she didn't tell you?"

"Oh, thank you," John said with a large sigh of relief. "Please have her call me when she returns."

"Yes, I will. Thank you for calling," Herr Liebert said, but his sense of dread was increasing despite the calm tone with which he had answered John. He had already been unofficially advised by consulate staff that he should look into removing himself and his family from danger. They had even suggested to him the option of buying his marks on the black market. But the bottom line was that he didn't want to leave.

That evening John and Ilse met at one of her apartments and held each other tightly for hours. "I was so worried about you," John said softly.

"You do not have to worry about me," Ilse answered naîvely, not truly understanding the dangers she was facing. No one really did at this time; their existence was more precarious from one day to the next.

"Yes, I do have to worry about you," John replied. "You are very important to me. Do you not see the Jewish pogrom that is obviously about to happen? You must leave Germany, you and your father and brother, the sooner the better. Sell everything you have and just go somewhere, Africa to see your daughter, or Australia. I can make it happen for you."

"We cannot leave here," Ilse said wearily. The true realization of her predicament was starting to sink in. "This is our home and we have discussed it many times." She was showing signs of fatigue from the stressful situation, the look of fatigue enhanced even further by the unusually casual clothing she was wearing. "Why are they doing this to us John? Am I so terrible?"

"It's not you, Ilse; it's that madman Hitler."

The fear started to show on Ilse's face now, but she fought it off. "I am a little scared," she quietly whispered. "They were so mean to us in Frankfurt, and they are usually so nice there. It was degrading."

She looked as if she would burst out crying, "I have never been so humiliated."

"You should leave Germany," John repeated himself. "You can come back after this silliness is over."

Ilse burst out crying and fell into his arms, "They will leave us penniless," she sobbed, "and Father will not have it. It's just not right. We don't know what to do."

"There is the black market," John quickly sat up. "If you sell everything, I am sure we can arrange for you to get eighty per cent or so for it. That is still very good, Ilse. You should go. Please, talk to your father about this, promise me."

"Yes, I will," she said, "thank you, John, I do feel much better now."

A little smile came over her face, and she said, "I really don't think we will need to worry about it anyway; we have sufficient funds and friends, all living here in the Kaiserallee. I am sure we will be fine."

John shook his head, "I hope so, my dear. I will be worried nonetheless, so be sure to ask your father about leaving, and talk to him about the black market."

Then, quite unexpectedly, Ilse looked at John very sternly, "I am quite sure we will not do that."

"Why not?" John asked confused.

"Isn't it illegal? You said yourself it is cheating our government. Would that not make us as bad as them, liars and thieves?"

"You are not murdering people, Ilse. Do you not see the danger here?"

They held each other, and John hoped that the meagre four per cent allowed by the government would not be their downfall. If not tonight, he hoped he could persuade her before too long.

Chapter 24
GETTING INTO TROUBLE

Back at the consulate, Captain Haysley was pacing back and forth in his office, when John, who had been urgently summoned, arrived.

"There you are," Haysley yelled. "You have gotten us into a fine mess this time," he said a little calmer now that he was able to look John in the eyes. "Your enquiries about this Dr. Liebert got a lot more attention than we like around here. We had the office of the Chancellery here on our own doorstep. Here," he yelled again.

"I have a direct message for you from Captain Foley, and he is quite upset. He wants you to have no further contact with this Dr. Liebert or any other German big knobs for that matter. Stay out of trouble now, John, or you know the score. Do you have it?"

Captain Haysley went over to his barrel area and poured them both a sherry. "You must be far more careful with all of the Jewish people from now on, John. We cannot seem to be so involved."

John let his head drop and did not say a word. He knew he had been foolish, but the thought of losing Ilse had driven him to it. He snapped out of it quickly when Captain Haysley offered him the snifter glass saying, "I think you should disappear for the day; I don't want Captain Foley to bump into you. Maybe it's a good day for the press club. I hear it has been quite the spot to be in this summer heat. Cheers."

John put the glasses away for Captain Haysley and said, "Yes, sir." He was afraid to say much more, and then he was off. Shortly later he was seen ducking out the back door towards the press club as suggested. It was quite early in the day and only a few men were there. John ordered breakfast, a rare treat compared to the sandwich that he usually ate, and then later he sat off to the side, enjoying a cigarillo and a coffee while reading the newspaper.

Herr Rommel entered with two younger men in tow. One was burdened with various camera apparatus and the other was in full uniform. Herr Rommel himself was in casual dress and smiled when he saw John. "Hello, John," he paused for a second on his way by. "I'll see you on Sunday."

"Very good," John answered, nodding in compliance.

The two younger men were quite interested in Herr Rommel, and he ordered a round of beer for them, which made them slow down a notch. Before long they were loud again and seemed to be having a lot of fun for still such an early time of the day. John could hear Rommel stating his usual comment, "When I am in uniform, I am a soldier, and it is my duty to fight for my country; but when I am in civilian clothes, I am just a man and I must serve men."

Just then Admiral Canaris entered the club with another man at his side, both of them in full uniform. The club had gotten busy now in time for lunch and, momentarily, there was a respectful silence in deference to the Admiral's rank and uniform. The two men with Rommel both stuck out their arms saying, "Heil Hitler."

Erwin Rommel smiled at Admiral Canaris. "Guten Tag," he said. The Admiral nodded and smiled in return, continuing on with as little pomp as possible and quickly disappeared into a large empty booth. John could see Rommel talking quietly to the young men now and could just imagine his words. "Watch what you say, and remember, for just thinking and listening, no one can ever hurt you." Moments later they were on their way out the door and before long the entire lunch crowd was dissipating.

John wondered if he looked out of place, having been there for so long but he was really enjoying himself, officially having a beer on the company's quarter. After a while, Admiral Canaris sent one of his men to fetch John over to his booth, and they ended up talking for hours. Admiral Canaris loved the theatre, and when he found out that John had some early connections with the stage, he had become instantly intrigued.

He asked John, "Have you ever heard of Max Miller, the 'Cheeky Chappie,' with his off-beat stories?"

"Yes," John replied with a big chuckle. "His jokes raised many eyebrows. He really was a cheeky fella and he used to tell cheeky jokes.

"Then there was Gertie Gatana; she was a very nice singer," John added.

Admiral Canaris didn't know whom he meant and shook his head curiously saying, "Is she also an actress?"

John replied with the lingering affection of a young boy's first love, "She was the young Miss of Alice Blue Gown."

He took a deep breath thinking back, "She was a very polite and reserved kid," John paused and momentarily his mind went back to 1912. "I used to pull up the ropes for her and set up her stage props." Then blushing a little, he added, "We used to sit together and talked quite a bit. She taught me a lot about girls."

"You must have been quite young then?"

"Oh, I was about fifteen or sixteen then. Yeah, those were happy days at Southend-on-Sea and, as a prop man I was able to meet many famous people."

Admiral Canaris sat up straight again. "You were so lucky. How about Charlie Chaplin? Did you ever meet that fellow?" he asked inquisitively.

"Yes," John answered, taking a sip of his beer and searching his memory for the right words. "The first time I saw Charlie Chaplin he had a part in the play 'The Mumming Birds' with Fred Karno.

"He was an easy man to remember, a very humble man, delightful. One of the very nicest persons I ever met," John said. "He was always ready to listen, a wonderful habit that more people should try."

Admiral Canaris listened intrigued as John spoke. "Yeah," John said, exhaling a large puff of pipe smoke away from the table but it swirled back again and made Canaris cough.

"Charlie Chaplin was a great friend of Fred Karno and often appeared in his army. Fred had a troupe of men they called 'Fred Karno's Army'. He was quite a character that Fred Karno. I met him a few times too."

Laughing out loud, John explained, "He used to come on the stage with a sports car that he would gradually pull to pieces until it would all fall down. Then they would try and build it up again, and they would get all mixed up. They would have a car one week and then maybe a fire engine or a cab or something else the next week — that was Fred Karno, a really funny chap."

"But Charlie Chaplin, he always had a smile and good word for everyone around him. I admired him very much."

Admiral Canaris sat listening intently. "Times sure have changed," he exclaimed.

"They sure have," John sighed. "There were so many on the stage then," he said with a big smile. "George Elliot, the 'Chocolate Coloured Coon,' who made his name with the song, 'By the Light of the Silvery Moon.' He was one of my favourites. He was actually a white person, you know?"

"Yes, I have heard of him," Admiral Canaris beamed a large smile back at him. John sat up straighter then, as if thinking about leaving but instead he went on with his story, only a little quieter. It was fun to reminisce about those happy days.

"Another one who was a favourite in his day was George Lashwood, who made famous the song 'Burlington Bertie.' He was a very quiet man and never had much to say off the stage.

"Also, there was Jack Pleasant with his song 'Watching the Trains Come In.' He was just a fellow, just a man about town. He'd sit at the railway station, and watch the trains come in and the trains go out, and that's what he used to sing about. There were many others, too numerous to name."

"Did you have a favourite?" Admiral Canaris asked.

"Well, I guess my favourite of them all was the one and only George Formby Sr. He may be forgotten today, but what a character. I met him many times and came to know him very well. He was a lovely chap, very nice. Old-fashioned you know, nothing special about him, just an ordinary person. A person you could talk to."

John leaned back and took another sip of beer. "When we met, we used to talk together and he would discuss with me the songs he was going to sing. I was all for 'When I'm Cleaning Windows.' George was very fond of 'Limehouse Blues' because he liked to strum. The last time I saw him was on the stage of the Old Theatre Royal at Newcastle-upon-Tyne. He was on stage singing, 'If I can't have a nice young lady, a big blood orange will do,' when he suddenly collapsed right there on the stage; he died right there. I often wondered if that was the way he wanted to go, right there on the stage."

John paused and a profound sadness crossed his face, "I lost an old friend that day. He was a favourite of many people. I often wondered if he was 'cleaning windows' in heaven? He'll certainly be singing it, he was that kind of a person."

Later in the day, John was teaching his new friend Gerry Fulton shorthand in his flat when she asked him, "Where did you learn short-hand, John?"

He was feeling very nostalgic when he answered, "At Southend-on-Sea in England." He was reflecting how curious it was to think of it again, and how much he had enjoyed living there.

"It was a very interesting and pleasant seaside town," John said, "famous for its seafood and pubs. That's where I attended Southend's High School of Modern Business, where the standards were very high and everyone had to work up to those high standards. The classes were considered equal to some universities. I learned business and office routine there, shorthand, typewriting, bookkeeping, and other sundry subjects."

"Is that right?" Gerry was surprised, and so John explained.

"Of course, a business class was almost routine in those days, because all they had to work with were typewriters; they had no business machines of any kind, and you had to do it all by hand."

Gerry gave a big sigh and shrugged her shoulders. "That sounds fairly tedious."

John raised his eyebrows. "It was. We had to learn Carterson's Advanced Accounts, and they were hard. Then we also had to learn two systems of shorthand, Pitman's and Gregg, the latter being the one I liked. Pitman's took me a year, whereas I learned Gregg in only six months."

John leaned forward and scratched a few marks on the paper. Gerry pulled the paper towards her and tackled the sentence as if it were a cross-word puzzle. Mumbling at first, she slowly deciphered out loud, "These skills have proven extremely useful over the years."

"Very good," John said. "You really are catching on."

"Yes, I studied hard at Southend, and those schoolmasters back then were pretty strict. But in the end, I attained a Fellowship Degree for Bookkeeping from the London Royal Society of Arts."

"Well, no wonder you're so good at it," Gerry said, yawning. "Hey, do you want to go to Wannsee with me this weekend? One of the fellows I work with said that it's beautiful this time of year, and I just have to see it now."

"That would be grand," John said, suddenly excited. "If I can get a car, do you want to drive?"

"Sure," Gerry said as she jumped up, "It's a date, so to speak."

⁎⁎

Wannsee was a very popular beauty spot quite near Berlin, much used by the German people as an escape from the city. It was very scenic there with its Hanging Gardens modeled after the Hanging Gardens of Babylon and its avenue of tall poplar trees about a mile long in which all the trees appeared to be of the same height and shape.

Wannsee was a large and spectacular lake with gorgeous beaches jam-packed with people in the summer, and numerous piers to accommodate all of the sailboats. There were two islands and a boat trip around the lake, a Rundfahrt or round trip, in which they would go to each island for a snack. It very much reminded John of Lake Windermere where he used to take Betty, his college sweetheart, and it was still a very popular form of entertainment with a young lady.

While at Wannsee, they went to see the castle, Sanssouci, in Potsdam, where Frederick the Great used to entertain his French friend, Voltaire. It was rumoured among the locals that the two were lovers. Whatever the case, the rooms were fantastically designed and made quite a love nest, John thought.

Gerry and John went to Wannsee on many occasions after that, and once they stopped at an outdoor café for a meal.

The waiter could hear them speaking in English and was curious to try out the English skills he had been practicing. He asked them, "Are you visiting Germany and if so, are you having a good time?"

John explained to him, "We are just secretaries working at the British Consulate in Berlin."

"Oh, my," the waiter replied. "That is interesting."

He introduced himself as Philipp, and they ended up talking with him for quite a long time. Eventually, Philipp had to go back to work, but before saying goodbye, he said, "It has been a real pleasure to meet you. I would very much like to go to England one day. Do you think I could get a visa?"

"I am not sure offhand," John replied, "but you should try and next time I am here, I will check and see how you've made out."

"Oh, thank you so much," the waiter said again. "Thank you, good day now."

On the drive home, John could see the construction beginning for the new Olympic Stadium and the exhibition grounds for the upcoming 1936 Olympics.

Gerry looked over at him and, as if to read his mind, she said, "This government sure has been good at getting people back to work with all this construction and all the new roads, don't you think?"

"Yes, that's a good thing for Germany, but at what cost?" John replied.

***

The following Sunday, John met up with Herr Rommel at the English Church. His wife Lucie was not with him, and so they had a much longer talk with the minister Jacob Strauss after the service. Erwin Rommel was commenting on all the construction everywhere and what a bother it was, and the minister was saying how that was modernization and they would just have to get used to it.

John changed the subject entirely. "That was a great service today. I have to agree with your philosophy about standing up for what you believe. It really got the crowd going."

Jacob thanked him, and Rommel shook his head in agreement.

"I laughed my head off though," John snickered, before he quietly said, "when a man who was sitting a few people down from me let out a huge fart. Did you hear it, Jacob?"

"I think I might have," Jacob replied, "and I certainly noticed people pulling some funny faces around you."

John was trying not to laugh as he said, "It reminds me of when I was a little boy at church in Australia." He paused and looked at the expression of the two men, who were smiling with curiosity, so he continued. "There was a Reverend Lloyd Jones there who was a Welshman with a strong, loud voice and he was a good singer, well, quite naturally, being Welsh."

John chuckled, "He was scary to us as little kids, but he was good, and during one of his sermons one Sunday, someone in the congregation suddenly emitted a loud expulsion of air, a fart. As the reverend said afterwards, 'Someone has partaken of too many beers or beans.'"

John continued, "The minister was silent for a few seconds, then said in a very quiet voice, 'According to the good book, wherever thy be, let the wind go free,' and then proceeded with his sermon."

The three men had a good laugh over that story until Jacob Strauss asked John, "Was church a common thing in Australia?"

John perked up again, "Oh, yes, it was. It kept us busy and out of trouble, and there were many interesting things to be learned."

"Isn't that wonderful," Herr Strauss commented. "Well, good day to you, gentlemen. Enjoy the last of our summer weather."

John looked towards Herr Rommel and exclaimed, "I usually go over to the Adlon Hotel for lunch after church. Would you like to join me?

Herr Rommel instantly said, "Yes," and so they walked over towards the hotel.

"The food is spectacular there. Have you ever been?" John asked.

"Ja, once," Rommel said, "with Lucie."

As they entered the dining room, they could see Joseph Goebbels, Hitler's propaganda minister, preparing to leave. Herr Rommel instantly went over to pay his respects to him, and John, unsure where to go, shyly followed and was introduced once more to Herr Goebbels, officially this time. John stood there quietly trying not to be noticed, but Rommel and Goebbels did not have much to say and they soon went separate ways.

A few weeks later, John met Joseph Goebbels once again, right next door at the German Press Club, and as always he was eager to provide Captain Haysley with any useful information from within its walls.

"I thought he was a really interesting man," John said.

"You think everyone is interesting," Captain Haysley replied critically, eager nevertheless to hear more.

"He is Hitler's propaganda minister."

"Yes, yes, I know that already. Anything else," Haysley said, obviously in a hurry.

"Well," John said, purposely taking his time. "He's not a bad looking man, short in stature but with a firm build and very well dressed."

Haysley gave him a dirty look and shuffled around impatiently, so John quickly continued, "But he had a very serious look on his face, that of a thinker. He seems to be a really clever man, that Goebbels. He could be a lot more dangerous than we think. He is a man of many languages, too – well educated, well spoken, well acquainted with the arts, and, above all, he is a good listener as well as a good speaker."

"Well, I don't trust that guy; I want you to steer clear of him from now on." Captain Haysley said. "Do you hear me, John?"

"But I might be able to find out some useful information," John replied, with disappointment.

"No," Haysley shouted, as he impatiently held the door open for John. "It's too dangerous; he's too high up in the echelon for you, just leave it alone for now." Their eyes directly met for a moment, and Captain Haysley knew by now that, from the look on John's face, his advice would probably not be heeded.

Chapter 25

FACTORIES TO EXPLORE

Many were the Sunday mornings after church when John would wander over to the American Bar in the Adlon Hotel and meet up with Joseph Goebbels, complete with his little dog and his famous hat.

The Adlon Hotel, now in its full glory, was usually crowded with people, including numerous beautiful models who could be seen at any given time, posing for one thing or another, in the grand lobby or up against the majestic pillars with little swarms of camera men surrounding them.

Herr Goebbels and John both enjoyed being away from the crowds and would rather have a quiet lunch, in order to spend their time discussing a variety of things and speaking of the many places that they had visited.

Goebbels spoke many languages and once John asked him, "How many languages can you speak?"

He replied with a little smile, "Anything but Greek."

Then John asked him, "Do you speak Afrikaans?"

Goebbels reply was: "That is Greek to me."

"That's a very good answer," John exclaimed with a laugh.

It was obvious from the newspapers that Herr Goebbels' faithfulness to the Führer was steadfast, and yet he never spoke of it. Despite his diminutive stature and the limp caused by a clubfoot, he was a known Lothario, although John considered him to be just a romantic at heart. He was also a very smart dresser, and many were the days when he was accompanied by a vivacious young lady, a starlet or a young beauty hoping for some advancement or advantage. John's head was turned many times by the ravishing women on Goebbels' arm. Personally, he liked Goebbels at the time and had no inkling of his intense hatred for Jews.

⁎⁎

A horse of another colour was Herr Himmler, the chief of the Gestapo or SS. John never had much in common with him and often crossed swords, as it were, through paperwork in the office. He thought he was a creepy little fellow with his circular glasses and pyramidal moustache. They did not often meet in the flesh, and when they occasionally did, it was usually through the consulate, where the staff had a number of altercations with Himmler regarding visas.

The girls would talk among themselves for days or even weeks about these visits. John was never able to confirm that Heinrich Himmler was at one time a chicken farmer and a taxi driver, although his workmates said it was true; it was always a running joke. This rumour likely arose because Himmler had studied agronomy and had done a brief apprenticeship on a farm.

Although John was only an acquaintance of Himmler, he never liked him nor his attitude towards the German people, especially the Jewish people. Himmler was more overt in his opinions than Goebbels at the time.

His attitude towards the Jews became even worse when the Nuremburg laws were introduced in the fall of 1935. It had already been a very rough year for the Jewish people living in Berlin, with the physical brutalities increasing dramatically. Now, with these new laws, all of the Jewish people in Germany lost their citizenship.

Even more laws were passed on German citizenship for the protection of "German Blood and Honour," laws that banned marriage between Jews and Aryans. It was also declared that sexual relations of any kind between German nationals and Jewish people had become illegal. Now one could by law be sent to a concentration camp for sleeping with the wrong person. Sex could officially be a crime.

Most of the Jewish people had already lost their jobs, but now the doctors and other wealthy people were also being ordered to resign. They were denied voting rights and were even forbidden to fly the new German flag adopted at Nuremburg. This new flag for the Reich's national people was a right facing Swastika, an ancient symbol of life, sun, power, strength, and good luck; the red and black colours were meant to symbolize blood and soil.

*
**

At the British Consulate in Berlin, it was busier than ever. The pressure was on, and the passport applications were pouring in; many people wanted out of Germany. Scores of the older generation Jewish people left through consulate channels, and they all wanted their children to leave with them. Many of the young men, however, wanted to stay and fight this oppression, not understanding what they were up against nor realizing they would all be slaughtered. They were in a state of disbelief until it was too late.

People were constantly queued up outside the front door of the consulate and everyone in the passport division did whatever they could to help them. Confidences were stressed to their limits, and the secrecy that was required from all staff members of consulate business was imperative. Miss Avery was trying her best to keep up, but more staff was needed to manage the crowds forming in the consulate building, and so additional people were sent over from the UK.

John knew he was not to see Ilse Liebert anymore, direct orders from the boss, but he was terribly worried for her and her family. Late one evening he walked over and quietly knocked on the door. Ilse's father opened it cautiously. "Oh hello, John, come in, come in."

"Thank you, Herr Liebert. I am so glad you are all right. Is Ilse OK?"

"Yes, she is, thank you. Just one minute, John and I'll call her down to the drawing room."

Ilse was already at the doorway holding out her arms for a hug, which John eagerly stepped into. "I thought I might not see you again," she said, "and I would have understood."

"I am so sorry," John replied, "but I am afraid you are right; I will not be able to see you anymore."

He felt so sad that he almost cried right then and there, until Ilse lovingly tipped his head up with one finger and kissed him on the lips saying, "It's OK; I would not want to put you in any more danger than necessary."

"It's not just that, Ilse," John said with a worried look on his face. "If I go to jail or a concentration camp, I will not be able to help any others.

"I hope you have finally decided to leave Germany," he quickly added. "Have you talked with your father?"

"Yes, but he does not want to leave," Ilse quietly answered.

"You cannot stay here now. It's just too dangerous." John gave her a little shake. "Please, please consider it," he urged.

Ilse puckered her lips, "Don't worry," she said. "I'll be safe here on the Kaiserallee."

John shook his head. He knew that she hardly left her home any more and was not seeing the complete impact of the Nazis. "I am very afraid for you, my lovely Ilse," he softly squeaked out.

"Freddie and his wife Lili Solinger are having a small party tonight," Ilse said with a pause, changing the subject. "Do you want, or think, you can come with me?"

John smiled and looked deep into her eyes. Even though he knew he should not go, as usual he did, feeling boldly confident that it was safe enough. The Solingers were protected on a very high level with their uniform factories, and the horrible effects of the new laws did not seem to apply to them as they did to many others; "seem" being the operative word, of course.

Herr Berhandt, the draftsman, was at their party and was very happy to see John. "It's good to see you, John, how are you?"

"Getting by, thank you, and yourself."

"Not so good," Berhandt replied. "I lost my job with the government this week, and it is going to be very difficult to find any work. Good thing I have some savings."

The two men sat on the couch with a brandy in one hand and a cigar in the other, completely encompassing them in the smoke, like a cocoon. They had a long discussion about leaving Germany and how John could help him and his family.

Berhandt commented, "This is where I was born, John. My whole extended family is here. How could I leave all of them?"

"Even for the safety of your immediate family," John answered plainly. "All of you should be going, for that matter."

Berhandt showed distress at John's words, as if the reality was suddenly true. He was instantly mad at John for such a blatant comment and banged his glass down on the table and loudly stated, "I feel sure this government will not last long, and soon this hatred will be over."

After gathering his composure a little, he added, "I sure hope so at any rate. My family will need to be fed wherever we are and so what I really need now, John, is to find some sort of work."

Then he quietly added, "I will consider your offer, John." He shook his head. "My children are having a hard go of it, too, and they have to put up with this discrimination. They're outcasts, and not allowed to use the same bathroom or playground as the other children."

Ilse Liebert was sitting very quietly and listening, when some of her German national friends suggested to her that she leave Germany with them. She still preferred to stay, saying, "As long as the government needs me, I stay." Apparently, the only reason she was allowed to move freely around Berlin in the later years was because she owned quite a number of shares and interests in many factories and stores.

Freddie invited John over to their house a number of times before it got too dangerous for him, and when he visited, Freddie's wife Lili was always trying to get him drunk on the rum. She was capable of consuming quite a lot of it and they became quite friendly. She was a very useful contact for John.

Since the two brothers Freddie and Karl still had the free use of their Mercedes Benz cars, travel was not difficult for them. They often took John to some of their factories and let him see the people working at these places. He noticed, however, that they were not only making uniforms but other things as a side line – armaments of different kinds. John passed this information on to Captain Haysley but, surprisingly, this was classified as unimportant.

The Solinger brothers often allowed John to use one of their cars, and he frequently made use of this offer. Sometimes he would get away with his new girlfriend, Gerry Fulton the Canadian girl, and sometimes with other friends. They were still able to visit places like Wannsee, Potsdam, and Frankfurt.

*
**

Life in Germany also had its funny and embarrassing moments. An occasion arose when John was assigned to attend a function at the British Embassy, as the regular staff was tired of this kind of function. He was asked to escort a niece of Dr. Ley, the German Minister of the "Strength through Joy" movement, or Kraft durch Freude, which was meant to boost tourism for the masses. He was also involved in the movement called Lebensborn, established on order from Adolf Hitler in December 1935. It was reported in the United Press that Hitler had decided the country needed more Aryan babies, and illicit sex was condoned and encouraged between "racially pure" men and women. The Lebensborn program was intended to bring the Aryan race up to scratch.

Dr. Ley's niece was a beautiful girl, who wore an extremely provocative dress that evening and whose behaviour was very shocking. John was quite embarrassed to be with her and, also felt very uncomfortable in his suit, with its long tails and high collar. It was just not his style. It was a difficult evening for him, especially trying to talk to that young lady. There was a complete breakdown of communication, from their different accents, and ages, and, soon he wished he wasn't there at all.

Later in the evening, John asked her, "Do you like cocktails?"

She said, "Yes, please tell me some."

John had to chuckle at her misunderstanding.

*
**

John's Canadian friend, Gerry Fulton, with her curly red locks, was still working with the German officers. What Gerry did not know was that the Brits knew all about her and her activities. They were able to watch her movements and the people she mixed with. John could give her information, which she unknowingly passed on to the German officers. Gerry was a very valuable contact in that sense for spreading false rumours, and the British made use of her from time to time.

Gerry and John often visited Potsdam and Wannsee together and when the factory moved from Siemens town, John used to go there with Gerry, because maybe she knew a "fella" who was making a gun barrel or something like that. Then John would talk to them about it and if he played his cards right, he could go into the factory with them and watch their machines. This had eventually become his primary task.

On one of their day trips to Wannsee, they bumped into the waiter Philipp again, and he asked John straight out, "Could you get me a visa?"

John explained to him, "At this time, I can't be sure if that is possible, but I will look into the matter for you." This year was 1936.

On his next visit John asked Philipp, "What do you do in the winter months when you're not working as a waiter?"

He said, "I'm a machinist, working at a factory quite near Wannsee." With this information John naturally became interested.

He wanted to encourage the young man and said, "It might be possible for me to obtain a visa for you." On other occasions, John returned to Wannsee, sometimes with a German girlfriend, and talked with Philipp. John eventually asked him, "Would it be possible for me to visit this factory?"

At first, he said he didn't think it would be possible for him to get John a pass, but after a period of time, with a few special gifts from England and the possibility that John might get him a visa, he did finally get John a permit just to look around the factory.

He explained to John that it was a secret factory making commercial goods in competition with other factories in the area making the same type of goods, and hence it was difficult for him to obtain a pass. But John discovered that it was just a sham factory hiding a real factory. The real factory was in a disused railway station where they were making shells and bombs and other kinds of munitions. This site for the factory was later destroyed in 1938. John duly reported this information back to Captain Haysley.

*
**

Every day John reported to Captain Haysley. There was a lot of activity going on now in the city, not all of it in the open. John noticed that, in an effort to hide their arms and airplane production, the German government would hire a farmer or someone to build maybe a wheel or part of a wheel or a strut. They would do that and then send it back to an airport or someone in the next town, who would make some other part and so a circle of farmers unknown to each other would all make a part of an airplane. When the parts got to the factory, they could be assembled into a complete airplane. These clandestine airplanes weren't on the list of production from the factories. All that was reported to the German papers was the planes being made in the factory, not outside the factory. John gradually realized that the Nazis had many more fighters than were being reported.

Looking at Captain Haysley very sombrely, John stated, "Of course you see, since last year they have been building up their resources for a war, for instance ..."

"Enough of that war talk," the Captain interrupted.

"I know you're sceptical," John insisted, "but now I know for sure that they mean war." He let out a huge sigh and continued before Captain Haysley could object. "When Gerry and I stopped for a beer in a country Gasthaus on the way home from Frankfurt, we had a long chat with a farmer there. He told us that they had a foot and mouth disease outbreak in the area and that the government had butchered all the cattle, but instead of burning them, they sent men to come and take the infected cattle away. Gerry and I were speechless, and then the farmer pointed out of the window and in the distance we could see the goings on. The farmer continued, 'They told us they were going to tin all the meat and save it for emergency rations during the war.'"

"Oh, that's just hogwash," Captain Haysley said, shaking his head.

"No," John added, his voice hollow, "that was a fact."

After a moment he persisted, "Of course, the German people, they wouldn't mind if they were starving, because they wouldn't even know, and they would be happy to have it. They would never know or think there was any foot and mouth disease at all, but I was there, and I saw it."

"Ooh, that's ridiculous!" Captain Haysley repeated.

John mumbled under his breath, "That's not ridiculous."

After the war arrived, many people realized that John had been right from the beginning.

Haysley changed the topic. "I don't want you to go back to the café in Wannsee where Philipp worked."

"What, but that's my favourite restaurant there! And it's quite large; they don't usually even notice me there," John pleaded.

"No, and that is it," Haysley roared at him. "There are too many people paying attention now, and we just don't know where we stand on that one, so just don't go there."

John left the office annoyed. "English people are so conservative," he said on his way past the secretary. Down the hall, he mumbled under his breath, "You can't do this, you can't do that. What a bloody nuisance they are."

John did return to Wannsee later but was unable to locate the waiter or find out what happened to him. He was never issued a visa in the name he had given, but then it was possible that he had used another name. There were many ways of leaving the country, but they were never talked about. That was where this particular assignment ended. It was a case where his engineering knowledge had been useful.

At the time, Winston Churchill was thinking the same way as John, that the English were a bloody nuisance. He had been warning the English people that Germany was preparing for war, but no one was listening; no one wanted to believe or hear anything about war. Most of the ordinary people in Britain and France were just trying to get a job or to feed their families. To them, the thought of Adolf Hitler rearming and sending marching troops in to reoccupy the Saar Valley and the Rhineland in March of 1936 was like a bad dream. So, as Hitler expected, there was no retaliation.

With these acts, he had obviously followed through on his threat to defy the Treaty of Versailles. Hitler had also ordered Hermann Goering to establish the Luftwaffe, the German Air Force – another direct defiance to the treaty from the first war.

Many of the German people were also scared at the thought of war, yet most were secretly happy among themselves to have reclaimed their once German land and their strength as a people. In Berlin they were celebrating, and life was becoming more normal as they began preparing for the Olympic Games in August.

A giant façade had begun by Hitler's Third Reich. Behind this mask of hosting the Olympic Games and the "Strength through Joy" holidays, Adolf Hitler was seriously and methodically rearming. Many of his officials were working very hard behind the scenes now to propagate this pretence and to try to please their great Führer.

Adolf Hitler was now 47 years old and peaking in his power. Thousands of men were now raising their arms to him in adoration. "Heil Hitler," they would roar.

The great Führer's response was very eager, but his arm was not quite as stiff and energetic as it used to be. He was already taking his soldiers and his people's appreciation for granted, which could be seen in his responding salute back to them with his arm now bent at the elbow and with his hand eccentrically waving off to the side in a queer almost feminine fashion.

⁎⁎

The majority of German citizens were not nearly as concerned about rearmament, but far more concerned over their daughters' welfare and how immoral the new sex laws were. The media was ruthless to anyone caught breaking the laws of Aryan purity, and it made many headlines. They were particularly hard on priests for breaking foreign currency laws and also a number of trials hit the newspapers where priests were charged with sexual perversity. Sex was once again a hot topic in Berlin.

The Strength through Joy movement had become literally "free love," where the boys and the girls were told to sleep together at the youth camps. There were special homes for the young blonde, blue-eyed Aryans, where they could stay until the girls became pregnant.

There was an article in the British press at the time about one of the youth camps named New Venice. It was a series of canals and campsites, complete with its own bathing pool. Thousands of Aryan babies were born under the Lebensborn program, and they were treated like a commodity, raised in camps and bred only for the future of the Third Reich.

Chapter 26
The Spy Within

Joseph Goebbels ordered that all anti-Jewish propaganda was to be halted until after the games. A campaign was started to take down the anti-Semitic signs and to fix up the storefronts. All the while, secretly, the Sachsenhausen concentration camp was opened 35 kms north of Berlin. It was headed by Heinrich Himmler, and it was where they trained his newly created division, the "SS Deaths Head," or Totenkopf unit, which had also been secretly started to guard the concentration camps.

At this time, Heinrich Himmler was always accompanied by two or three special Gestapo guards in threatening black uniforms. They presented a sinister atmosphere that moved with them like a cloud of poisonous gas. When they approached, all men froze in their tracks, submissive to Himmler's orders, which were very rarely questioned. In February, Himmler had his Gestapo officially placed "above all law."

At the consulate office, there was a new man, Mr. Mullins, a commissionaire sent straight out from England. He only lasted three weeks. His duty was to supervise the people of all races and nationalities who were applying for visas and also to supervise things on the outside of the building, on the grounds of the consulate. Mr. Mullins spoke very little German and was not blessed with too much knowledge of the world in general.

John and Mullins went out for supper together a number of times and the first night, when they brought the menus, John said, "I'll order off the menu for you."

Mullins said, "Oh, I can order, I know how." But he didn't know what he was ordering and his plate of food arrived, just the one plate of asparagus. He said, "I got what I wanted," but he sat there playing with it for half and hour.

John said, "Aren't you going to eat something or order something else?"

"I've got it here," Mullins replied.

"You wanted steak, didn't you?" John queried.

"No, I've got my order," he stubbornly said, and he sat there all that night eating that asparagus. He wouldn't let John do anything for him; he knew what he knew. He was a stubborn man.

The new rules on sex were explained to Mullins on the first night and like all the staff, he had to sign a paper, stating that he understood there was to be no fraternization. He was warned to be very careful in what he did and said, but sad to relate in spite of the warnings he attempted to rape the caretaker's daughter, Adaleena, who was a German national. With anyone else, he might have gotten away with it, but this resulted in an awful mess.

People in other countries probably did not understand the attitude towards sex in Germany in the late thirties. Here is the way it worked. To commit rape of a German national was considered a crime against the German government. One would be liable to be imprisoned, or if they were lucky, given their passport and made to return to the country from which he came.

To attempt to rape a Jewish person was considered a slur on the German state. The rapist and the victim could be imprisoned and, in some cases, both would be executed, so one was caught both ways.

Mullins was sent back to London and discharged from the corps or so they thought. But later on a holiday in England, John went to his home to visit Mullins, but his wife didn't know where he was. She thought he was still in Berlin, but he wasn't. John couldn't tell her any more. And John never found out what happened to Mullins.

Later, John was telling Gerry Fulton the story. "They can be very hard on people for breaking the Secret Service Act and he probably will be sent to prison in England. Very hard, you see once you marry a person or get into a relationship with another person like that, you get friendly with them and, well, you're liable to tell them something."

John shook his head, "It was disgraceful. Poor Alfred our caretaker, remember he was the one who looked just like Hindenburg. Yeah, he had the peaches for cheeks and everything. He's a very nice old fella, we get along together and he is one of the few people who doesn't look down on me, but treats me as an equal. And his poor daughter Adaleena," John continued with a huge sigh. "This Mullins fella came over, a commissionaire, and after a few weeks, he tried to rape her. It was really awful."

*
**

The press club next door was bustling nowadays with reporters and officials, so John had to be considerably more cautious than before. He received a few unwelcome looks, but overall it was still fine.

He would still sit with Herr Rommel if he was there, and one day Erwin had a good laugh when John said to him, "A smile means the same thing in every language."

In one indiscreet moment at the press club, Erwin Rommel once said to him, "John, Germany could never win a war against Great Britain."

John was befuddled over that remark, because he knew what was happening in the Middle East and that the Germans were storing up ammunition all over the place. Everything was being made in advance, and they had built up all their forces to prepare for such a war, whereas the British were not up to date with war machinery because they never had a head start. John asked him, "How do you arrive at that conclusion?"

Rommel's reply was, "If you have read the book Herr Hitler wrote while he was in prison, Mein Kampf, there you will find the answer."

This is an extract from the book Mein Kampf that Rommel might have been referring to: "The British can be counted on to carry through to victory any struggle that it once entered upon. No matter how long such struggle lasts or however great the sacrifice that may be necessary, or whatever means that they have to employ, and all this even though the actual military equipment at hand may be utterly inadequate when compared with those of other nations."

*
**

Admiral Wilhelm Canaris, the chief of the German Secret Service, was also still cooling himself down at the press club from time to time. John was always afraid to talk to him first, but Canaris would go out of his way to speak to him.

Wilhelm Canaris discussed a lot of things with John, particularly secret codes that he would find useful in later years. Canaris specifically liked to use expressions of the day or famous writer's quotes.

One day Admiral Canaris asked John, "You told me that you met Harry Houdini once. What was that like?"

"Oh, yes," John said happily. "We met a number of times and became quite friendly over the years. He was the well-known escape artist, yeah. Houdini was a very pleasant man and was very dedicated to his profession, and to his mother. He was then known as the handcuff king and jail breaker. He was very sincere, except when he was on the stage and then he was the ultimate showman and a good one at that."

"On one occasion when he was in London, he asked me and other people from the audience to come on to the stage and asked them to examine the milk churn that he was going to use in his act. So then I proceeded onto the stage with the other people and began to punch the milk churn. Houdini turned to me and for the benefit of the audience he said in a very loud stentorian voice, 'Sir, I said examine it, not test it.' That went over very well. He was a truly remarkable man." John took a pause to sip his beer and reflect. "He was well-noted for his churn trick.

"One day I was sitting with him at the South-End Hippodrome, and Houdini was telling me this story. He said it really happened. In London, after his performance and returning to his hotel, he discovered he had left his front door key in his suite. To gain admission, he had to call the manager. Rather embarrassing for an escape artist and we used to laugh about that.

"Houdini really used to laugh when he was telling me about being on the stage when he had the handcuffs on and there would be a policeman there. He would tell the policeman how to get out of them, and the police-man would just laugh, because unlike Houdini, he just couldn't get them off. A simple little act, but he was a nice fellow, a very likeable man."

Admiral Canaris loved hearing John's stories of the theatre. "That Richard Tauber is quite the singer," he said to John one day.

"Oh yes, quite entertaining," John replied. He knew right away that that comment was odd, thinking back to his encounter with Tauber on the train when he had first arrived in Berlin, and how Tauber was close to Captain Foley. Again John had to wonder, whose side was Canaris on?

During the war Churchill and Canaris were enemies, but before the war, they were still good friends. Admiral Canaris was a man of many colours. As chief of Germany's foreign intelligence, he later became known as "The Prince of Shadows."

*
**

The British Consulate in Berlin seemed to be the only place that didn't change over the years, although there were a few shake-ups from time to time. John's memory training came in useful on one occasion, when an application was received for a visa by a young lady who wished to visit some friends in West Ealing, London. Nothing unusual in that, except that it so happened that the address that was given for the purpose of the visit was an address where John had stayed years before with the retired postman and family. The coincidence struck him as very odd, particularly as she had not given the name of the people who were living there while he was there.

They were old people in Ealing, and this made him quite worried for their wellbeing. They were so nice and had been really so good to him as a lad that he would never forget them. Even later, when he was studying in London, he used to go back to live with them. He would go to the various theatres every chance he got and help their son Tommy with the props. They had made such an impression on him, that when he saw the address on this card, he wondered what had happened to them.

So he went to see Captain Foley and asked him, "I want to make an inquiry about the address on this application. May I put a note through to

London?" He proceeded to explain, "When I was only a child, I stayed with them for many years, and I knew their house like it was my own house."

Captain Foley's reply was, "Oh don't worry about it; she's all right, don't be bothered about it." But John couldn't get it off his mind, and it did keep bothering him. He kept asking Haysley and then asking Atkinson until finally he sheepishly asked Captain Foley's secretary.

"Captain Foley said to ignore this, but I'd like you to put a note in the bag for me."

That got a result and finally Captain Foley agreed, "OK, we'll do it for you." The application was put through to the London Office with just a query about it. There was a short wait for the response, and John had a vague idea that there might be something not quite right about this application.

Meanwhile, he began to worry again for Dr. Ilse Liebert and her father and brother, as he had not been in touch with them for some time. So that evening he walked over to their home. He wasn't going to go in, but just wanted to see the lights on. It was dark, and no one was there, and so he went home, none the wiser.

Back at the consulate a few days later, John's "just a query," produced the following results. The London office had discovered that their own Miss King, the beautiful petite girl with blonde bobbed hair who had been working as a desk clerk for years at the consulate had been issuing visas to many people using that address in West Ealing, London, and also using an address in Wales that did not exist.

John was completely floored at this news. "Not our Miss King," he thought. "She was so nice, and everyone liked her." It was so hard to believe. Miss King used to type up the cards before she would give them to John or another clerk and, in that capacity, she had access to all of their records.

Captain Haysley was quieter than usual when John arrived in his office. "Pour us a sherry won't you, John?"

He put a report down on his desk as John sat down, "That was jolly good work. I still cannot believe it," he said. "Do you know it turned out that Miss King was not even her real name, and that the little lady was putting through German agents? People were passing through to England and then some of them were going on to the United States."

"I thought something was fishy," John said, wrinkling his forehead.

Captain Haysley took a sip of his sherry and remarked, "At the address she provided them with in North Wales a number of Germans were found and imprisoned."

Captain Haysley leaned forward looking very serious. "There are a lot of double spies out there, John, people who are working for both sides with no direct loyalties. It's a confusing world we live in."

John nodded in agreement. "Is a friend really a friend or is he your enemy? I mean, they say they are your friend and that's how they get away with it, simple." He took his last sip of sherry, "Well, the same goes for me, really; I don't know who my friends are any more and they don't know me."

In the end, Miss King was suddenly returned to the London office. The staff and John did not know, nor did they ask what became of her. What bothered him was the fact that all of them in Berlin were run through the mill once again taking all the foreign secret tests.

John was left wondering as well about the coincidence of Miss King having used that particular address in West Ealing.

*
**

It was a funny thing that their consulate building on Tiergarten Strasse backed onto Bendler Strasse and from their back window, while sitting there, they could see across Bendler Strasse and into some of the German government offices. They could see the people moving about in their different rooms and things happening, but of course they didn't know what the people were doing, and the Germans in those offices didn't seem to mind that they were being watched.

The Tiergarten, the fabulous park in which the consulate building was located at the south end, was a wonderful place – especially the beautiful rose gardens that John frequented regularly. After the Olympics were over, however, there was a sad note on each gate into the beautiful gardens. An affixed sign said JUDEN VERBOTEN, Jews forbidden. The same went for the lavish Victory Lane; Jewish people were excluded.

The anti-Semitic propaganda had started up once more, and this time with even greater fury. John suddenly began to fear for his friend Ilse's safety and that evening he went to her home again, not really knowing what else he could do. This time, however, there was someone home, but not Ilse nor her father or brother. John could see a man in military uniform leaving the ornate front doorway and kissing his wife goodbye.

John was crouching in the shadows behind a Citroën in the neighboring yard, when he fell backwards on his bottom and just stayed there until the officer drove away. He could tell the German officer was high ranking due to the number of medals on his lapel, but he had never seen him before. John felt sick and scrambled to his feet, suddenly not wanting to be there at all.

Almost frantic and fearing the worst, he hightailed it back to his flat. "What has happened to them?" he questioned himself. His mind raced a mile a minute as the worst of his fears seemed to be coming true; "They're missing, just vanished," he was thinking aloud. He knew the office would not, or could not, help him anymore, and he just didn't know what to do next.

Chapter 27

A Passport Application

Captain Haysley sat comfortably reading in his chair as John entered his office. The new yellow curtains on the long windows allowed more light in than before, and John could see the signs of age more clearly on the captain's face. He was so afraid to speak about Ilse for fear of losing his job, but in the end, from somewhere deep beyond his control, he was compelled to. He and the captain had grown close over the years, and Haysley was really the only person that John could talk to about everything ... well, almost everything.

Captain Haysley had become more understanding of John's nature and had resigned himself to the fact that John would get into trouble while he was out and about, but thankfully so far John had also been able to bring back good information and to get out of the messes he fell into.

John whispered to Captain Haysley as he leaned forward over his desk, respecting the fact that he shouldn't even be talking about the Lieberts. "Their house is occupied by a German officer, all of a sudden, and her brand new group of flats has German soldiers living in them now."

The captain felt great pity for John, but as usual was not able to show it. "We have no news, John, but I will let you know if I hear of any," he whispered back. "You know, we cannot save everyone if they do not want to leave the country."

John dropped his head and agreed, but it made him feel sick. Instead of returning to his office he went out front to see Miss Avery and the office women, and to hear the buzzing of typewriters and to listen to the people chattering away, and sure enough the distraction did soothe his mind a little. One of the young women came over to talk to him and very quickly another one followed.

"It sure is busy today." The first one smiled at him. "Hello, I am new here; my name is Gillian." She held out her hand for John to shake, an unusually brazen gesture from a woman.

"Hello," John answered. "It's very nice to meet you."

"I have heard lots about you from the other girls." She smiled as if she knew more than there really was to know.

"Oh, is that so?" John laughed. "I hope it wasn't all bad."

Marjorie, one of the girls who John knew fairly well and had been working in the front area forever, or so it seemed, announced to John: "We have some news today."

"Oh?" John titled his head with interest.

"Miss Avery told us that she read a report on Adolf Hitler and supposedly his father changed their last name only a year before Adolf was born, from Schicklgruber to Hitler." She couldn't wait for a response. "How crazy is that," she shrieked out, trying so hard not to laugh.

"Can you imagine everyone going around saying Heil Schicklgruber." She wiggled her arm in the air mocking a Nazi salute and laughed so contagiously that all the other girls had to laugh with her, and a little ripple of giggles went around the room. John's huge smile was an obvious reflection of his improving feelings. He knew the girls would cheer him up.

Marjorie continued, "We had such a good laugh over this at lunch," and then she laughed even louder with a dainty little snort at the end.

Miss Avery came over on that note and, of course, she knew what the girls were on about. "That's enough now," she said much more quietly than usual, and yet sternly.

"Good day, Miss Avery," John said with a smile.

"Good day, John, I see you have heard the latest rumour. I guess someone is poking into Hitler's own ancestral identity. Now, because of this, they're wondering who his real grandfather was, and they are even speculating that this man might have been a Jewish person. That should distract Hitler for a while or at least make him mad," she smiled. "I'm sure it isn't true."

They both gazed out over the busy women at their desks, and the hum of their typewriters seemed to disappear. Miss Avery looked down at her feet "I am still quite shocked over our Miss King being a spy," she said in shame. "It was just a real coincidence that you found that out, too. How odd that is, don't you think, and after all this time?"

"Yes, indeed," John replied, "How odd."

All of a sudden his thoughts drifted back to a talk with Admiral Canaris, and how John had told him the story of the old postman and his wife and their son Tommy who worked in the theatre. He wondered now if the connection between Miss King and the address of the postman's family in Ealing could be attributed to Admiral Canaris. Canaris's name had not been mentioned in connection with Miss King's spy ring, but that still didn't mean he wasn't involved. John was also remembering now how Miss King always wanted to know what was happening at the Press Club.

"John," Miss Avery's voice shook him out of the re-enactment going on in his mind. "I feel so stupid for not seeing it or even suspecting it," she said, almost starting to cry.

John could see the pain on her face and how defeated this made her feel. He put his arm around her for the first time ever and gave her a hug. "No one saw it coming," he whispered reassuringly.

They straightened up and pulled themselves together quickly before the women could see them. John tried to comfort her, "She was like one of the family here, and it was quite a shock for me, too. So don't you feel bad! Our little Miss King was very good at what she was doing, and we know what to look for in the future."

He could see a little relief on Miss Avery's face. They had grown so much closer over the years and wiser overall by working together. He wished he could talk to her about his dear friend Ilse Liebert officially; however, he had broken the rules and so, as always, it was best to say nothing, particularly if sex was involved.

"Do you think you could help me with this one application, John?" Miss Avery asked.

"Yes, what is the problem?"

"Well, it's usually the type of application I would give to Atkinson directly, but he said he was too busy to take any more at the moment, and this nice young couple seem to be in quite a hurry. Her sister is getting married in Manchester in a fortnight."

"What's the delay?" John pressed.

"There is just no information on them," Miss Avery said, "and we were so busy when they were here that we didn't get much from them. I just told them someone would be in contact."

She looked as if she was about to cry from sheer exhaustion, and John said, "Come on now, come sit down. Here let me take that application and don't you worry about it."

He had never seen Miss Avery show such emotion before. The tension and uncertainty of the times were starting to show up everywhere even in the sturdiest of souls.

In his office John pushed through as many applications as he could, and then he sent a few over to Captain Haysley to be double-checked. Soon his desk was clear except for that one file. He never spent much time in his office, but he liked to keep the paperwork completed and his desktop empty. After looking over the application forms they had for Klaus and Brigitte Lehrer, John decided to pay them a surprise visit to update the passport office file which was, as Miss Avery had pointed out, oddly blank for the most part.

So John went home and quickly changed into a casual suit to make the young couple feel more comfortable, but he still carried his briefcase to appear official. When he got to the address, he noticed it was a very nice little house with a tiny fenced-in front yard and flowers up against the brickwork. Brigitte Lehrer hesitantly opened the door, a gorgeous woman with a checkered apron on and extremely long legs sticking out from under it. "Hallo," she said curiously.

"Hello, Mrs. Lehrer, I presume," John said after a pause. For some reason, he had been expecting someone much older, and he had an equally curious look on his face to match the size of the butterfly now flying around in his stomach. "I'm John Harrington from the British Consulate. I was wondering if I could ask you a few questions about your application to visit England. I hope you don't mind; I was in the area and I've heard you're in a hurry," he stated straightforwardly.

Brigitte Lehrer was a little surprised but happily said, "Yes, of course, come in." As her big blue eyes looked him up and down, she took his coat and said, "Please have a seat. Can I get you something, a coffee or a glass of wine?"

"Yes, a coffee would be wonderful," he answered with a smile.

She came back from the kitchen holding her husband by the hand. "This is Klaus, my husband," she declared and edged him towards John before turning back and going down the hall. John couldn't help but notice her long brunette hair that showed signs of having been tied up all day but now just lay relaxed on her back like an alluring, shimmering piece of art. Her voluptuous, full figure was accented by her extremely sexy walk, all of which came quite naturally.

Klaus had seated himself and was watching John's expression. He knew he had a beautiful wife and that scared him a little. Every day Klaus looked in the mirror and realized he was a scraggly-looking character, tall and thin. He had large eyes that never seemed to close and big dimples that made him look even younger than his twenty-six years. He always wondered what his lovely wife saw in him.

John quickly pushed opened the little bronze clasps on his leather briefcase and retrieved their application form along with a large pad of paper. "Sorry for the inconvenience, Mr. Lehrer," John said. "I just have a few questions before I can put your application through. The rules are so strict right now.

"Have you and Mrs. Lehrer lived in Berlin for very long? We don't have much information on you," he asked curiously.

Klaus sat upright and then squirmed back down into his chair, "We are both from Peenemünde," he said. "We moved here a few years ago, so that I could go to college."

"Oh well, that explains it," John exclaimed. "What do you do for a living, Mr. Lehrer, if you don't mind my asking?"

"Oh, just call me Klaus," he said, loosening up with a smile, "and my wife is Brigitte. A beautiful name don't you think," he remarked as she appeared in the room carrying a heavy tray with a full coffee pot and three cups.

"I'm sorry we have no sugar; it's so expensive," she said with plain honesty.

Klaus spoke instantly, "I have a good job now. I work for the City of Berlin as an electrical engineer." He leaned forward to pour the coffees. "It's a new job, and I've only just started. The city has many projects on the go right now; I am very fortunate to get taken on there." As Klaus passed the first cup over to his wife, he said, "And my honey bun Brigitte is a waitress at a restaurant nearby."

After a few more questions, John put his personalized nib pen away and instantly the conversation became more relaxed. He soon realized they were just a nice young couple, proper German nationals, who like most young people wanted to travel for the thrill of it and to see the world, much like himself in his younger days. Before they knew it, they had consumed a bottle of wine and chatted for a few hours. John was telling them stories of his childhood in Australia. They were amazed at such things and soon wanted to visit the land from down under.

On his way out, John happily remarked, "I don't think there should be any problems with your visa; hopefully, someone will notify you quite soon and if not, be sure to come and talk to me."

The next day John filed his report, fully expecting it to be pushed right through; however, when they put the application to the German government, it was turned down, for reasons that nobody seemed to understand at the time.

John was flabbergasted and went to see Captain Haysley who directed him over to Atkinson, who now primarily dealt with the German passport division. "They are from Peenemünde," Atkinson murmured as he looked over the report. "Well, that's interesting anyway," he said with an inquisitive look on his face.

"What is," John said, trying not to show his frustration.

"Maybe they will take you with them on a holiday there, to Peenemunde that is, if you ask really nice." Atkinson grinned at John and winked. "Or if you offer them a consideration or two."

John stared back at Atkinson with a blank expression, completely confused. "But they…"

Atkinson cut him off. "Then maybe you can find out something interesting from the people there," he mentioned as he rushed John towards the door. "Try to make friends with them if you can, but damn well watch out for yourself and be alert."

Atkinson turned back towards John as he rushed off and waved the file folder in the air. "I'll look into this," he yelled back to him, already on his way down the hall as the words echoed back to John.

"Got to go now. Keep up the good work, John."

John walked back to his office thinking, "What the heck was that all about?"

Outside the weather was bleak, somewhere between rain and snow, as John left the office later, and he could see Frank sitting in the consulate car out front. He hopped in. "Got time to give me a lift?" he asked hopefully with his cutest little pleading smile.

"Where are you going," Frank asked as he started the car up.

"To visit a couple over on Kirch Strasse, the Lehrers. It's about their passports."

Frank turned almost completely around to face John as he was driving forward at a good clip. "Oh yes, I heard you were with them last week. Was it fun? Was I not invited?" he said, moving his eyes down to look sad.

"It was business, Frank," John said with a nervous smile, while watching the road ahead on Frank's behalf. "You were nowhere around, and how did you even know where I was?"

Frank finally faced forward again, "Oh, ha-ha-ha," was his response. "The all-seeing and all-hearing Frank knows more than you can imagine."

John sat back; he was hesitant about the idea of telling his new friends, Brigitte and Klaus Lehrer, the bad news, and considered leaving them to find out officially through the mail. On the other hand, he did at least want to tell them what he knew in person. He was deep in thought when Frank, who couldn't keep quiet for more than a minute, roared, "Have you met a Fräulein yet, John?"

His pungent cigarette smoke was drifting back like a sheet in the wind towards John, who snapped out of his thoughts. "Very funny," John replied lifting his eyebrows with a troubled grin.

"Do you know the way to Peenemünde," John continued after a pause. "Have you been there?"

Frank pulled up to the curb and came to a quick stop, tensing up his body and looking straight ahead. "There's nothing there," he said. "I wouldn't be bothered with that place, not for now anyway."

"Do you want me to wait for you, John," he asked quickly, to change the topic. "I have the time and a good book, and if you want, I'll stay."

"No, I think I'll be good," John said while stepping out of the luxurious Rolls Royce. "I'll probably go out to the cinema tonight or somewhere else afterwards." He smiled back into the car at Frank with that look of just you try and keep up with me!

"Thanks though, Frank, really this is great. You have a good weekend, too," John said, barely getting the door shut before Frank tipped his hat and sped off.

John stood fidgeting on the doorstep, brushing the slush off himself and off the large package of sugar he had brought, while balancing a bottle of brandy. He'd brought the gifts to help make amends for the consulate's decision. Brigitte opened the door and held her arms open, "John, come on in," she said, reaching to help him with the packages.

As John handed her the brandy, he couldn't help but notice how stunning she looked, flamboyantly dressed for a night at the clubs. "Klaus," she called, "John is here."

"This is just a little thank-you for the other night," John mumbled. "And I am afraid I have bad news," he reluctantly said, as he watched both of their faces go from being very happy to becoming very serious. "Your application was refused by your own German government and we don't know why," he explained. "Of course, I will still look into it some more for you, and another superior is also on it," he said with an uncomfortable smile. "Can you think of any reason it would be refused?"

They both looked at each other and shook their heads. "No," they said in unison.

"We travel all the time, that's what we love, what we work for," Klaus said. "This was just a routine visa application."

"We went skiing in Austria last year with no problems," Brigitte remarked.

There was an awkward moment until John realized that he was still holding the sugar and quickly passed it to Brigitte. Klaus then lifted up the bottle of brandy, and said, "It's Friday night, we won't worry about it now."

They had a short drink and then Klaus helped Brigitte on with her coat. It was lovely to see their amorous gestures relaying the true depth of the love between them. Outside their Opel Olympia was parked on the street and, as they were getting into it after saying their goodbyes, Klaus looked back to see John standing there. He had a rather forlorn look on his face, not sure yet just where he was going himself that evening.

"Sorry again," John said with a little wave good-bye and turned to walk away.

Klaus spoke loudly while leaning over the top of his car, with a mischievous smile taking over his face, "Would you like to come to the club with us, John?"

"Are you sure?" John instantly replied with a teenager's glee.

"Hop in," Klaus said, and soon they were off.

John had a lot of fun times with the Lehrers after that and they became quite good friends. Klaus enjoyed talking about engineering and Brigitte enjoyed cuddling and listening to the bands. She loved to dance and usually had to look elsewhere as John felt too clumsy and Klaus didn't enjoy it either. John continued to visit them from time to time, with more gifts from the "Diplomatic Bag:" coffee, butter, whiskey, or English cigarettes, and other little things that they liked. Many of these things were in short supply or completely unobtainable in Germany.

John continued to be very friendly with them for a reason. Often in the summer months, they invited him to accompany them when they visited such seaside towns as Peenemünde, Swinemünde, and Gdynia. These were lovely country towns that reminded John of Richmond, Yorkshire England.

The office expected him to find out what he could about this district along the Baltic coast. Haysley always said, "See what the people are like." That was the most important thing. They always wanted to know what the people were thinking or what the people were talking about, and John didn't blame them. That was the whole idea of him going, and it really paid off later when he went back to Peenemünde.

Gdynia was a border town, part of the district that surrounded the port city of Danzig, and watched over very closely by both the Germans and the Russians, who were always squabbling over it. Gdynia's name was later changed by the Germans as well as Swinemünde, which originally had a Polish name. An extensive radio communication installation and bomb factory existed there.

No matter how far one travelled, one never forgot the current malaise throughout the country, as the numbers of Jewish people trying to leave Germany were increasing daily. It appeared to John that their little passport office was like a funnel for them to step into and be seeped out of the country. His physical presence in and around the office had become less and less, while the newer recruits were dealing with all the applications that were still pouring in. Instead, John was sent on many errands around the city because of his language skills and his, by now, flawless Berlin accent.

Chapter 28

BERLIN 1937 – SIGNS OF WAR

The manager of a German bank that John sometimes used had a very fine home in the Kaiserallee District. He invited John to his house for supper one evening. John discussed this with the office, and it was decided that this time he should accept his offer. The banker sent his car to pick John up, and they had a very elaborate meal – English style, complete with butler, and followed by a cigar, coffee, and brandy. All, John assumed for his benefit.

His daughter also dined with them. John thought she was about twenty years of age and certainly good looking. She seemed to be a very nice person, or so he thought at first. She invited him to join her in her sitting room for a coffee and to speak with her in English. She was looking for help with the language and wanted John to teach her some of the English habits and expressions.

What she really wanted, however, was to obtain a visa to visit some friends in England and, in fact, the address she gave him in Wales, which John checked out in the following days, once again did not exist. The coincidence of Germans liking Wales was beginning to become odd to say the least. She offered John many things in advance, as one could imagine: a sleeping partner and of course money, it was always money. John told her simply, "I'll make some enquiries at the office."

They had been advised not to use one bank all the time, but instead to switch from one bank to another, apparently to confuse the Germans about just how much money or property they owned. John did not go to that bank again. It is easy to understand why the consulate had rules about sexual relationships at a time like this. One mistake and they had a hold on you. Her female companionship might have been very nice for John, but had he taken her up on this, his career would have been finished.

⁕⁕

His lust was soon dampened when he went to another of the Nazi party rallies, held in the gigantic Sports Palais. These party rallies were still a highlight for most people and were truly something to see. The furor created in the crowd was electric, as thousands of people roared Sieg Heil, and raised their arms in unison. It would tend to make people instant believers in the party policies, even if they hadn't been before.

John was able to attend two of these unbelievable rallies with his German Diplomatic Ausweis; however, on the third attempt, he was stopped at the entrance by a sergeant of the Black Guards who refused to let him pass saying, "Kein Ausländer, kein Eingang." No foreigners were allowed admission by this time. He told John that he would be well advised to go away. John felt that it was unusual to be told that he could not go in. The guard said to John, "There are three more sentries of the Black Guards Unit whom you will have to pass by and who would be ready to arrest you."

Later John discovered that the guard who had stopped him from entering the Sports Palais was, in his civilian life, a clerk working in a well-known store in central Berlin. This is where John had been in the habit of buying his English tobacco and other goods from England that they could still obtain at this time. The strange thing was that John had been served by him so often in the store in his working clothes and yet he didn't recognize him in his military uniform.

John never talked to him again. Had he reported him to the German government or even to his own office, he would have been in a lot of trouble. One had to be sure of one's ace in the hole, as it were, because instead of being refused admission, John could have been arrested. This was very important, as the British Foreign Office would have denied any knowledge of his activities.

On the other hand, the clerk, in not having reported John and someone having reported him for not reporting John, could also have been in very serious trouble. It was apparent that he and John both could have been sent who knows where. It was also apparent that John had made some good friends in Germany.

"You must have done something right for someone," Captain Haysley said after hearing the story. He put his newspaper down and got up to pour the usual two glasses of sherry.

"Thank God, we can still get the real news in through our diplomatic bag," he said pointing to the British newspaper on his desk, "and not that hogwash that Hitler is force feeding them."

They both started to talk at the same time, both hot on the issue, but John was the loudest this time; it was a topic he was adamant about. "This is just like in the First World War, you know, when Earl Grey was warning of war and no one was paying attention. Grey then, Churchill now," he said plainly, his shoulders raised like that of a soldier stepping onto the field. "Well, I'm listening, and we have to start being even more fastidious around here."

Captain Haysley's face showed a little smile, "Finally, you may perhaps start listening to my warnings."

John looked leery, and Captain Haysley quickly said, "Yes, yes, you are right; there is a very good chance of war now, but I still hope it can be avoided."

"Of course," John lamented as he took a large sip of sherry and sat down. "Hope is good, but tanks would be better in this case."

"Indeed," Captain Haysley replied lifting the paper off the desk. "It's a volatile time right now. Just read this: Italy is fighting, and Japan is at war with China, now Spain. No one back home even wants to hear the word 'war' and yet with all this fighting going on around us, it seems almost inevitable now."

John was almost in a trance as he spoke, "I still remember this feeling quite well, the disbelief that lead to a massacre. It is like we are all precariously balanced on a leaf floating in the water and waiting. Perhaps the world could change overnight, moving us one way or another in a breath of time, like a gambler waiting for that one lucky roll. Or perhaps not," John said snapping out of it.

"Well, that was that," he added standing up again. "What's on for today?"

Haysley shook his head in confusion, "Yeah, okay, I guess you and Churchill are going to be right after all." He squirmed in his chair. "But don't you forget; no one wants this to turn into war. You know we're not popular when we send them this information of all the atrocities and the goings on over here, and now these exorbitant propaganda tactics being used by the Nazis. The people just do not want to hear it." Haysley flung his arms up in the air. "What am I supposed to do?"

John looked bewildered.

"Sit down again, John," Captain Haysley said in the serious military voice that he only used for special occasions. "We have direct orders from Captain Foley here," he said tapping his hand on a manila folder. "He is running some kind of special operation right now and needs us to stay low key, hush-hush, so to speak. He doesn't want to hear from us at all.

"So, don't go raising any eyebrows in our direction, all right," Captain Haysley said very adamantly, making sure to get an acknowledgment from John. "Is that clear," he demanded of him.

"Yes, okay," replied John with a nod. "I'll lie low," but that was not quite so easy, as it turned out.

Everywhere John went, he began to get the cold shoulder. Many of his favourite watering holes were now closed, and he got the heebie-jeebies just looking at some of the empty buildings. The German Press Club next door was no longer a friendly place for the British or for any foreigner for that matter.

He found out the hard way that the restrictions had become much worse when he couldn't just walk into the press club one day because a black guard stood inside and asked him for his papers before refusing him entry. It caused a little kerfuffle as John had already rushed passed him and was already ordering a beer, when the guard came after him. In the end, he had to abandon the beer.

No, the English were not as welcome as they had once been. It was obvious again the next day when John was walking down the street on his way to get a cigar or some cigarillos from a little machine. He put his mark piece in, and this day it stuck. A man came by and said to him "Was machen Sie hier?"

John told him, "The coin is stuck."

The man said, "Ach, you're a bloody Englishman, you are all the same." He didn't like John because the machine stuck, and John couldn't make it work. Well, John never got his cigar and he walked away disgusted, but he'd meet those kinds of people more frequently now.

**

War was in the air again and the soul of the city was becoming darker. The remaining nightclubs and hotels were emptying out as all the young men were joining the army or had just vanished. The airwaves were buzzing with reports of people being shot in the streets for as little reason as not giving the Nazi salute.

At the British Consulate where John worked, there was always a man on duty patrolling the grounds, but one night a bomb was thrown into the consulate building. Nobody was hurt, but it destroyed a lot of papers and property. Acts of violence like that were happening quite frequently at this time.

Thinking about the destruction from bombs would sometimes leave John with a powerful nightmare, thankfully a rare occurrence. He would wake up from these nightmares in a frenzied state, bathed in sweat, thinking he was back in the trench warfare of France.

The next Sunday he would make sure to go to church and, when he was in Berlin, it was the English Church he would attend. The priest Herr Jacob Strauss had become a confidante over the years, and they always chatted briefly after the service. On many occasions Herr Rommel, later to be known as the Desert Fox, would appear from the crowd to give his greetings to both John and Herr Strauss.

Strange as it may seem to some, Erwin Rommel at the time was a very gentle man but, after a while within the Hitler regime, he changed.

After the many hours over the years that John spent in his company, he realized that Field Marshal Rommel wasn't really like all the others but, instead, he was all for the getting rid of Hitler.

Rommel, with his rough voice, would often say about Hitler, "What he says, goes." They weren't friends, that was clear to John, although on the surface they appeared to be.

*
**

Captain Haysley was very quiet for a long time after listening to John's recent exploits. He was considering reprimanding him, John thought, but in the end, he didn't. Instead he began to speak softly with great concern. "Word has come through that your friend, Ilse Liebert, and her family may have escaped to a place in the country, but there is no way to be absolutely certain. We have seen no records of her in the work camps or any ghetto, or of having left the country, and so it is most likely they have made it to her uncle's farm."

"Thank God," John said, deflating his chest with a big huff.

Captain Haysley pointed his finger at John, "You know, John, this will have to be my last inquiry on this matter."

"Yes, of course, thank you so much." John felt so relieved. It was finally some good news.

Chapter 29

1938 – The People Change

Going to the Adlon Hotel after church was now a familiar routine. John didn't see Joseph Goebbels there anymore, and he was very thankful of that. He had begun to see another side to this man. On their last encounter, John would never forget the twisted smile on Goebbels face as he told a very sick story of Jewish children being shot in front of their troublesome father at a work camp. It had made him feel so nauseous that it had been difficult to hide his emotions.

Since then, Joseph Goebbels, the minister of public enlightenment and propaganda, had been brilliantly fooling the average German into believing whatever the party wanted. He arranged to have cheap radios, mass produced, so that every home could have one, but they only had enough range to hear the local Nazi German stations. This was an act of war in John's eyes, even though he could still receive London on his set. His dislike for Goebbels grew as the various reports became known. John eventually considered him to be an evil and sinister man, the deadliest of foes with his insidious propaganda. He relentlessly promoted what the Nazis stood for, and to John, that was an abomination.

*
**

Early one day, while dining at the Adlon, John once again met Dr. Burns, Karl Solinger's close friend from the party, who worked for the Kranich Company of Berlin.

"Dr. Burns," John said as he stood up and extended an arm. "It's good to see you again."

"Yes, hello" he said, "John isn't it, Herr Harrington?"

"Yes, yes, please join me if you are alone."

Over a drink and a chat, Dr. Burns informed John about his position at the well-known German photographic company — a subject that John held dear to his heart, as it was also his father's business in Sydney.

"Do you think there is any way I could get in there to have a look around," John begged out of pure interest and a little curiosity. His skills in persuasion seemed to be improving with age and the young man soon agreed.

He took John through the factory that very evening and showed him what they were making. John was absolutely thrilled, looking around at all of the machines in use and the various processes that were under way in the huge Kranich building. Everything looked very normal to him on the surface, nothing out of the ordinary workings of a photographic company.

It appeared that Dr. Burns was elated to see John so happy and laughing, and reminiscing about his early days. The two were having a really fun time in the echo-filled, empty factory when John asked Dr. Burns if there were any beverages, and Burns disappeared to find some. Meanwhile John was able to take as many photographs with his miniature camera as he could before he had used up all of his film.

It turned out the factory was not so ordinary, as they discovered after John reported what he had seen and what he had surmised, and they had developed his photos. It was ascertained that this special tissue was not only being used for making stamps, it was being used to produce bank notes of foreign currencies – English, American, French, and other countries — as well as stocks and shares, and other such documents.

At a much later date, John learned from the British news that somehow, someone managed to blow up the whole factory. He never learned what happened to Dr. Burns.

Captain Haysley came storming into John's office the morning after. That just never happened. John stumbled to his feet and stood at attention while Captain Haysley waved his arms wildly about in the air as he rambled on about the factory that had just blown up.

"The Kranich Firm is gone!" he said. "You had something to do with that, I know you did." He went on to say, "Captain Foley called and wants to see our reports on this, right away."

John's jaw dropped. "That was ages ago, and I gave you everything," he said deeply concerned. "What reports is he talking about?"

In anguish, Captain Haysley said, "Someone else had an eye on that place; we weren't supposed to be there and you're in big trouble now."

"I am so sorry," John said sincerely. "It was just so easy, and I thought discreet."

"Everything is such a mess," Captain Haysley shook his head, looking forlorn. "Come up to my office after lunch" he said. "I'll have some news for you." He turned to leave, clicking his heels together by accident in his desperation. It was an instinctive habit from his younger life as a soldier and was now making a rare and unwelcome appearance.

John could not wait until after lunch. He lasted about two hours and was begging Margo to let him in to see Haysley. "I am so sorry," John said, his head held low. "I didn't mean to get involved with someone else's business. I was just curious and I didn't mean any harm."

Soon he was sitting quietly with Captain Haysley, but there were no drinks offered. The air was stiff with tension and John feared the worst – that this time he had gone too far.

Captain Haysley finally said, "If London hadn't been so pleased with your information, you probably would have been let go. You do know that?"

"Which means, I'm good?" John asked worriedly.

"It seems that way," Captain Haysley sighed, the signs of great relief showing on his aging face.

John never found out what became of Dr. Burns.

*
**

At the consulate, all of the staff members were instinctively becoming more vigilant than ever. It was around 1936 -1937 when one of the young fellows noticed that the Italian embassy was being moved from where it had been near the Tiergarten to another location, and then in 1937-38, it was moved again into a new building very near to the British passport control office, from where they could easily see it.

The young man explained to them, "They built a big block, a huge basement right under the ground, I saw it. I bet that is going to be a bunker for Hitler." Most of the staff believed that it was where Hitler's bunker was going to be.

Other people still maintained that the bunker was on Wilhelm Strasse, where the German Chancellery was. Wilhelm Strasse was an ordinary city street with a sidewalk on either side and one or two stretches of homes, but there were chancelleries on this street. The newspapers maintain to this day that the bunker was in Wilhelm Strasse, but according to John and the consulate staff, it couldn't have been. There just wasn't enough room for it. The official story was that they were building a new Italian embassy in this spot on Tiergarten Strasse, but they weren't; they were building a bunker. No one outside the consulate ever talked about it however.

It reminded John of a funny thing that happened at the Chancellery (or German government buildings where Hitler had his office in the early days).

John was sitting in the lunchroom telling stories, as he reached over to put his cigar in the ashtray, exhaling the smoke high into the air so that it lightly hovered over the regular staff of girls and a few gentlemen recruits who had joined them.

"There used to be a huge statue outside of the chancellery," John began. "A great big thing it was, a beautiful historic statue with kind of an angel on top with spread wings." Everyone was listening intently and some had their heads tilted in curiosity.

John smiled wryly, "And sitting in the Chancellery, the shadow used to fall into Hitler's room, so he had the massive thing moved to the Tiergarten." Everyone laughed at the eccentricities, but it was true. They had it moved back again afterwards.

The Tiergarten itself had changed quite a bit since the early days. It had once been an enormous, elegant lush park for all to enjoy, but now in the later 1930s it was changing. People all over the city were restricted as to what they could see and hear and do. There was garbage everywhere and no one seemed to care. Of course, there were still big signs that read Juden Verboten, but by now there were no Jewish people brave enough to wander freely in such a barren place.

One evening John was reading an English newspaper, The News of the World, while at the Adlon Hotel. A young man seated at his table asked him in perfect English, "Could I have the loan of your paper?"

John said, "Yes, of course."

After having a drink with him and some conversation, the young man suggested that John might like to join him and his friend at a party that they had been invited to attend that evening.

It turned out to be a very nice party. Pleasant people, good food, (English style), and drinks. The conversations were wide ranging and covered a lot of topics. Some of the guests spoke English. John found it to be a very enjoyable evening. However when he reported for duty the next morning, he was told that the chief secretary wished to see him, not an uncommon thing. Entering the office, he was told to close the door.

The chief secretary then scolded him saying, "You were with Jewish people last night. Do not let it happen again." Then he was curtly dismissed. This was in 1938 and he had been instructed before this date that the staff at the British consulate was not to mix with the Jewish people. John however had not even thought that he was "mixing" with Jewish people when he had attended the party the night before.

Later, John wondered, "How did he know where I was on that night and so quickly?" Germany at this time was indeed a strange country. One had to be very careful where one went, and even then one might not have been careful enough.

The ways and means by which they sometimes resorted to obtaining information were at times funny, yet often tragic and dangerous. Such was the case with John's new friends, Brigitte and Klaus Lehrer.

It was possible at times to get valuable information for a little consideration, and "consideration" did not always mean money. John speculated that others on the staff must have had similar incidents as the following story of his was just one of many.

Some months had elapsed before John suggested that he might like to accompany Brigitte and Klaus Lehrer on a visit to Peenemünde. After some time, they agreed that it might be a good idea. He was about to learn something very funny about this couple.

They had decided to travel in their brand new Mercedes Benz, so the trip was a smooth one. Both Klaus and his wife insisted that John ride in the back seat of the car with her. He found out en route that the reason they wanted him in the backseat with her was that Klaus was sterile, and they could not have any children. They were both interested in his sexual prowess. Well, it ended up being a case of "combining business with pleasure" — John the business, they the pleasure, or John the pleasure and they the business.

Brigitte was very attractive and she used to cuddle with him all the way. John didn't really like the idea, since he had been told he wasn't to have any contact with them, but what could he do?

Arriving in Peenemünde they introduced John to many of their friends living there. Peenemünde was a peninsula with a small island on the tip, and the firm of Leica had a factory on the little island. There was also a hotel there, the Three Feathers Hotel, in English, and when they stayed in Peenemunde they would stay there. The son of the hotel owner, Gerhard, was good friends with Klaus and worked in the Leica factory. This chap was a technical engineer and was interested in engineering stories and, of course, that was one of John's great interests.

John got talking to him and asked, "Look, can you get me a uniform, you know, overalls, so that I can go in?"

Gerhard answered, "No, I don't think I can."

"Ah, that's too bad," John said with a little twinkle in his eye.

John didn't get in right away, but he knew this fellow suited his purpose for getting into the Leica factory there, although he also knew it was very dangerous.

Often in the summer months after that, Klaus and Brigitte would invite John to accompany them when they visited these seaside places.

**

This was a time beyond deception. Germany had invaded Austria in March of 1938, and Hitler proudly roared victoriously through the streets with no opposition, the Nazi banners waving high with the Blut und Boden Swastika on their flag.

The Hitler Youth organization was now compulsory and kept a steady flow of young people in training to be the "Super Aryan soldiers" of the future. Anti-Semitism was now being taught in the schools and was in their textbooks.

A family that John often visited in Berlin had a little girl about ten years old. She was a member of the German Girl Guides, the Mädchen Bund. As such, she attended the weekly meetings that were held in a large hall along with many other girls. At each meeting, the girls were expected to take 15 pennies. On one occasion, her father, not having enough change, said to the little girl, "Never mind, I will give you 30 pennies on your next meeting." The little girl demurred but went to the meeting, only to return later accompanied by two policemen.

The police always worked in pairs since the beginning of the Hitler regime. One of the policemen demanded the 15 pennies and said to the father, "Should this happen again, you will be in serious trouble." As there were usually about 100 girls at these weekly meetings, one wonders what happened to that collection.

One day John was walking along the Tauentzien Strasse in Berlin with a young native German. This was a very busy thoroughfare in the heart of Berlin, something like Oxford Street in London. In this street was the K.D.W. or the KaDeWe department store. This Kaufhaus des Westens or Merchant House of the West was one of the largest stores in Western Europe and was known worldwide before the war, just like Harrods of London.

As they passed this store, a large Mercedes Benz car drove up and stopped in front of the store. An elderly gentleman stepped out of the car and with his gold-tipped cane proceeded to smash every window on the street level. He smashed at least ten or twelve windows and then returned to his car and drove away. A small crowd gathered, but no one seemed too concerned about this.

John's companion put his hand in one of the broken windows and picked out a beautiful diamond studded wristwatch. He put it on his wrist and said, "Do you not think it suits me?"

John said, "You're not going to keep it, are you?"

He said, "Why not."

"You cannot keep it; that's stealing," John said to him. He was thinking they might both be in trouble.

The young man then said, "It's all right; it's only a Jewish store." The German government was continually raiding the Jewish stores and warehouses. This was one of those stores.

John's acquaintance invited him to his home to meet his family. Upon arrival, he introduced John to his father and proudly showed the watch to him. His father asked where he had bought it.

The son replied, "I didn't buy it, I took it from the K.D.W. store window."

His father was shocked and said, "You must take it back. Taking it like that is stealing."

The son then said, "Not on your life, I am going to keep it."

"If you do not take it back, I will call the police," the father then threatened him.

The son yelled back in a thunderous voice, "You will call the police! No, I will call the police," which he did right away.

The police arrived, two of them, and the son explained the whole situation to them. One of the policemen then said to the young man, "My son, you may keep the watch," and turning to the father said, "Come with us to the courthouse."

Later, the judge said to the father, "I am fining you 500 marks, for having Jewish sympathies. You are lucky to be so lightly sentenced. Do not let this happen again."

It was hard to believe that in 1938 a son would turn on his father just like that. This was an instance where the Nazi influence had reached the son, the younger generation, and not the older generation. This was the Germany that John was coming to know.

The German people had changed. As Captain Foley would say, "This whole situation has happened because Hitler has promised the people something, and he does it by hurting the Jews." Foley was very upset at what was happening because he considered himself a friend to the Jews.

It was a big mistake for Foley to get too close, too involved, as far as the British authorities were concerned at the time. Still, he never faltered and instead began to spend even more of his time helping the Jewish population leave the Third Reich.

His cover was eventually blown over a fellow called Rosband when he was trying to help his organization. Paul Rosband was deeply engaged in Jewish activity. Paul never knew that his own father, Franz Heiniser, was a Jew. It was through a connection with his father that Captain Foley and Rosband met. The relationship between these two men grew more trusting. Paul passed along scores of information, sometimes important, sometimes not, but then came the danger signal. The Captain's aid to the refugees had become known to the Gestapo.

When MI6 and the Air Section of the British Secret Intelligence Service required an insight into the German Air Force research, Captain Frederick Winterbotham was sent to Berlin. He carried out his observations by openly mingling with the highest levels of the Nazi officialdom. The reason for this was that Captain Foley had done much to compromise himself with the Germans.

Back in November of 1937, a law had been passed that forbade Jewish people travel visas or passports of any kind. Captain Foley was a great humanitarian and could not bear to see what was happening to the German Jews. Even with discipline forced upon him, he increased his efforts in using the passport office to help the Jewish people leave Germany.

John could see what was about to happen with Captain Foley, and he had also been warned by Haysley to avoid him for that reason. The other consulate staff couldn't understand why John wouldn't attend certain functions or be around for introductions, and they were cross with him; it seemed to hurt their pride. Yet he was doing things that they couldn't do, and he couldn't explain. It had become very risky to sneak around in factories and to explore places where others would not go, but that never stopped him, and so they had to find new and different avenues for him to explore.

Chapter 30
PENNEMÜNDE

There were times when the expression used by the German nationals, "Heil Hitler," was a little disturbing for John. Such was the time, when Mr. Chamberlain, the British Prime Minister came to Munich to meet with Adolf Hitler. John arrived in Munich that day from Berlin to assist with the Chamberlain-Hitler conference early in the morning. He was hungry so he went to a restaurant for some breakfast. The waiter refused to serve John until he gave the Nazi salute.

John said, "No way," and he refused to leave the restaurant, so the waiter called the police. The police were very nice and asked for his identity card, his Ausweis. They were satisfied and ordered breakfast for John, for which he had to pay. So, at that point, still in the restaurant, all was well.

When he got back on the street, it was a different kettle of fish. At this time, things were difficult for an Englishman. So many people gave John the Nazi salute, which he would not return, that the police had to follow him around, explaining that he was an employee of the British Embassy. Many were the emphatic comments of the people they met; they were not amused, and some threatened bodily harm to him.

However, all was not yet lost. As soon as the result of the meeting of Hitler and Mr. Chamberlain was announced, it was different. After Mr. Chamberlain was escorted to his plane, the same policeman came up to John and said, "Everything and anything you may require is absolutely free to you. The money you paid for your breakfast will be refunded."

As you may recall, the result of that meeting was questionable. What really happened? Did anyone really know? Hitler knew little if any English.

Chamberlain knew little if any German. True, some of the British attachés also spoke German, but remember that Hitler spoke a dialect of German, so things could have been said that were not totally understood

Herr Smitz, the interpreter, spoke both languages, but did the British attachés understand what was being said? John also wondered in later years what was on that piece of paper that Mr. Chamberlain had waved at the airport, when he'd stepped off his plane in England. Did anyone ever see it, and is that paper still in existence? John's belief was that it could have been just a blank sheet of paper.

As John departed the hotel near München, he noticed a cemetery being built and beside the cemetery was a soap factory. The horrific turn of events that had now begun had John fearing the worst. He wondered why they would have a soap factory right there and questioning around was sickened to learn later that it was to get the lard.

On that same trip home to Berlin, he noticed various places on the way where there would be a little church with a little church yard, and then a new little factory had popped up next door with maybe 20 people working there. "Making candles," they said sometimes, but again – where'd they get the fat? That was the question that tormented John. He sank a little deeper into cautious mode. Such atrocities were so appalling that no one in the office wanted to hear it, so ghastly that most people would not believe him.

November 9, 1938 was a horrific night for Berlin, one that was to become famously known as Kristallnacht or Crystal Night. The great city was on fire with a total frenzy of destruction, as thousands of Nazi soldiers amassed at Hitler's bidding. All of Berlin's famous synagogues were destroyed that night, burned to the ground. Hundreds of Jewish people were killed in one evening including rabbis, many of whom were beaten to death. All of the large Jewish stores were broken into and looted, and many of them were set ablaze by Nazi soldiers, celebrating as the flames flew upwards. Dead people were strewn around in the streets, and anyone who came to mourn them was taken away – all at the hands of the government.

The streets were filled with so much broken glass that it was as if it had snowed diamonds and had left the ground layered with glittering fragments of all sizes, all shimmering in the flames that were lighting up the entire city. It was as if a massive candle chandelier had fallen down on Berlin and left a reflection that was so intense, it was named forever after as Kristallnacht.

Many of Berlin's Jewish people who were not killed that night were arrested and taken away, along with many others the Nazis found undesirable, including the sick and the homeless. Jewish people who were allowed to stay were forced to pay for the considerable city clean up or to do it themselves.

Klaus Lehrer called John on the telephone the next day. "We are on our way up to Peenemünde for a few days. We just have to get out of here, John. Isn't it horrible? I was wondering if you wanted to come with us for the weekend."

Klaus always drove, and all that John would see of him from behind was his thick chaotic mahogany brown hair. Brigitte persistently wore provocative clothing and would quite often unbutton her blouse. "How many children would you like, Klaus," she would say openly.

He would reply with a shake of his head, "Five or six would be about right I think." They would continue to talk about the pressures that were now being placed on young couples to have a family; it was expected of them.

Brigitte was a very sensual woman. Her long brunette locks would blow gently in the wind from the window. She talked most of the way there and back, and sometimes she cried a little, but she enjoyed showing off her body and cuddling John, which made it really difficult for him to resist.

As soon as they arrived in Peenemünde, John saw to it that he encountered Gerhard, the son of the hotel owner who worked in the Leica factory. He had been working on a relationship with him in the hopes he would take John for a tour of the factory.

John would say to him, "Well, okay, would you do it for a consideration, could you do it then?"

"What do you mean," Gerhard would reply.

"Well, do you like English coffee, cigarettes, or butter?" John would say. "If I can get you some of these things, can you get me a pass to go in?"

Not money, just considerations, and most people were quite happy. John would explain to him, "I have some knowledge of engineering. I am interested in seeing the machinery that is being used there."

To all the people who knew John in Peenemünde, he was just a scruffy kind of fellow. They found him to be an ordinary English fellow in his rough clothes, and probably not very intelligent. It took months and a lot of coaxing with goods before Gerhard managed to get him a pass to go in. But Gerhard finally took John around the factory, where he was able to talk to the machinist and exchange information on the various machines in use.

Gerhard asked John later, "What do you want to know all this stuff for?"

"Oh, I'm just interested, you know," John would say. On the surface, everything was just as it should be, but on closer inspection and after a couple of visits, it appeared to John that they were making dial sights for guns, range finders, aircraft parts, and different kinds of scientific instruments, besides cameras. Many of these were far in advance of what was being made in Great Britain. John reported what he had noted, of course, and the Embassy found it was valuable information.

Klaus and Brigitte didn't know what was going on, nor that John had gotten to know a lot of people in Peenemünde. Gerhard, who was single, befriended John, and they went into the Leica factory two or three times afterwards in their working suits, but the visits didn't last long before there came the danger signal. The Germans got suspicious of people going in and he was barred. Suddenly the factory and the grounds were declared out-of-bounds. This was to all nationals, and especially foreigners, strictly forbidden. Just after that, they moved the Leica factory inland to make it less conspicuous.

John's interest was, in fact, further increased while they were staying at the Three Feathers Hotel. He could see that a lot of building material was being brought through to Peenemünde, and onwards from there to a small village about 15 miles away. He was told that it was for houses, for people working at the Leica plant. This John also reported when he got back.

He told the boss that they were building something interesting there, and Captain Haysley said, "Oh it's probably nothing, don't worry about it, it's not your business." Another time he was told, "We already know all about this at the office." They certainly didn't think it was anything very exciting. Later John was to learn that it was the base that was being built for the ramp used to shoot the V1 and V2 Rockets. This fact was reported after the war, and it was then that John realized that it was the secret structure that he had seen being built between Peenemunde and the new factory.

Unfortunately, the story does not end there. John was immediately flown to Hamburg, where they stated he had supposedly already been for several weeks. All the way there he was picturing his last contact with Captain Haysley, who was in a flustered state not typical of his usual patient nature and had yelled at him, "Now you have to go to Hamburg! Today! For two weeks."

So John spent the next two weeks in Hamburg while they waited for it to blow over. The Germans had found out that somebody had infiltrated the factory, but they didn't know who that person was. They had some inkling though about the chap from the consulate in Berlin, who had been known in town, but of course John being just an employee, a clerk, they would not have been certain just who it really was. They must have had other suspects.

John was in trouble at the consulate, because he had been sent to Peenemünde to talk to people and learn what he could that way, not to explore the factory. He was told again and again to go just so far and then stop, and somebody else would take over. John knew they were using his information, but still he wasn't supposed to go into the factory.

"Not on your life," he would grumble to himself.

He had gone too far since the factory was closed to everyone in 1938, even German nationals. John knew darn well that he was taking a big risk, but he didn't care. He had no family to worry about.

***

When John returned to Berlin, he decided to call on Klaus and Brigitte and found, to his dismay that they were missing. Their little house was empty and all the furniture gone. John inquired around, but no one could or would tell him a thing, merely shrugging their shoulders.

The people at the hotel in Peenemünde also suddenly disappeared. John could only guess what had happened to them. They had found out what he was doing and closed the hotel and dispersed the people. Much later John learned from a private source that Gerhard had broken the German Secret Service Act by allowing a foreigner to enter a "special factory." He was told he was lucky to get out of that mess.

John felt sick to his stomach with fear, worrying about the fate of his young friends Brigitte and Klaus Lehrer, but he never did learn. It reminded him of the old saying, "All's fair in love and war." This was the really tragic part.

Chapter 31
The Factory Triangle

It was not long after that that John was called up again to Captain Haysley's office. He dreaded being summoned, because it meant the news was coming down to him instead of going up.

"Unfortunately, I have some bad news for you," Captain Haysley reluctantly said, as he picked up a report, paced a few steps and put it back down again. "Your draftsman friend, Herr Berhandt…" There was a chilling pause.

"Yes, what is it," John said impatiently, picturing instantly Berhandt's beautiful family, his wife, and children.

"They are thought to have been with a large assembly of people from Kaiserallee and other streets throughout the city core who were rounded up and taken to Charlottenburg. There they have a section of the city where a group of streets had been barricaded off, and it's meant to contain all of them."

"Charlottenburg, those poor people," John repeated almost in shock. "But that means they are still here," he hesitated, "in Berlin." His eyes widened as he stared at Captain Haysley in earnest.

The Captain stared back at John with a seriousness that was comforting, "We are trying to find out what we can do for them," he spoke sternly. "It's best for you not to be involved; it's far too dangerous."

John was deep in thought and nodded at Captain Haysley, who looked John right in the eye as he spoke, "Do you hear me, John, leave it alone for now."

John had to be sure, he had to see for himself, and do his own research. First, he went to Herr Berhandt's house pretending to be an official of the German Government, only to find that it was eerily abandoned, ransacked of anything light and visibly valuable, including all the food from the cupboards. The children's toys lay untouched, abandoned as they were when last played with.

On the street it was obvious that all of the residents were gone; most of the doors were open and some belongings were scattered on a few of the lawns. Partway down the street, there was a group of four soldiers standing around trying to look official, and they stood at attention as John rapidly approached them. He was fuming mad, but he dared not show it. He raised his arm in disgust, "Heil Hitler," stopping on the spot and stamping his foot down.

The soldiers immediately straightened right up, becoming inches taller and returned the full salute. "Heil Hitler."

John started waving the clipboard in his hand and yelled at the soldiers in perfect Berlin German, "Where have these people gone! How am I to record this?"

"They have been taken to Charlottenburg," the young soldier quietly answered, fearing reprisals.

"Charlie's Dump," another lad bellowed out with a laugh, no fear in the world.

John threw his hands up in the air, "Charlie's Dump, why do they not tell me these things," he complained loudly. "Danke," he added grumpily as he carried on down the road, not needing to turn back to imagine the snickering faces of the young soldiers.

John had to summon a ride there as it was too far to walk, and once there he could see inside the tall wooden gates that had been recently constructed. There was a large group of people standing around as if in shock, tightly holding onto their children and some personal belongings. Outside of the gate there were plenty of soldiers milling around, and a large empty truck was just leaving. John stayed back for a while, watching in disbelief. Soon the soldiers went inside and began walking the group of people down the street.

John went to the gate, furious again, and it was even harder to hide it this time. "Who is in charge here?" he demanded.

Both of the remaining soldiers looked at each other, "I guess I am," one of them piped up.

"Well, then," John said a little calmer gaining his composure back, "where are the logs for this camp?"

"Here we have some lists," the youngest one said as John grabbed them from his hand.

"This is it! Where are the logbooks?"

The two soldiers shrugged their shoulders, their eyes wide.

"Very well then," John stated. "My officials will be coming in shortly to make the proper records," John stomped his good foot down and raised his hand.

"We must not miss anything. Heil Hitler."

In response, the young soldiers snapped to attention, kicking their heels together and throwing their right arms up, in the typical Nazi salute.

"Heil Hitler," they said in unison.

John continued, speaking sternly, "Precision record keeping is the key to keeping control here."

The young soldiers were speechless, just the way John liked them. "I will look inside for myself then," John shouted at them and waved the list, "Dismissed."

He briskly turned and went through the gates, and then proceeded to walk down the street. As John perused the list, he saw the names of Herr Berhandt's family, his wife Maddie and their children. He dodged two soldiers coming his way by ducking into a building, but as soon as they had passed, he located the building that the Berhandts were housed in.

The Charlottenburg district was a very poor area to begin with, and that was why it had become known by the locals as Charlie's Dump. It was a complete shock to see the whole Berhandt family, even his parents, and many other families that had been forcibly moved here by their own government, the Nazi Party.

They were put in a very old building capable of housing about four families under normal circumstances. Now, there were more than twenty families. Each family was allotted just one room, where they had to sleep, eat, and do all their toilet necessities, all in that one room. To live under these conditions was humiliating and very uncomfortable.

"Can you believe this?" Herr Berhandt asked John as he gave him a quick, manly hug. "It is so good to see you," he added, tilting his head and questioning with his arms. His wife Maddie stood up and gave John a hug also, but the children stayed huddled in the corner.

"I told them I was the census taker," John smiled, holding up the list.

Berhandt smiled briefly, "It's so atrocious here," he said in anguish. "All of these families in this little area, and we are only allowed out at certain times of the day or night. Each family has a different time."

"I don't even have a chair for you to sit on, John," he said mournfully as he pointed to the filthy floor.

"I am afraid I cannot stay, but I had to come and see what was going on and to find out if there is anything I can do." Both men looked at each other sympathetically.

Berhandt shook his head in defeat, "There are guards everywhere."

"What do you eat," John asked eventually, "and where do you get water?"

"We obtain our water supply from a stand pipe in the street, and we remove our garbage at the same time."

John shook his head, "I just cannot believe this. It's insane." A tear rolled down his cheek as he looked over at the children, "I am not sure what I can do, but I will talk to the boss."

They embraced once more, Berhandt squeezing John hard and then promptly pushing him away.

"Goodbye," he said, and John slipped away into the night.

The next day, Captain Haysley stomped around his office as he and John talked. "This is unacceptable, but what can we do about it?"

John was thinking a little more clearly but he was not yet resigned to the situation, "Does Captain Foley have the connections?" he asked in desperation.

"I have asked him," Haysley responded quickly, "and he is working on it, but I was told that it was best if we didn't know."

John slouched back in his chair, "I was afraid you were going to say that."

'It's chaos right now," Captain Haysley said very quietly, as he exhaled a large puff of smoke that seemed to hold its shape for an unusually long time. "I have heard of a few different escape plans going on from the ghetto, some more obvious than others."

"It's very dangerous now," he said shaking his head in resignation. "Many people are being slaughtered for any attempt to leave and there are some reports of men and women who were shot in the streets just for running at the wrong time."

John felt helpless, as he was being kept in the dark about any plans to help these people. Still he continued to hear vague things from Alfred the caretaker and felt comforted that someone was working on it.

"Berhandt was of great help to the British," he would tell everyone, and he would never let them forget that.

*
**

John immersed himself in his job; he felt like a combatant against the impending war machine. He knew that the Germans were starting to build up their arms and wanted to do whatever he could to shut them down.

Over the years and the many trips to his favourite golf course with Gerta Hoffman and Gerry Fulton, he had acquired considerable knowledge about Siemens Town. By now he knew that the town was concealing a really huge factory making war material, such as gun carriages, machine parts, and other armaments.

During the years of 1937-38, the Germans had decided that, as there was "talk of war" in the offing, they would segregate the various machine shops all around the golf course. These were an enigma for only so long, as John soon discovered just exactly what each shop was making. He would plan to be there during lunch and tea breaks, and he would stop and talk to the men. He got to know many interesting things. Each factory was producing a different part of something, a part of a shell or a barrel, a gun carriage and things like that. It smelled of war.

It was stated to the general public that they were making baby carriages and Volkswagen parts. There was a story going the rounds when they were there that one of the workers wives was expecting a baby. As baby carriages were in short supply, it was decided that each man would secretly take out a part of the Volkswagen and build her a baby carriage — which they did, and when they had assembled the parts, the result was a gun carriage.

278

"Some joke," John said to Gerry the last time they played golf, but it was a funny tale they used to tell often.

John was still living with the stiff leg of course from the first war. Wherever he travelled in Germany, the people used to think, "Oh, he's only an old Tommy, maybe he's on a rest, he's nobody," and John could go to places that other persons couldn't go, just because of that. He could talk their slang and the other officers couldn't do that. He got along pretty well with the factory workers, but he was really lucky too. Many times his education saved his bacon, many times.

John really loved walking and, over the years, it had become an important part of his guise, being able to blend with the people on the street, becoming unnoticeable when he wanted to be.

In his travels around Berlin, John had located three large landmarks that formed a triangle. The idea of locating these landmarks was actually how he had found the golf course in the first place, so many years earlier. One of the points was a big sports field with large iron gates, and there was a huge copper barrel to mark the spot. There was also the radio station Nord Deutscher Lloyd, with its large tower, and then the famous Wilhelm Church. John used to visit these places on occasion, and he got to know the exact distance between these points, counting off the steps as he walked and calculating the angles. He had walked it so many times that he had it memorized, which turned out to be very important in the future.

*
**

At the consulate Captain Haysley patiently listened to John.

"Anything I can do to shut this war machine down, just count me in," John expressed firmly and then with greater force, "How can I not get involved?"

"Now that would be impossible."

In 1938-39, Field Marshal Rommel was on a safari in South Africa. In fact, many members of the consulate, including John, saw his entourage of four or five caravans after their return. They were standing in full view in front of the German Press Club and in full view of anyone passing along the Tiergarten. The caravans were painted with signs that said, "this entourage had just made a safari in Africa by Herr Rommel." It was quite a sight.

It was discovered in later years, but not from the Germans, that the reason for Rommel's safari was presumably to survey the land they were interested in and to displace people, such as the Jewish population. That was never mentioned in the British press.

Yet, there they all were, these big caravans all laid out. John walked home and came back again with his camera to get a few pictures of the spectacle. Later at the office, he asked Captain Haysley, "Why didn't the press mention it?"

"Well," Captain Haysley said, "Diplomacy, diplomacy."

**

At this point, John had met Erwin Rommel many times. He always recalled very vividly what was to be their last meeting, although he did not know that at the time.

When meeting a friend or greeting someone in German, the expression is: Wie geht es Ihnen? meaning, "How goes it with you," to which one would answer, "Es geht mir gut," meaning "Good" and perhaps add, "See you at the Club." John had not been in the German Press Club since his last attempt in 1938. Nowadays you definitely could not go in there unless you had authorization. You had to be invited in and, when they were talking of war, you really weren't very welcome.

It was on a foggy Saturday morning and becoming bleaker by the minute when John encountered Herr Rommel, who was also walking on Tiergarten Strasse. The mist had thickened so quickly that it was hard to see any distance, and the strong winds made the microscopic droplets feel like a drenching rain, creating a sense of urgency. As they drew nearer to each other, the shadow of each man in the thick mist slowly turned into a person, alarming both of them until they realized who it was, and silent relief showed in the happy look on their faces.

As they would often attend church on Sunday, John politely said, "Guten Morgen, wie geht es Ihnen?" touching his hat while tipping his head in a friendly gesture. "See you at church," John smiled.

Field Marshal Rommel stopped in his tracks and looking John right in the eye replied, "No," shaking his head from side to side. "See you in heaven," he smiled.

John often wondered later, "Was it fate or did he know something?" Erwin Rommel was a person that John liked when he was not a soldier, but he was certainly a Prussian and he was definitely stubborn. He used to call John stubborn, too, but he was even more stubborn.

*
**

Captain Haysley motioned for John to pour the two glasses of sherry that had now become a welcome tradition with their afternoon reports. "How was your weekend," he queried, as he leaned back in his chair and cupped the burning match in his hand to light his pipe.

"Very interesting" John replied as he placed the sherry on the desk and sat down, but staying at attention in the chair. "I took the train down to Peenemünde on Saturday and had a look around there."

"You what!" Captain Haysley jerked forward and spit out a little sherry with his words.

"You know bloody well that you weren't supposed to go back there," he yelled, his body seeming to swell to twice the size with his words.

"Hold on," John burst out.

"There is a new railway there and the train was full of people," he quickly explained. "No one even noticed me."

Haysley slouched back into his chair a little and took a deep breath, "That's not your business anymore. I want you to stay away."

There was silence for awhile. "They are definitely building something there," John continued to prod. "I followed these trucks to a location where they were unloading materials like cement, wood, iron joists, and stuff like that," John said hoping the Captain would be happy with his discovery, but instead Captain Haysley just glared at him.

John quickly expounded. "They said it was for building houses, but those certainly aren't houses they're building there," nodding his head as if to reinforce his own words.

Captain Haysley shook his head back and forth letting out a full mouth of smoke, thick with frustration, "Okay that's fine," he finally said with a sigh. "But I don't want you going back there again, are you listening, John? You just take your holidays somewhere else from now on."

With one eye closing as his smoke drifted into it, the Captain looked a little sinister as he very seriously insisted once more, "You must let someone else take care of that one."

And that was that for Peenemünde, or so John thought.

Chapter 32
A New Generation Emerges

In 1938, buying a ticket to go anywhere in Germany or any other country was no problem for the staff of the British consulate. However, German nationals and the Jewish people who wished to travel by train or air, had to prove to the authorities "where they had obtained the money" to buy the ticket and "what their reason was" for the visit.

On the other hand, if a German person wanted to go to some place in Germany, members of the consulate could, unofficially of course, buy a ticket and give it to them, enabling them to travel by train or air. This was traded for a consideration, normally a little information.

Later in 1939, this was altered. The German government must have been tipped off, as when John or embassy staff or any other English person bought a ticket, it had to be signed on the reverse side of the ticket and the reason given for the journey.

It was still possible for a Jewish person to apply for a visa in 1938-1939 to visit other countries. They really were forced to leave because the government said the Jewish people were eating Aryan people's food and wearing their clothing. The Jewish people were given a chance to get out of the country if they had enough money; if not it was a different story.

Before passport control could issue a visa, clerks would go through their Black List. If that person was clear, they would then have to make a request to the German passport control and, if that request was granted, they could then issue them a visa. The German government would still hold back ninety-six per cent of their total assets.

Early in 1939, when the threat of war was in the air, John's bubbly athletic, Nova Scotia friend, Gerry Fulton, came to the office to see him. They had one last trip to Potsdam together, when she asked John for the loan of enough money to buy her fare to London. Of course he was more than happy to oblige.

A visit to Potsdam was always an event. Potsdam in the thirties was a typical Prussian stronghold in more ways than one. A German national living in Berlin had to wear a party badge, which distinguished him from foreign and Jewish people. When a German national left Berlin, they had to remove the badge and wear it again when returning to Berlin. Everyone entering Potsdam had to have and show proof of identity, including John. He did not, however, have to wear a party badge, but in Berlin and other cities, he was often questioned by the police, just as a matter of form. John had the impression that the police enjoyed asking people for their identification.

John liked to visit Potsdam and on this latest visit, John was interested in seeing the grave of Frederick the Great. It still was surrounded by its high iron railings – "to prevent him from escaping to worry the world again," or so it was said by the local gossip.

Many things seemed strange to John at times, but one thing that did not particularly seem strange or interest him much was at the zoo in Potsdam. Here at the base of a large tree near the entrance to the park was a small kiosk or hut where one could buy trinkets, picture postcards, candies, and other small items during the summer months. Often John stopped and talked with the owner, who had been there for years. He was an older man and seemed to be a very pleasant person who spoke both perfect English and perfect German. John never thought any more about him at all, at the time.

The newspapers meanwhile were on fire with action-packed stories of how Hitler had easily invaded Czechoslovakia, and the German people were really getting pumped up, ready once again for war. You could just feel it in the air, like a play where the people on both sides are waiting for the curtain to open.

Yet, out of respect, many people were still pretending and hoping that it wasn't the case, that it was still avoidable. But there was Nazi propaganda everywhere. The radio broadcasts spoke of glorious victories and brave soldiers, while the theatres and posters everywhere brought it visually to life. No one smiled anymore in Berlin – or shopped or carried-on and drank like "in the good old days."

A new generation was eerily emerging. The first of Hitler's young soldiers, who had been raised for the last ten years just waiting for their very moment, were now finally grown men with supreme missions. The German war machine was bursting to fight.

In the years 1938-1939, it was no uncommon sight to see a Jewish person lying dead by the roadside. One morning, when John went into work, he saw three bodies impaled on the nine-foot high iron railings in front of the consulate. They called the police, who sent along a fireman with a hosepipe who washed away the blood but left the bodies there for three days. Three bodies, for three days, Nazi humour.

Some things that were happening at this time gave John food for thought. It was Adolf Hitler's 50th birthday, April 20, 1939. Hitler issued a proclamation requiring every German National in Berlin to display a Nazi flag in a prominent place or window in every house or in every apartment. This may seem odd to some people in other countries, but it was really very smart, because if a flag was not displayed, it would mean that those people were either foreigners or Jewish people. Again it was a kind of sifting the corn from the chaff.

As stated before, John's apartment was at 33 Kluck Strasse, which was a part of the Tirpitz Ufer. It was known as being ex-territorial ground, like a piece of the British Empire. That being the case, as a bloody fool, John thought it might be a good idea to display in or out of his front window a Union Jack flag. The result was surprising.

When he returned to his apartment at mid-day, John was surprised to see waiting at the front entrance of the building a queue of people – not a sound of any kind, just silent people. As he approached the building, two soldiers of the Black Guards came up to him. One of them asked John if he could enter his apartment. He said, "Of course."

Once inside, one of the soldiers asked John, "Did you place the Union Jack in your window?"

John said, "Yes, of course," explaining that he was a member of the British Consulate in Berlin.

The soldier then said, "Young man, this is 1939, it is Herr Hitler's birthday, what would happen should one of the staff of the German Embassy in London display a Nazi flag from a window in Whitehall, London, on the occasion of your Monarch's birthday?"

"You know what would happen!" The volume of the soldier's voice increased radically. "There would be a riot. The people would be very mad, but we do not do things like that here in Germany," the soldier continued straightening up and trying to calm down.

The older guard then asked John to remove the flag, and said, "Well, let us forget all about it."

John felt very foolish and embarrassed. He realized that he could have been in a lot of trouble had this been reported to the office. More was to come. When he returned to his apartment later in the day, the sidewalk outside the building was absolutely clean – not even a matchstick or piece of paper could be seen – but that was not all. When he returned to his apartment again, even later in the evening, what did he see? Immediately beneath his front window was an anti-aircraft gun with an apparently broken wheel. The muzzle was pointing directly at John's front window. Accident or design, he thought again, he must have made some good friends in this strange country to have survived that blunder.

Many strange things were happening to him at this time. Take the case of the application made by Herr Heinrich Himmler, who was now the German Republic's Commissioner for the Consolidation of German Racial Stock. To many people, he was known as the director of German frightfulness. Himmler and his black-shirted SS were already feared and loathed in Berlin and all throughout Germany.

One day, Himmler applied for visas for five German air force officers to fly over all British Territory, meaning of course Great Britain. This was refused by their department but then granted after a direct appeal by Hitler. This approval for a visa came directly from London, and it was not an isolated incident.

Take the case of a young German air force officer who applied for a visa to visit some friends at Clacton on Sea in Essex, England. John gave him a pass to go, but when he arrived at Harwich, England, the port for disembarkation for steamers from the continent, he was turned back and not allowed to land. You see, he already had in his possession a coloured leaflet advertising the beauty spots and sights of Clacton on Sea. Their department was reprimanded for issuing the visa. Contrast this with the five German flyers. John thought it was all very strange

*
**

Freddie and Karl Solinger were still out and about on the street, and very busy with their uniform manufacturing. Back in 1938 when things were beginning to look uncomfortable, through express instruction from the office, John suggested to the Solinger brothers, "You would be wise to sell out to the German government and leave Germany while the going is good."

They said, "Why should we? We still have our factories, and as long as the government still requires us to make uniforms, we stay here."

John pointed out to them with emphasis, "As long as the government requires you."

*
**

To see his other friends the Berhandts, John made a second trip to Charlie's Dump and discovered their dilemma to be even worse than on his first visit. Food was scarce; everyone was afraid, cold, and depressed. On this visit, he snuck in some tobacco for Wolfgang and some cheese and chocolate for his wife and children, which was greatly appreciated. He tried to give them hope that something had to change.

Herr Berhandt spoke of the trouble facing his children, and his face was taut with anxiety. "We have received instruction from the police about the children, and they were very threatening." Herr Berhandt wavered a bit on his feet; the obvious lack of food made him appear much weaker than John had ever seen.

"They will only be allowed out in the street to play at a certain time and place." He sighed, defeat welling upwards through his body.

"It is just not enough, John, and I don't know what else to do. The children are suffering with no daylight."

John shook his head and didn't know what to say, "Oh, my God, this is so horrible."

Herr Berhandt took up his regular position in the room, a little path he walked back and forth on, back and forth. "What can we do? The police told us that if this order was ignored, there would be reprisals.

"What will they do to us, John? Do you think they would actually shoot the children?"

John answered very despairingly, "You must follow their rules for now. We are still trying to get you out safely."

Back at the office, John was informed that a plan was already in motion to get the Berhandt family and others out of this Berlin ghetto and that he was to cease his visits at once. Alas, it was too late. Children will be children and, as such, they frequently broke the curfew rule. After many warnings, the police came and blocked up all the exits with piles of wood and other burnable materials and they set fire to the whole building with the people inside. The building was completely destroyed, with all its contents.

No one outside of the ghetto seemed alarmed, with the exception of the consulate staff, that is, and John, who was absolutely devastated when he heard the horrific news. In the privacy of Captain Haysley's office and with a stiff drink in his shaky hand, John let it show for the first time how torn up he really was.

"The Berhandts were friends of mine," he said through his tears.

Chapter 33

RUSSIA 1939 – THE COMINTERN PACT

The following week, Captain Haysley was sauntering around his office when John got there, talking to himself and gesturing with his arms as if practising for a part in a play. "Oh good, you're here," he said with a smile.

John felt instant relief that he probably wasn't in trouble, but it began to fade as they stood facing each other for a moment too long. Suddenly, Captain Haysley broke away, "Do you think your Russian is good enough to make a trip to Moscow for us?"

"Of course, it is," John replied enthusiastically, feeling younger by the second – as if a few years had been unexpectedly lifted off his shoulders. Many years of language training was finally paying off, he thought.

"What for? When do I go?" he asked in almost perfect Russian, and then repeated himself in English.

"Sit down, John," Captain Haysley motioned to the chair as he walked over and sat down behind his desk, now bulging with papers. John was too excited to sit down and instead wandered over to the corner shelf with the radios. Being unable to bear a moment's silence, he instinctively turned one on, deep in thought. It instantly crackled its response.

"Turn that off," the Captain yelled so loudly that Margo could hear him outside. John turned and faced him, his eyes wide and ready for action.

"Do you think you can be packed and ready to go on Thursday?" Captain Haysley asked.

"I can be ready in an hour," John replied. "What's the job?"

Captain Haysley leaned back and rubbed a hand through his thick white hair. "They want you to tour a factory as if you are to be a potential investor in it."

"What kind of factory is it?" John asked curiously.

"It's a metal sign factory, nothing of importance really, but I think we are some sort of a diversion," Haysley replied.

"That's the point, I suppose, why they haven't told us much."

Captain Haysley tilted his head down and looked over his glasses, "You don't have to go, John. But if you do, there's a fellow from London who will be meeting you there, and he knows all the facts. So you just have to meet him a few days before and then go to the factory together." He shoved a manila envelope across the desk.

"I'll go pack," John said as he willingly picked up the envelope.

"Thank you, Captain Haysley," John raised his hand to his head in a military salute and rushed out, leaving the Captain in deep thought.

*
**

While John was in Moscow, he and the Londoner toured a factory where they were making metal signs of all sizes. The manager showed them all the machines in use on the floor, and on one of them in particular he pointed out the specific drop hammers that the British were quite interested in.

Then the manager said, "This machine is producing fifty parts per minute, but if necessary it can produce one hundred a minute." He was very proud of himself, and of his machine.

Everyone shook their heads in agreement and interest. It sounded very impressive, until just casually John asked, "What is on these plates?"

The manager looked over at the sign and read out loud, "LIFT NOT WORKING!"

He looked up at them blankly; his face was a picture. Everybody burst out laughing. Afterwards, when John was talking to him, he really had to try hard not to laugh again; it was so funny at the time.

*
**

John's second trip to Russia was a very important one. It was the signing event for the Comintern Pact, a non-aggression pact between Germany and Russia, held in Moscow. At this event, they decided the fate of Poland, clearing the way for invasion and dividing it up to suit themselves.

It was a kind of "feeling each other out." As what happened afterwards proved, neither party had any thought of carrying out the pact they had made. The whole thing was a complete farce, as was soon known by everyone in the world.

The Comintern Pact between Germany and Russia was a pact establishing their friendship. They agreed not to fight each other, but that was a lot of balderdash on behalf of the Germans, who had a big contingency there. As later events proved, it appeared that Stalin had believed in the pact he made with Hitler.

The German contingent consisted of Joachim Von Ribbentrop, the former wine salesman, the man who, when presented to the king at Buckingham Palace, gave the Nazi salute and was straightaway sent packing. There were senior officers of the German air force, navy, and army with them and also members of the Nazi hierarchy. The Germans put on a good show.

The British were invited as guests, so they immediately sent Mr. Strang, a man straight from London on a special assignment, and John was assigned to go with him. Strang was just one man, but he was the ambassador for the whole of the British forces. He was pretty much kept on the outside, so John didn't have much to do; he was just an escort and he didn't hear much of the conversations, but both he and Strang were good listeners when allowed.

To give the consulate staff their due, it was understandable to send John, their most discerning linguist with his Russian language skills, and with rumours of war in the offing, they wanted to be sure not to miss anything. It was an experience that John enjoyed. It gave him another outlook on life in Europe at this time, and he was glad not to have missed it.

***

Captain Foley was now in big trouble, and his job in Berlin was over. John was in Russia at the time and sad to hear the news. He had always thought Captain Foley was a decent fellow and really liked him. When the Gestapo caught Rosband, the Nazis knew all about Captain Foley. On August 21, 1939, the Captain was quickly moved out of Berlin and back to England with his wife, his secretary, and his cipher clerk.

The Foleys had maintained a home at Stourbridge, near Birmingham, but they didn't remain there long as they were later sent to Sweden. From there they were sent to Oslo, where he was once again a passport officer. John thought it was a really odd assignment for Major Foley, as he was the top MI5 German expert in the world. John thought he would have been more useful in London. Instead, the story was told that he was sent to a post already staffed by two men equal in rank.

*

John was posted to Warsaw towards the beginning of August 1939, to replace the secretary of the consulate general there, Captain Shelley. His wife, who had previously been his secretary and cipher clerk, had been killed by a German shell on the first day of August. War had not yet been declared, but the Germans had already been bombing Warsaw.

Some days later it was announced on Polish radio that war had been declared. John was called back to Berlin and he immediately made tracks with his diplomatic pass.

At the border everyone was strip-searched, even women and children, and all together in one big room. It was very embarrassing but in the end, there was no real trouble.

Arriving back at the Zoo Station in Berlin, John didn't know quite what to expect, but it was surprisingly calm. He was met by two policemen he knew quite well. One of them said, "Well, Johnny, you'll soon be leaving us, so let's go and have a drink and a chat before you have to leave."

Afterwards, they escorted him to the consulate and they parted as good friends. "Who knows, we may meet again sometime, somewhere," John said.

Well, that was what he thought at that time.

*

The last occasion on which John met Heinrich Himmler, the arrogant sadistic leader of the SS, was in the British passport office as they were packing up to leave. There were boxes sitting on many of the empty desks and a few of the men were there with John, quietly filling them with office supplies as Himmler appeared through the door. He was dressed to the nines in a long black leather cape, with six Gestapo soldiers in black uniforms crowding in after him. As usual, his presence was like a bad smell that had just drifted in, so horribly toxic that it was already too late to run.

"Leaving so soon," Himmler bellowed and laughed sarcastically. His soldiers all stood unflinchingly at the ready.

The remaining consulate staff also stood motionless, not knowing what to expect. Reichsmarshall Himmler had everyone's attention now, "What if I want a visa to England right now, can I get one?"

One of the younger consulate clerks responded quickly, to everyone's surprise, and honestly too, "I'm afraid we cannot issue visas after office hours. The office safe is always closed on the stroke of four o'clock."

Himmler was stunned and almost laughed, but didn't.

The silence was like ice cracking in a glass, intense and uncontrollable. John came forward, "Can I help you Reichsmarshall Himmler?"

"You," he said, "why have you not left yet?"

"We are leaving immediately, Reichsmarshall," John replied apologetically, having succumbed to the fear of Himmler's presence, knowing that he could be shot in the head at any second.

"See that you do!" Himmler put his arm up in salute to his Führer and stomped his foot down. Turning to leave, he had to pause while the group of men behind him slowly rearranged themselves in order to follow behind their leader. That was when John, with a last bit of bravado, asked him, "Why have you mounted anti-aircraft guns on the roof of the Shell building on the one side of Bendler Strasse and on top of the electric power plant on the other side of the street?"

Of course, everyone knew that all of the important offices of the German government were on Bendler Strasse.

Himmler stopped in his tracks and coldly replied, "One for the clouds and one for the crowds." One for the clouds, meaning it was for the enemy aircraft, and one for the crowds, meaning to shoot the people of Berlin should they start a strike.

Himmler then took a few steps towards John and the soldiers shuffled around once more. He shook his finger at him and warned: "Should you ever come back to Berlin after the war, I will put you in the Tiergarten and give you grass to eat."

In other words, assuming John would be a prisoner if he ever came back, Himmler would starve him to death. Not a very nice fellow.

*
**

There was still time for one last, large drink in Captain Haysley's office. He was trying to empty the little barrel in the corner. After that final drink, John was allowed to return to his apartment one more time. There he was met by his old landlady, Mrs. Hammersmitz, Anna, who had always taken such good care of him, looking after all his wants in Berlin, whether it was his laundry or food or tending the flat in his absence.

She came running to the door as soon as she heard it open, and as John entered he could see that Anna was in tears and had been crying for some time. She ran up to John and they gave each other a long hug, "Johnnie, Johnnie, how are you? We hoped you would come back."

She was calm for a moment but soon broke down again, and as the tears streamed from her eyes, she said in broken German, "Der Krieg kommt. The war has come, heaven help us."

John's heart was breaking to see her in such pain, and he never forgot that feeling. Her elder son was a pilot in the German Air Force, a flyer. But her younger son was only sixteen years of age and had been called up for service on the Russian front. Such were the fortunes of war. It was heartrending, that those who stayed behind also fought.

*
**

It was now the third week of the war, and all of the remaining British consulate staff left for England together, including Captain Foley's pet dog, who had been left behind when Foley left Berlin. The female staff had already been sent back as soon as war had been declared. Now just five of them were left – and Chester, the white Scottish terrier.

John said good-bye to the American and Irish people who took over the property along with the supplies that they had to leave behind. But the Americans were the next to go and followed them out of the country not long afterwards even though they didn't join the war until later. Of course when the Americans left, the Irish took over. The Irish were still very friendly with the Germans. John never found out what happened to the consulate building on Tiergarten Strasse after that.

**

The men of the consulate were quite apprehensive as they approached the frontier at Osnabrück, but there was no trouble, quite the reverse. The German border control officers were really nice to them.

"Well, gentlemen, and Chester," the young customs officer said, as he reached down to scratch the little dog's ears, "I see that all your papers are in order, just as we knew they would be."

He smiled at the group, "We were notified in advance of your passage.

"The only thing," the young officer hesitated and looked right at John. "We have been asked to remove all film from your cameras and to quickly check your luggage."

John watched sadly as the young officer took his camera off to the side and opened it up, taking the film away. It was a camera he rarely used, mostly on holidays, but he mourned the loss of some undeveloped pictures he had on it of Rommel's safari entourage. They also confiscated a few pictures that he had packed in his grip, and some were photos of the Reichstag burning – which they told him they wouldn't let out of the country.

Soon everyone was relaxed, and they were invited to a special area where it was suggested they wait for their departure.

"We can change your German currency now if you wish to English pounds," one of the officers suggested. Another officer got up and gave them a cup of tea and talked to them for a couple of hours, making a lot of jokes. Some of them had just been in England and were talking about what was "in" at the time.

They mentioned that the Germans had already been bombing London, apparently way back in July and August, but Germany wasn't getting bombed yet. The English planes were just dropping leaflets over Germany, telling the German people not to fight, to stay friends, and all this kind of stuff.

The customs officials all wished them "good-bye," and then this young lady came over and gave John a kiss goodbye. That was really nice.

It was the end of a wonderful experience for John, who never really knew until much later just how lucky he was to be alive. He hoped that one day he would be able to pay a visit again to that beautiful country and knew if he ever did, it could be quite an exciting experience. So, it was good-bye to Germany after many exciting adventures and many tragic events.

Chapter 34

BLETCHLEY – THE SECRET MACHINE

Getting back to London was exhilarating for John. People were bustling to and fro, all scurrying about with a strong purpose in their minds. There were military jeeps and trucks on the streets with young women drivers, a very welcome sight indeed. Everywhere he looked, John felt more at ease; there was no more sneaking around, he thought, now that he was back in England.

The cool wind was so refreshing on his skin, and the air felt so much lighter than the weight of Berlin air, with the tension it had always carried in its cool continental breezes. Every single breath came easier now, even as the fog seemed to be dancing across the roof tops of the historic buildings, and the visibly heavy air hung between the many spires, sagging in pockets full of moisture. Here John felt like he was coming home, at least it was the closest he had to that feeling of coming home. Australia would always run in his blood, deeply buried but never forgotten.

John was given two weeks' holiday and then posted to Bletchley Park, Buckinghamshire. He spent his holiday in London and other places nearby because he didn't have any special place to go to or anybody in particular to go to see. He hadn't bothered much about friends or family.

They sent him a railway ticket by courier, and it didn't cost him a cent to get there. It was late one evening when there was a knock on John's hotel door. He opened it to see a very official yet secretive looking fellow wearing a long coat and a Trilby hat slightly turned up at the back.

"John Harrington?" he queried.

"Yes," John replied wondering who he was.

"I have your pass here, to Bletchley." He looked at John for a response, but there was nothing but surprise and curiosity.

"Everything you need is here, all your instructions," the stranger continued. "You must catch your train on time; they will be waiting."

John took the papers, "Yes, good, I'll be there."

"Good evening then," the mysterious courier said and then slipped away.

That was it; all routine by now. It all sounds rather funny in hindsight, but it was very serious to John at that time. He didn't know what was happening but he was ready to follow orders.

Bletchley was just a quiet village and likely still remains a village. It was a station on the main L.M.S. Railway from London to the north of England and Scotland. In the magnificent park stood Bletchley Hall, a fabulously ornate Victorian mansion. The deep red bricks of the hall were elegantly adorned with delicate white woodwork, and very elaborate Victorian trim with numerous doors and windows. John thought it could truly be called "one of the stately homes of England."

It may now be told that Bletchley was the headquarters for the British Secret Service, then known as MI5 and MI6. Also, there was the Code and Cipher Departments, which housed the code-breaking machine known as Ultra, which superseded the Enigma and others.

Arriving at Bletchley Railway Station, John was met by an officer, (not in uniform) whom he had met on many occasions before the war had started. He knew him quite well, as you would know a neighbour. He asked John for his identification papers and so he produced them. After satisfying himself, the officer then escorted John to a private car.

John was a little taken back that, even though this man knew him personally, he still wanted to see his papers, but after he was satisfied, they drove down to what John thought was, or had once been, a country stile. In England hedges border the fields and every so often there is a gap in the hedge where you could climb over a little fence, or step up, or walk over it, but the animals couldn't, and they called it a stile. Here, they were greeted by a man who looked like just like a farmer who'd come right off his field. He also asked for John's papers.

Well, John produced them for him, but only after satisfying himself that he was really a member of the service. John gave them his papers only after he got some information on who they were, that they had some official status. He didn't give just anybody his papers. Nobody couldn't just up and say, "Oh, I want to see your papers."

He was in England now, and he wanted to know why this farmer had requested to see his papers. Soon they were both satisfied and the first officer drove away leaving them together.

The farmer was armed with a rifle and, after checking his papers once again, he led John to a small hut concealed among some trees. Here there was installed a black telephone sitting on a little table on which the farmer made a phone call, but John was unable to hear what the conversation was all about. After a short wait, a soldier came along. He asked to see John's papers and, when he was satisfied, he asked John to accompany him to a small house. Here he was checked over, searched, fingerprinted, and then passed on to another soldier. When John told the story later he knew it sounded stupid, but security was very tight.

This soldier escorted him to the entrance of Bletchley Hall. Here again he was searched and stripped naked while all of his goods and chattels were examined, and then he was allowed to dress himself. John was given new clothes and, at the time assumed his other clothes were destroyed. They also gave him a new passport and identity card that very day.

He was informed at this time that, when entering or leaving by car, one had to get out of the car for a physical examination, and the car also had to be thoroughly examined by the soldiers on guard.

This introduction had taken nearly five hours, from the time that he arrived at the railway station to eventually arriving at Bletchley Hall. He was informed later that he was lucky that all his papers were in order; otherwise, he might still be at the railway station or even be in jail, a gloomy thought.

John still didn't have any idea as to what was going on there at Bletchley, not yet. He just thought it was very, very funny indeed. You see, there were four guards to go through before he even got to the main door.

This procedure of showing one's identification papers was strictly observed at all times when entering or leaving the park. This applied to all persons, irrespective of position or rank. No matter who it was, unless they had a very special pass, a military escort such as Winston Churchill or the king, or members of the Royal Family. It was once reported that gaining admission was "just like falling off a tree, a big tree someplace."

As mentioned before, once in the building John had his photo taken and his old photo and pass destroyed. New ones were given to him and he was informed that he must have them on his person at all times, and he always did. It was part of his daily morning routine to make sure that he had them on him, always. Everything else was destroyed. He was like a new person. All that was old was gone and replaced by everything new.

Everyone entering the main building for the first time received a number and a location. It was explained to John that names could be doubled, such as Smith or Jones, but numbers could not be. During his stay John's number was 47, but he wouldn't ever have written that down normally. If at any time, John was required and wherever he might be, his number would be announced on the intercom or PA system, and he would have to report to his allotted location immediately.

To visit any other location other than one's own, one had to possess a Special Pass and know the password for that location. All the passwords given to them were changed every day and again at night. This did not apply to the chiefs of staff, generals, admirals, and special personages. These men had their own quarters to which all of the decoded messages pertaining to their department had to be delivered by a "special messenger."

It was officially pointed out to John that Major Frank Foley, who of course was his chief and the consulate general when he was in Berlin, was the chief of the MI5 for the whole of Germany. John remembered, that Foley had a German wife and the caretaker Alfred was a German and that the chief telephone operator on the main switchboard at the British Embassy had a brother in the German Air Force. At that time, John did not know what to do or think of this, and it was just one of those rare occasions when he had decided to do nothing about the situation. It was lucky for him as it turned out, because they were Captain Foley's "body-guard of lies!"

When John was posted to Bletchley, he met all the people with whom he had worked at the consulate in Berlin. The captain and his wife, the caretaker, Alfred, the telephone operator and his brother – they were all there at Bletchley. It was quite a memorable reunion, and it turned out this had been a big unknown spy ring. They were all British agents or spies, despite the fact that they were German nationals. They were born in Germany and trained by the British. John was amazed, and he didn't know what to say. He had had no idea that they were in the secret service. He knew he himself had been doing strange things like getting into factories to look around, but it never struck him at all that other people in the consulate were spies.

He just couldn't believe his eyes when he arrived and walked into that room at Bletchley to meet none other than the man who had sold trinkets at the kiosk under the big tree at Potsdam and learned that he was a member of MI5.

It momentarily brought joyful tears to his eyes when he walked in; he just couldn't help it. As one can imagine, they had quite a chat. The fellow was a native of Oldham, England. That made John wonder and think back, and hope that he had not transgressed in any way. Apparently he had not, as the man so gently put it, "If you had, you would not be here today."

Often John wondered what he would have done had he known then what he found out later. Just how near he had been to trouble, he would never truly know, because he always seemed to duck out in the nick of time. All was well that ended well.

Nevertheless, John had many questions and worries about possible transgressions that he might have committed in Germany and realized in hindsight that, right from his very first day on the train to Berlin, even the encounter with Richard Tauber had been planned. This brought to mind the many questions that John had about Admiral Canaris, but no one was talking about him in England.

The story of Miss King and her spy ring was a popular topic and, when John returned to London, he was congratulated for his work in that connection and also informed that a member of the London staff was an accomplice of Miss King's. It could have been much worse.

In Berlin, John had met a young lady who said her name was Rosie Lee, not her real name of course. She was a very good singer and a strapping young lady. To John, she seemed a typical German girl, a typical Fräulein.

She was employed by the German government to sing songs to the German troops on the radio and on stage. She did it very well and had a good following. Rosie Lee had excellent relations with the German officers, and she had introduced John to many of them. So much so, that he was on his guard as he had thought she might be a Nazi agent.

Again he was wrong, as after the war had begun and he had been posted to Bletchley, who met him with open arms? None other than Rosie Lee. She was also a member of MI5 in Germany.

They had a very, very long talk at one point. John could hardly believe his ears as he poured himself a little shot of Scotch whisky. "What are you doing now?" he asked her.

She brushed away a large feather on her hat that was tickling her face and said, "What do you think? Singing, of course."

As Rosie Lee got up to leave, she pointed out to him, "I am doing the same thing here, Johnny, except I'm singing to the Allied troops now instead of to the Germans."

He then asked her, "How did I behave myself in Berlin?

She put her delicate gloved hand on John's wrist and said with a smile, "You helped me in what I was doing, by being suspicious."

He let out a sigh of relief. "I am just so surprised to see you here."

John often wondered what was to become of Rosie Lee. She was born in South Africa, shades of Rommel, he thought.

*
**

John had tried to keep tabs on some of his old contacts from Berlin, and he found out, that in February of 1940, Erwin Rommel was sent to the Rhine Valley with a panzer division. This same year, Hermann Goering was made Marshal of the Realm by his good friend, the Führer, and was now in charge of the entire German Air Force.

Bad news hit John hard when a cable was handed to him about four weeks after the war had started when he was just barely back in England. It was from Fred Solinger, who was in the Hague and asking for help. His plea was probably ignored by the office, and John, unable to help, never knew what became of them. The fortunes of war had struck another cruel blow. John felt especially bad for Mrs. Solinger, Lili; she was quite a dish, a beautiful woman with whom he had become good friends

"What a waste," John tearfully remarked when he got the news.

"Imagine risking one's life for money. But what could I do?" John pondered aloud. He was only a very small cog in a big wheel.

Gerry Fulton, however, John's friend from Nova Scotia, was alive and well and now living in London. The loan of three hundred marks for her passage was paid back to him in 1940 by her father, who was living in Canada and owned a steel plant in Sydney, Nova Scotia. The last time John saw Gerry, she was in London driving a Red Cross ambulance. John was greatly worried for her safety as the bombs were falling heavily on London at the time.

Chapter 35

ULTRA

Winston Churchill had become prime minister of Britain on May 10, 1940, and it was only a short time before he would give name to the famous Battle of Britain during which Goering's air force, the dreaded Luftwaffe, filled the skies over England with their unrelenting Blitzkrieg. A fast and hard-hitting tactic of attack designed to catch the opponent off guard, the Blitzkrieg was manifest initially by German bomber planes aiming for Britain's shipyards and airfields.

Hitler's war was now heating up. After invading Poland, he originally wanted peace with the British, but that didn't last long. He invaded Denmark in April and then the Netherlands and soon Belgium. Hermann Goering was so proud and impressed with the large numbers in his modern air force that he swayed Adolf Hitler to attack England by air and convinced him that they would soon be glorious victors.

With that, the bombs began to rain down on London and many other blameless towns; it was like nothing they had ever seen before. Innocent people were dying by the thousands. Night after night the German bomber airplanes, the mighty Heinkels and Junkers flew over, while helpless people lay in their beds or crouched in their cellars or shelters – many of them counting the bombs as they dropped and listening to the increasing roar of the engines as the giant birds of destruction approached.

"1, 2, 3, 4," they would mouth, holding their breath for the longest time while waiting to hear that fifth bomb explode, wondering "will this be the one to hit us?" The lucky ones would hear that horrible yet comforting sound of the bomb dropping past them; "five," they would whisper with another breath of life that was allowed them.

In the city of London, masses of people from every walk of life gathered in the undergrounds or designated air raid shelters; sometimes the people were packed so tightly that they had to stand all night long. The British morale was so strong though that, even with the city of London burning all around them, most never gave up.

"They will never get us, they can bomb all they want," was on the lips of most Brits, except of course for those who had lost a loved one and were still in shock. It was in their British nature to be strong willed and it was what kept them going.

They desperately needed all the hope they could muster while the bombs showered down with horrible devastation. As the flames leapt higher, they were ripping British cities apart as if the hungry beast of hell itself was eating them up.

The air battles were phenomenal and had never been seen to such an extent before and by so many spectators. The British Spitfires and the German Messerschmitts were fighting constantly, literally chasing each other around the clouds outlined against a crystal blue sky, climbing then plummeting, performing spectacular manoeuvres in the air until a winner emerged. Scenes were unfolding in the skies above that were breathtaking for those on the ground and would live forever in history.

Eventually the Blitzkrieg was over and Britain had survived, unconquered but with great losses. Over 40,000 people were killed in the Battle of Britain, and half of them from London.

Hermann Goering was devastated and ready for another breakdown. Adolf Hitler was very disappointed, but just gave up on the plan to invade the British. He never really thought it would work anyway and told his top officials that it was really just a distraction while he planned his empirical crusade on the Russian Front.

Hitler was now fifty-one years of age and starting to show every second of it, with a new seriousness that had recently crept across his face. He was at war, full out. His armies were invading every country on Germany's border in a series of Blitzkriegs, and as Germany's borders expanded on the map, it looked like a flower opening up, with each petal unfolding to reveal the new shape of Germany.

The more land that Adolf Hitler conquered, the more he wanted; but doubt was creeping into his gaze. How long would the bloom last on this flower? It was like a death sentence; suddenly, he could see it had a lifespan, an expected demise.

His lack of participation, of being on the front line, was like a thorn in his side, and he stood quite often with his hand behind his back now, just an observer. He could often not even be bothered to give the Nazi salute but just a nod of his head — when he had to.

*
**

Back at Bletchley, when reporting for duty in the mornings and upon entering the park, John would give the guard the password that had been given to him when he last left the building. Again, this was changed every day. If you were away for a period, upon returning you would have to produce your special pass for the guard to see and then he would call security to get you clearance.

One morning when John tried to enter the park, the guard asked him for the password for that particular day. The password for that day was "caramel" but he pronounced it cameral. It was a simple mistake; you wouldn't normally detect it, but this guard did. He knew John fairly well; they used to go out and drink together and yet he detained him while he telephoned security for information. Eventually, after receiving clearance, he allowed him to proceed, but John was reprimanded, again.

The guard explained to him that the reason that he would not let him enter the park was that if he had let him in on the wrong password and someone had noticed this and reported it to security, both he and John would have been in serious trouble.

John asked him, "Why a password instead of a pass?"

He answered simply, "A pass can be forged, but a password cannot." That seemed quite logical to John.

It must be understood that there was more than one man on "the guard": one on the outside but always a few more coming behind. It was some time after John's arrival that he was officially informed that all of the guards were fully trained officers and not just ordinary soldiers. Even the farmer on the first day was an officer, and all of them were fully armed right down to the bayonet.

It was here at Bletchley Park that the wonder machine, the Ultra was housed in one of the many huts in the park. It was said to be capable of breaking almost every known code, in any language. John was amazed by this marvellous machine.

The Ultra machine was invented by two Englishmen, Alfred Knox and Alan Turing. These two men were specialists and the best in their field, and the machine was first known as the Turing Machine after the man who first invented it.

Bletchley Hall itself was like an old castle, a big old hall full of history and memories for many. John never found out who owned it or how it came into the possession of MI6. They even kept animals there, just munching away in the yard, part of the cover. John thought it was pretty funny, when he first got there, to see cows and sheep and geese wandering around the yards. He was quite astonished at all these little things.

Various huts outside in the park were wired up, with the wires running all around outside, and there were guards at every hut, each of which had some particular purpose. Some were for German instruction, French instruction, or whatever kind of instruction was necessary. Many others housed different political staff.

The Ultra was housed in Hut Number One, the only one that John was really interested in. To make the machine, they used a special screen with "connections" on it. The fellows didn't make them normally, so they asked John to go out and explain to them how to make these customized parts. His machining skills came in handy.

If John had to enter, or attempt to enter one of the huts, he had to have a pass and know the password for that particular hut. The pass and the password were given only to the guard of that particular hut and to the people concerned with that hut. When he had to go back out, he had to get the password from the guard there. This may seem very confusing, but it was a routine that had to be strictly observed at all times.

The Ultra Coding Machine was made up of many parts from many places, and even from different countries. The reason for this was that it would be impossible for any one person or country except the original inventors to copy it – or should it be said, to perfect it.

On more than one occasion, John was sent on a mission to obtain a certain part for the Ultra machine from a specific factory. The machine was working constantly and some of the parts were apparently wearing out.

Entering the huts, one could hear the machines at work. The operators were wearing headphones as the messages came through, and no words were spoken about the message. When it was finished, the operator would hand it to John or some other person for the message to be decoded and translated, scrambled they called it, and then it was delivered to the officer or department concerned. There were some surprises at times, for instance, messages from one department to another in a foreign language, where some people would be discussing their sex problems.

*
**

It was stated later that Winston Churchill sacrificed the city of Coventry to save the secret of the Ultra Coding Machine. Just how that evolved was quite the secret. The order to bomb Coventry came through clearly over Ultra; and yet, if the city had been evacuated, the Germans would have figured out that the Brits knew their strategy. No other country knew about Ultra, as far as they could tell. MI6 explained to Winston Churchill what was needed, and he had to do that. On November 14, the Germans attacked as planned, and Coventry was demolished.

John saw Winston Churchill only once, and it was there in the Bletchley dining hall, but he didn't have the opportunity to talk to him. The dining hall was a very long room, where he would go to get his lunch at a certain time each day. He would sit next to anyone, and he never knew who his neighbour was. No one ever discussed his or her work, and he would just say "Hello, how are you doing?" John never knew what that person was doing or who he was, and that person never knew who John was.

They would just announce 47 on the PA, John's personal number, and he just got up and walked over. It sounds dramatic maybe, but that was it. It was very interesting to be sure, but John knew he didn't truly understand what it was all about; he had no idea what the big picture was. All he knew was what he had to do at a certain time and place.

*
**

Life at Bletchley had its bright spots. One was allowed to go into the village one day a week on a rotating basis, on a special pass and under certain conditions. John soon became friendly with the local doctor and his good wife. The doctor was a bluff Irishman and his wife was also of Irish descent. He was an excellent sportsman. The doctor liked good food, shooting rabbits, and playing golf – and he was a good player of the game.

When possible, John would accompany him on his daily calls. Doing the rounds was usual in this part of the country and, after finishing his rounds, they were invited on occasion by the Duke of Bedford to play a game of golf on his own private course at Woburn Hall. The duke would play with them and, after the game, they usually ended up in the hall at Woburn for a very enjoyable evening. The duke was a good sport, and the trips to the hall were a very pleasant change. It was very lovely there, and John found those occasions to be quite special.

John only attended church on two occasions in Bletchley, as it was discouraged for obvious reasons. The friendly country people asked too many questions – who he was, what he was doing there.

*
**

On May 10, 1941, for reasons still obscure, Winston Churchill told the War Council that he wanted the "best expert" on Nazi officialdom, Captain Frank Foley, to interrogate Hess, Hitler's deputy, who had landed solo and clandestinely in the Scottish highlands. John was proud of Captain Foley and thought he was a truly remarkable man, a compassionate man who had saved thousands of lives with little concern for his own safety.

*
**

Hitler and his armies were in full swing now. In April of 1941 he had invaded Yugoslavia and Greece, and in June he sent in 3,000,000 troops to invade Russia. By December of 1941, and after Japan attacked Pearl Harbor, Hitler was forced to declare war on the United States because of the Japan/German pact. Only a month later, when the famous conference was held in Wannsee, the plans were presented and agreed upon for the "final solution." It was a sickening plan to eradicate the millions of prisoners, particularly Jewish people being held in atrocious concentration camps, which were increasing in number behind the plague of Hitler's new Third Reich.

Now almost every country was involved and fighting in the war, and it was now officially the Second World War. The British were really starting to pump out the airplanes, as were many other countries, and these new airplanes with the young flyers in control of them, gave people hope to think that this was a new age, with new advantages. It was a constantly changing defence strategy, and aviation was on the leading edge of war technology.

⁎

While at Bletchley, John was shown maps and photos of Germany from the pre-1914 period. These were all out of date and, in many cases, the locations had been altered or completely moved.

"I hope our air force isn't using these old maps," he said to his commander-in-chief one day.

The commander looked at John as if a light bulb had just lit up his thoughts. He pointed and shook his finger at John saying, "You know, with your knowledge of Germany and all the cities there and the locations of the factories that you've been to …" He lingered, deep in thought, "Maybe you could be of value to the Air Force, an observer or something like that. You know, to help with the identification of those specific points that you have been mentioning."

"Yes, that could be interesting," John replied, with his large brown eyes opening wider, forcing one of those little curls on his forehead to mischievously pop up.

Chapter 36

PATHFINDERS – 1942

A very tall, redheaded soldier entered Hut 3, and everyone momentarily looked his way – and then, just as quickly turned away again, continuing on with his de-ciphering production.

"Harrington," the soldier inquired looking around the room. "Captain Haysley would like to see you."

The two men walked over to Bletchley Hall and up the main staircase into a beautiful room with large arched windows that had a commanding view of the estate. Captain Haysley was standing in front of one of them, gazing out. He was holding a glass in one hand and a cigar in the other, appearing far more relaxed since his return to England than he ever had abroad.

A number of people were mingling about as always, but John went directly over to Captain Haysley, who had drifted away from a group of Royal Air Force officers.

"Good afternoon, gentlemen, and Captain Haysley," John said as he nodded his head politely with a smile. Unconsciously, even though he spoke English, John's Berlin accent came through strong and clear when addressing Captain Haysley, and the air force officers all stepped back together in a bit of shock.

Captain Haysley let out a huge bellow of laughter, enough to completely distract the officers. "Men, you are looking at the master of disguises here, a man who can change his accent or dialect or even the language, as quick as a flash."

The air force officers now looked a lot more closely at John, eyeing him up and down.

"Hello," one of them said with a grin. "Good lord, you had us going."

John noticed that these men seemed to always react as a squadron; even when relaxing, they simultaneously took a drag of their cigarettes.

Captain Haysley explained to John, "These men have just been telling me about a new group the air force is starting in an effort to pin point their bombing locations in Germany, so as to not kill as many civilians."

He took a sip of his drink, "They are called the Pathfinders."

"Pathfinder Squadrons," one of the older officers corrected him. "We are trying to achieve greater accuracy in our bombing raids and are using every means at our disposal. It would involve more strategic bombing."

"I see," John said, even though he didn't really see at all but didn't want to say so. Instead, he motioned to the whiskey bottle on the desk, and Captain Haysley gave him the nod of approval.

The RAF officer continued, "We have new navigational aids that are increasing our precision, and we have good aerial photographs now, but we are also looking for any specialists who have actually been to these particular bombing areas."

John finally understood what he was doing there, "Yes, good," he said.

Captain Haysley let out a large puff of smoke which was followed by a ghastly cough, "I thought you might be of some help to these fellows, you know, locating the factories on the ground, at least when it comes to the Berlin area." He looked closely at John's reaction, which was mostly surprise with a little excitement thrown in.

So John jokingly said, "If you give me a Pathfinder position, I could easily spot some of the locations for you."

Captain Haysley took the last sip of his drink and loudly plunked the glass down turning to the air force officers. "Well, you know I think you can give him a trial."

The RAF officers looked at John so intensely that he felt like they were peering deep into his soul to see if he could be trusted; it was the same way that he had felt when agreeing to the Secret Service Act upon arriving at Bletchley. They could not help but have a little distrust of him with his superb German language skills, yet it was this exact form of information they were after, and so it was decided to give John a chance to make a trip.

After the officers had left, Captain Haysley told John, "If anything happens to you, you will not be able to claim any compensation." He let out a big sigh. "You see, we can't give you a commission."

John was not really surprised, "In other words, I would not exist," he replied.

Haysley's age was starting to show by his slower movements, which were forgotten instantly when he roared loudly, "Well, if you go, it's on your own head."

He looked at John over his glasses the way he had so many times before. His eyes were very intense when he seriously said to him, "I mean if you get hurt or anything happens, we don't know you.

"We can't give you a pension either," he quickly continued on. "But you should be okay on that front because you are already entitled to one from the First World War."

✳✳

It was only a short while later that a commander in the Royal Air Force unofficially asked John to volunteer for a civilian air force. So, naturally he volunteered; John was so enthused and eager to help out. It was a real chance to be on the front line again, so to speak. So after his position at Bletchley was over and after a short break, it was off to new adventures.

John was never officially in the Royal Air Force, but they gave him a uniform and some wings as part of his camouflage and he remained with them until early 1944. Again he was told that there would be no records of this, but they gave him a Defense Medal for being there.

The Royal Air Force map room was enormous, with long windows going all the way around the room and with a very high, rounded ceiling that caught the light and intensely lit the room up. Maps and photographs covered any wall space remaining, and numerous large tables were scattered around that had photos and maps of different areas spread out over them. Groups of pilots were gathered at a few of the tables when John first went into the room, and their coloured uniforms caught his eye instantly, recognizing that some of them were from foreign countries such as Canada and Australia.

One man looked up from the farthest table and immediately recognized John. It was Mac Pierce, a Scotsman who had also been working at the British Consulate in Berlin.

"John," he yelled, waving towards his table. "Come on over here."

They shook hands, "It is good to see you again," John said. "It has been some time now, but you look well."

"Yes, and you," he said smiling. "I thought you might be able to help these fellows in locating a few of those factories that you always visited in the Berlin area."

The whole room seemed to go quiet and, in that split second it took to answer, everyone seemed to notice John, his tall thin demeanour, very well-dressed and clean shaven as usual — unlike their sorry lot, mostly a scruffy crew in their leather flight jackets, with the exception of their commanders who had shaved that day and were always in uniform.

"Well, of course I will. That's what I was doing it for," John said with a big grin, "I wasn't always just walking around for the sake of it."

The room began to buzz again, a little bit louder as the enthusiasm heightened. Everyone in the room seemed to be smoking something or another, and yet the smoke just drifted up and away leaving a surprisingly fresh atmosphere. One of the RAF men offered to show John around the room. Starting with their table he said, "These are the photographs we have of Peenemünde. We're interested in the Leica factory there."

John leaned closer and took a good look, "These are really good," he said happily. "Such a good view. How did you get them so clear?"

He looked in even more closely at the photos, pointing down at one in particular, "This is not accurate though — that's not the Leica factory."

The men stood back alarmed, but before it could be debated, the RAF man who was touring John around the room had moved on without him. John had to leave the first group of men and catch up with him for the ensuing introduction. They looked at some of the different map tables, and John was horrified at how old some of the maps were. Of course, they had no idea beforehand that the war was going to happen and they had no decent maps at all, or so John thought.

As they began to study the Peenemünde maps, one of the air force officers briefing the men said, "We know the Leica factory is situated in the bush so many meters from these various points."

He was pointing to the map, "From the station, from the sand, and from these buildings here."

John loudly contradicted him. "It's not in the bushes; it's right close to the shore now."

The officer looked at John sternly, "Oh, no. You don't know bugger all," he said point blank.

John could see the look of disbelief building on their faces, and he quickly spoke up, "You weren't there in 1938 and 1939, but I was there. I saw the changes, and it changed quite a lot." The men listened intently, while John raised his voice for the first time in a long time.

"When I first went there, the Leica factory was inland and there was sort of a narrow strip where you had to go almost through the gates of the factory to get to the Three Feather Hotel, and that's where we used to stay," he blurted it out.

John gained a bit of composure and began speaking to them in a stern, yet excited voice. "Then of course in 1937 they suddenly moved the factory to the shore, right up to the sand. They made it look a bit like a big sandy beach, but it was right there, along the beach," he chuckled a little, "too long for a bloke to walk."

Everyone leaned over the table and took a closer look at the aircraft photos they had laid out. They could just see this black thing behind the clouds, and they had thought that was the factory, but it wasn't.

"These maps here," John told them, as he tapped his finger on the date of the map itself, "are from 1936, and a lot happened between 1936 and 1939."

"The Germans have better maps of Britain than this," Mac Pierce interceded, his Scottish blood starting to boil, "and the Germans have better means of finding out about new changes and such things, too."

There was an awkward silence, until Mac Pierce spoke up again in his distracting Scottish accent. "Ach laddies, he'll know. If he doesn't know, nobody else will know, because he used to wander around these places."

John stepped back and shrugged his shoulders, "I just thought you should know," he said almost reluctantly.

Mac Pierce cut in, "He shouldn't have been to half the places he was at, but he thought nothing of it."

He backed away from the table and stood beside John, who was calmly putting a match to his pipe. The officers quietly discussed it, still not completely sure of these two new blokes.

John looked at Mac and exhaled his smoke, blowing out the match with the last little bit of it. The unusually sweet smell of his tobacco had a calming effect on those within its reach.

"That's true," John said with a nod, "I didn't just sit around and hope to go to these places like some of the staff; I went there."

Mac Pierce laughed and crouched in towards John, lowering his voice, "Remember some weekends we used to go to that little place called Uncle Tom's Cabin, Onkel Toms Hütte, they used to call it, right?"

John smiled, "Oh, yes, that was a beautiful little village on the outskirts of Berlin, and I used to wander around a lot there and talk to the various people. It was great," he said as he blew out a huge puff of smoke towards the RAF officers. "There were many tourists still in 1936. When we were there, it was easy to get about."

"That's right," Mac said quite loudly and then turning back to John. "We were welcome as tourists since we used to spend our money there and everyone was nice to us. I mean, we didn't have a lot to spend our money on anyway and it was just paper to the government."

John nodded his head in agreement and that was that. Soon Mac was on his way out the door and, as he passed by the RAF officers, he said to them again, "If he doesn't know, nobody else does."

John went back to the table and looked down very closely at the map again. "Is this where they are experimenting with those rockets?" he asked.

The commanding officer was quite surprised and for the first time he took John very seriously. John was piecing it together from the scraps of information they had received through Ultra and also because Werner Von Braun and his rockets were of a particular interest to him. John had feared their potential for some time and was quite devastated when the V1 and V2 rockets pelted down on England a short while later, causing horrible destruction and loss of life, but also thankfully missing most of their intended targets and blowing up many large fields where no people or animals were injured.

The RAF commanding officer circled the existing faint pencil line on the map, with the bright red pencil in his hand, and said, "We don't really know yet, but it appears to be in this vicinity."

"Where are those maps, MacDonald," he barked out his order at an unsuspecting pilot. "I ordered better maps days ago, and I want them right away."

The flight officer, who could not have been standing any stiffer, replied, "Yes, sir, we are expecting some tonight."

"Well, get more than that," the commanding officer insisted. "Get some people in here to make new ones up, now."

The men closed in on the map table again and began discussing all they knew on the subject. "In 1936," John said pointing at the map, "they began to build a railway from Peenemünde inland to here, and then to here."

"I took the train there twice and pretended I was worker along with all the others, because I could see truck after truck full of building supplies going there and I was curious."

All the officers were quiet now, and you could hear a pin drop. "I saw them building these huge structures. Of course, I didn't know what it was for at the time."

John stood up straight, "It could have been for the rockets, I can't be sure though. I was told to stay away by the office. Someone else could tell you more about this, I would imagine."

The RAF officers were confused, "We need more information; that's all there is to it. We cannot just bomb everywhere; we need actual locations."

Another officer said, "These photographs have been recently taken; we think this could possibly be the location."

John looked very closely and raised his voice really loud again, a rarity in itself, "I can see damn well that's not right. I've been there and this is a college, not a likely place to launch rockets at us."

"Blimey," was the only reply from one of the men in the background.

*
**

They mapped all of the coordinates that John gave them and took him seriously, but some of the men still didn't want to believe him.

"Who is this guy," John could overhear them talking in the distance.

"He's some kind of secretary for the secret service," was the reply as he watched the man shrug his shoulders.

"Just an ordinary secretary," John thought to himself. "If I'd have been someone special, a sergeant major or a colonel, it would have been a different story. It was almost an insult to the highly trained RAF officers, because they couldn't take the credit or the praise for what I did, because I did it," he mulled.

"What a bloody nuisance they are," John almost whispered out loud.

It was clear to him that they thought of John as just a secretary who probably worked a typewriter. He was such a little cog in their opinion.

*
**

It wasn't long before they found out that John's information was accurate. "Bloody good show there, John," one of the top RAF officers told him.

"We sent out a reconnaissance airplane to take more aerial photographs of your locations, with excellent results." He lifted some photographs off the map table and handed them to John.

"These are your locations and look, we now have a perfect picture here of the launch pad for the V2 rockets."

John looked closely and was thrilled to see numerous photographs of the Peenemünde area, including one of a launch platform itself that was as clear as could be.

"So that's it," John said lifting the photograph closer to his face with a huge smile. "I have always wanted to see the finished product, and now I finally have."

"Your information is greatly appreciated," the RAF officer said, smiling at him with the eyes of a conqueror who suddenly has the high ground and is ready for battle.

"Now, I was wondering," he continued hesitantly, "if you would like to go in the aircraft, to assist in locating some of these marks?"

John looked up at him, the thought of being in the aircraft as part of the aircrew was a little intimidating. He had only flown once before in his younger days when he was taking pictures for the Scottish Exhibition and that had been in a biplane that was much slower, and it was in the daytime and a considerably different experience from this proposal.

"I would be honoured," John said with a short salute, and it was settled.

"Good," the RAF officer smiled a little and unrolled a new map. "Show me again. We'll review the area once more."

Chapter 37
The Lovely Lancaster

The plane John flew in was a Lancaster bomber with a crew of seven, with John being the eighth. The first time he went to the hangar, the chief officer didn't like the idea of him being there. He was nervous in John's company, because of his many accents. To most of them, an Englishman is a man speaking English and an Irishman is a Scotsman – it all sounded foreign to them sort of thing. They couldn't figure out whether John was an Englishman or a German or something totally different. Fortunately, the Yorkshire men were there, too, with their strong northern accents, which John knew like the back of his hand and could easily mimic. That was how he got away with these things and was accepted – his deep understanding of their particular way of speaking, and their habits as well. In the end he was an additional asset to the RAF, when aircrews would arrive from abroad, and he could talk to these men from different nationalities in their own languages and using their slang.

There was not a lot of mixing with the crews off the job, just on the airplane. For the most part it was out of bounds, but John did have one picture of himself in the mess hall with his uniform on. He had a beer in his hand at the time, which he quickly ducked under his arm, leaving a silly grin on his face just before the snap.

The air force was constantly upgrading its systems on board the aircraft and had just installed a new radio aid that was achieving very accurate navigation. John attended the classroom and was taught how to use these various instruments that they'd need on the tour. Taking bearings, calculating angles, and range-to-pinpoint locations were all like second nature to him.

He was given no training for the aircraft, however, nothing at all. They gave him a parachute, and he just got on the plane. He had complete trust that the men knew their jobs as well as they could. It was a time of great reflection, of how many people, each with a single job to accomplish, can come together to achieve great results.

The Lancaster was a wonderful machine, enormous and powerful, the best bomber the RAF could have ever hoped for. John sat on a grassy knoll one day and watched as the pilot, so tiny in comparison, walked around the giant fortress inspecting it before the flight. Touching it with such gentleness, whispering positive thoughts to it as he checked for anything unhinged.

The engineers with their ladders and rags in their pockets were not as gentle, crawling all over the plane like ants and then slapping the cowlings down harshly, treating it just like the massive machine it was. "The oil is good, all clear," one of them yelled.

John was completely amazed with the huge airplane. From the front, it looked highly futuristic with the sun glistening off the greenhouse cockpit and the ominous nose turret waiting below that. The four gigantic engines, Merlin Rolls Royce, were hovering above the sleekest wings possible that managed to hold their massive weight. Even the shiny metal fuselage of the Lancaster was immaculate in its construction, as you looked down its long sleek sides – yet strong and sturdy. The large twin tail rudders appeared almost delicate behind the huge bird, if it weren't for the intimidating gun turrets positioned below them. The Lancaster was capable of carrying the largest bombs to date, easily, and had some of the most advanced equipment in the world on board.

As each engine began to fire up, the pace quickened for everyone around, and the aircrew quickly assembled. "Come along Harrington," the captain said, unexpectedly.

"This is Bertie," he said patting the belly of the airplane. "She's named after my sweetheart, Roberta."

"Just hop up here," he said, shaking the rickety steps that led up into the huge airplane, steps that were held on only by a cable and a hinge. It was then that the pilot looked directly at John's stiff leg, and he realized he had just stuck his own foot in his mouth.

He watched with a sigh of relief as John climbed the steps with relative ease and then, turning to his crew, with direct eye contact between John's stiff leg and their eyes, he said, "And these young chaps will show you around."

It was a beautiful sunny day with not a cloud in the sky, and the men were taking great pleasure in their training day on the home front. It gave them a nice change. They were testing the new systems installed and also testing their newest Pathfinder, John, who was exhilarated as the airplane lifted off.

"Amazing," he said to the man next to him, as he watched the ground quickly rushing away from them. He felt a surge of excitement as they raced up through the open sky like a rocket, with their bodies becoming pasted to the back of their seats.

Bertie now had John's complete respect, and the huge Lancaster quickly gave him a love for flying. It was such a wonderful day, and both of the pilots enjoyed showing him around the cockpit. He was amazed that they could just go all over the place, wherever they wanted, three dimensions up down and all around.

The Pathfinder Group that John was flying with were in a special plane that goes over and locates the targets and then drops flares for the bombers to come and bomb. For instance, if they were going to Berlin, and they wanted the bombs to be dropped at a certain spot, they would drop a white flare. If they dropped a yellow flare, they would not bomb it. The idea was to mislead the Germans.

"We may not hit it the first time," the pilot yelled to him once, over the engine noise. "But the second plane will usually get it."

John's first mission with the Pathfinders was to locate and bomb the Continental Tire Works. "Have you heard of it," the commanding officer asked him one day in the map room, while standing there in full dress uniform.

"Yes," John replied, and he went over to a map of Berlin that was pinned on the wall.

"Continental Tire Works used to be right in Berlin City, but in 1938 they had moved it here, to nearby Potsdam, out in a big open space." John tapped his finger on the wall map.

The commanding officer looked down at the photographs in his hand, which didn't show that at all. He knew they were outdated and just shook his head angrily. "We shall have to locate this with new aerial photos," he said putting the old pictures down.

"John, you will assist them," he ordered, before storming out.

*
**

On this, John's first aircraft mission, which was to the tire factory, one of the gunners asked him if he was scared, but he wasn't scared at all because he was on his own. He had time for reflection on that trip, and he knew if he got killed or wounded, there was no one to worry about him. It didn't seem to matter what happened to him, because there was nobody to give a damn. That was the way he looked at life and how it was lived, luckily. Even in Germany or wherever he happened to be, he was on his own. The government paid all his expenses, and all he had to do was to go there and do as he was told – perhaps investigate someone and find out what he did for a living, what family he had. That's all he had to do, and then he'd come back and report it and that was it; the next person continued with the investigation.

The crew onboard Bertie were all Brits, really great chaps, John thought, but they didn't like going across that sea. It was always so dark that you couldn't see anything.

When he got back from that first sortie, they had new maps laid out, and this time he was asked to pinpoint Siemens Town. This was the big electrical firm that had moved to a new location around the golf course where he used to play and where he would sometimes stop and talk to the men during their lunch and tea breaks.

John told them all about Siemens Town because on their maps at that time they had relocated it to an area that was entirely different from where they had actually moved it. The old place that they knew of was still there but was more or less just a ruin, a dummy. So he explained it to them, and they said, "Oh no, you're fooling."

John said, "No, it's true; they had a place just by the radio station in Berlin, but they moved it to Potsdam, 20-odd miles away." It turned out the officers didn't know that information and were dropping bombs on the wrong place. John was horrified.

The smaller factories were located around the nine-hole golf course where John had spent many days, but of course their maps didn't record any of this. There was a fellow who was doing them again, but they didn't show much. Unless you'd been there, you couldn't really tell, but he knew this time because he had been there and they hadn't been there. It was hard to convince them.

It was the same thing as in 1937, when John wrote a note from Berlin to the English newspapers, The Daily Telegraph and The Post, telling them about the Jews being persecuted. He wanted to warn people of the impending situation, but they wouldn't believe it. He got in a lot of trouble over that letter.

Captain Haysley had hollered at him, "You shouldn't do that; you are never to talk to reporters." They were really upset with him. The consul general in

Vienna lost his job for doing the same thing. It was just a few words; anyway, he lost his job. John was lucky to talk his way out of that one.

So once again John said to the RAF officers, "Give me another plane, the Pathfinder and I will pick them out for you."

How he got the locations was not from their maps but from three points that he had walked numerous times in Berlin, a triangle. First of all there was the church with its tall steeples and that was the first point. There was also a big sports ground, where they held the Olympics and other athletic events and it had a large tower with a big copper barrel on top, and that was their second point. Then the third point was the radio station, with its large tower, and that formed the triangle that was their point of contact.

John knew the exact distance from each one was so many meters, and then at so many degrees, he could exactly pinpoint the target. Well, again they wouldn't believe him. They thought it couldn't be true. Counting the meters or miles between locations and finding the bearings was a common pastime for John while he was in Berlin, and now it came in handy. It was so elementary, yet extremely precise.

This made the mission easier for all of the aircrew, as they didn't have to drop down to a lower altitude to see the target. All John had to do in the air was to set the screen to a certain degree and then adjust it accordingly, so many degrees left or right, and they could pinpoint precisely what they wanted. Then he would tell the pilot where to drop the flares.

This was to be John's last trip and, after successfully locating the town with flares, it had been agreed that they would try to do something that John would have liked to have done while living in Berlin. That is, they decided to bomb the hell out of the Central Generating Station, the same one that used to start up and block the BBC news every night.

It was a go, and they decided to drop flares over the power station, which they did. However, in doing so, they may have flown a little too low and were caught by the fire from the same guns that Herr Himmler had once described as, "One for the crowds and one for the clouds."

Chapter 38

HAVE YOU EVER BEEN TO CHURCH?

It was a vulnerable feeling, flying that low over the sleeping city of Berlin. Sitting in the Pathfinder right at that time reminded John of what it was like when he was in the observation post in France. It wasn't the big bombers they were after at the moment, it was that first Lancaster, the one that John was in. Then suddenly, POP, that was it! It just seemed that quick. The next thing that John knew, they were returning to England with the greater part of the Lancaster badly damaged.

He had been sitting on the left side of the airplane, and the Germans must have machine-gunned the other side. At first, they were knocked about, and there were lots of bullets, and then it quickly became like a sieve on the right side of the airplane. The fellow sitting on the other side of the plane was quite badly wounded and suffered dreadfully before he died. The poor fellow didn't have a chance.

The right side was completely shot full of holes. John could see flames flooding past the windows towards the tail until there was the distinct sound of only one engine running, but it was running hard and strong, forcing his body deep into the seat. Their undercarriage was gone, and in its place was a gaping hole in the floor where one of the fuel nacelle tanks had been ripped open and was now burning wildly. The smoke poured in and obscured the inside of the cabin, or what was left of the cabin on the great machine, and, with the smell of burning gas and oil, it was impossible to breathe. A most horrific few moments passed when John wondered, "Is this it?"

Fortunately, it was only for a short terrifying while until the smoke thinned out, siphoned through the many holes in the fuselage. It was replaced with fear itself, as John turned his head and saw blood streaming backwards from the cockpit onto the windows of the good side of the airplane.

John knew he had been shot through the legs as the pain was becoming intense, but he was so busy just hanging on that he was not really sure just how bad it was and was too afraid to look.

After awhile, the flames went out and they were flying quietly along at a very strange angle, so low to the water that John could feel the cool sea breeze on his skin. The co-pilot yelled back, naming all of the crew members one by one until he knew who was alive or not. He didn't call the captain's name, and three of the other men didn't answer.

As they approached the coast of Yorkshire, John felt such relief. He thought they were really lucky to get so far and hoped for a smooth landing. They were somewhere near Saltburn, he estimated. He looked forward through a little opening in the oil-streaked cockpit windshield and could see that the ground ahead of them looked nice and flat, just right for a belly landing, he thought. But looking backwards, John could easily see that was not so. The wheels of the undercarriage were not only missing, but the remaining struts also jutted out unnaturally like spindly, sick rudders. Through the large, jagged opening, John could see the one tiny wheel that was left. It was just a little tailwheel, clearly visible in the rear and flapping out of control as the plane gradually came down and down. Then, the whirring sound from the needle blade propeller suddenly got very loud before the engine backfired. The silence was deafening when that last engine quit.

"Brace yourselves," the young co-pilot screeched. A few silent prayers were said, and, just like that, they were on the ground. The landing was perfect; the pilot had done it. He had found a perfectly flat field and put it down, easy as can be.

They skidded along for some time, bouncing occasionally and sharp pieces of metal were breaking off like twigs on a dry tree. Suddenly, directly in front of them appeared a church, and that was all John could really remember.

When the plane crashed, two or three were wounded, but they were conscious and talking to each other. John never knew what happened to them after that. He was worried about where they had landed, and if they would get a beer or something when they got out of there. That was the sort of thing that worried his mind; not crying about getting killed, but just what kind of place was it down there, and could they get something to eat, could they make friends down there?

When they hit the ground, the airplane must have broken up and John was flung out of the giant serration. The crash left him with a very badly injured leg, for the second time. Split open with multiple injuries and gaping bullet wounds, but it wasn't so bad this time as it had been in the first war. It actually might have fixed the leg up a little better, he would joke. Yes, that leg got it twice; it was an unlucky leg.

Yet, John couldn't help but imagine walking around in Berlin for so many years without his straight leg. He wasn't much of a threat with that, and he wondered if they would have even employed him in Berlin without the stiff leg. That had become part of his cover-up and how he was able to get around so easily.

The war was over for John. They found him lying on a tombstone. Two ribs were crushed and his back was hurt but not badly and his good leg was gaping open and most of the flesh had been ripped off it. John never felt the pain and had easily drifted away into unconsciousness.

They took him to the hospital and, when he finally came around, the first thing he saw was a cute young nurse sitting on the end of his bed smoking a cigarette. Apparently he had been in a coma for some time, so when he moved and spoke, it scared the wits out of her. She jumped up, and started yelling, burning a hole in her outfit. John's first words to her were, "Can I have a cigarette?"

A little later, when he returned more to life as it were, John asked the nurse, "Where am I? What am I doing here?"

She said, "Oh, so you are awake. Do you ever go to church?"

John curiously said, "Yes, occasionally, why?"

She then replied with a smile, "We thought so, because you and the crew had gone to church and tried to take the aircraft with you." They did not tell him what had happened to the other members of the crew.

John spent a period at Queen Mary's Hospital in Roehampton. Things were different from his previous visit. He was a patient then; now he was a number. He read every newspaper he could get his hands on, and he was so pleased to read that Hitler was losing his war and that the Allies were fighting back hard, attacking the Nazis from all sides and angles.

One of the nurses had a large scrapbook full of newspaper articles, which she eventually left for John to peruse. "This is a horrible one," she said pointing to a page and screwing up her face. "It's about those death camps."

John read it to himself, "Near the end of 1942, all Jewish people held in German concentration camps were to be relocated to Auschwitz, Poland. At Auschwitz is located one of Adolf Hitler's largest death camps, which is still growing daily and whose primary objective is the extermination of every single one of these people."

A sick feeling came over John, and he thought of Ilse Liebert and where she might be. The nurse saw the distress on John's face and felt bad for showing him the article.

"It's probably not true," she said turning the page. "It's very hard to believe."

"Oh, I believe it," John said, his eyes welling up. "I'm glad that the reporters got these stories for the press, because even if we don't want to hear of such atrocities that are the reality over there, these stories show us just how perverse the Nazis are."

The nurse gave John another cigarette, and they smoked for a little while without talking. Then John turned the page of her bulging scrapbook, and she giggled at the article from the United Press on the next page.

"We get a really great kick out of this story," she said with a comical grin. "It gives everyone a laugh."

The story at which they laughed was the following and it was said to have been a true story, since it was once reported and published in the United Press and, also later John found out in the Winnipeg Free Press. The records may be checked, but very few of the German people knew of it.

"Hitler as a youth was said to be a daring kind of boy. He once made a bet that he could urinate in the mouth of a billy goat, while another boy,

Eugen Wasner, a classmate of Hitler's, held the billy's mouth open, but the boy released his hold of the goat's mouth. It was said at the time that the goat had bitten off Hitler's penis, but the truth was it had bitten off his testicles."

This embarrassing incident took place at Leonding, Austria, Adolf's boyhood home. The witness, Eugen Wasner, later became a soldier in Hitler's Third Reich. The German people were never told until much later that Hitler was probably sterile because of this bite from the billy goat.

The story continues that in 1943, on the Russian Front, Eugen Wasner told this story to some of his comrades and also said that Hitler was a crazy fool. When this reached the ears of Adolf Hitler, he ordered Wasner's arrest. When asked, "Have you anything to say?" Wasner cried out, "Jesus Mary, I swear on my life that it did happen."

He was executed. The story didn't circulate in Germany at the time, but it was published after the war.

*
**

The airborne attacks on Germany were increasing steadily, and their persistence was starting to wear the German people down. There were numerous reports of assassination attempts against the Führer, Adolf Hitler himself, and yet he carried on. With his arms now crossed behind his back most of the time, he was lifeless and tired, with a depressed face that very few would see.

Only rarely now could be seen an evil and twisted smile on Hitler's sinister face, on such occasions as when he was told of the V2 rockets that were devastating England once again. His evil grin was twisted even deeper; enhanced by the thought of his devoted young soldiers who still fought on fiercely for him.

It finally came to an end, when in January of 1945, the Auschwitz concentration camp was liberated, and the true stories began to flow back across the channel of starved survivors and far worse atrocities.

In April of 1945, three famous leaders perished: the United States of America lost their dearly loved President, Franklin Delano Roosevelt, who suddenly passed away from a cerebral haemorrhage on April 12.

April 28, Italy's head of government and well-known Fascist leader Benito Mussolini was summarily executed, and his body was publicly hung up, displayed for all to see the proof of his death.

Two days later, on April 30, the news came that Adolf Hitler had committed suicide in his bunker under the German Chancellery. No body was found, and the uncertainty of his death lingered.

Hitler's faithful soldiers, the youngest of the children who were the only ones still left, fought on and continued to die trying to kill the invading Allied soldiers for at least a week until May 7, when Germany finally surrendered.

There was a celebration in the streets worldwide, and many soldiers were left wondering, "Why are we the ones to have survived?" The lucky ones went home completely different men, changed forever. The war, however, was not over for everyone; and it was not until August 15, 1945, when Japan surrendered, that World War II was officially over.

*
**

John, meanwhile, after his release from hospital, had been posted to Parkstone, Dorset, England to convalesce. Parkstone and Poole are located quite close to Bournemouth, a nice seaside town, a Mecca, which is just a short trip from the Isle of Wight. It was just right for retired single ladies, such as schoolteachers or nurses and soldiers on rehabilitation leave.

While at Parkstone, John worked occasionally for a typewriter firm as a typewriter mechanic. They also got him writing a bit again, daily jokes and such, and he liked that. It was there in Parkstone that John decided that he was getting tired of being tied up all the time with all the restrictions. He was still supposed to abide by the Official Secrets Act and carry on with all the restrictions, but he didn't go back straight away. He was just biding his time, as he was still entitled to some rehab leave.

He lived on Park Street and went down to the beaches and played around, even while he was still getting paid by the Foreign Office. He didn't decide to move on until the money stopped. It was during this period, at Bournemouth, that he met someone who changed his entire life.

By a chance encounter in a cinema, he met Miss Olive Meadows, a beautiful young woman who simply took his breath away. She was as tall as him and quite thin. "Shapely," John thought, as he admired how smartly dressed she was, but what really got him was when she smiled at him with the most compassionate smile he had ever seen.

It's interesting, John would often think later, how little things can turn so easily into big things. He was just sitting there smoking in the lobby of the Pool Hill Cinema, and he offered Olive a cigarette – and he might have touched her leg or something, you know accidentally, no intention. They talked a bit before she said, "Well, I must go now."

John stood up with her and said, "Good evening, then, I'll come with you and see you to your door."

"That's all right," she said, obviously in a hurry. "Don't be bothered."

He walked her out anyway and, after passing through the front door, she began to do up her coat. She was wearing a Macintosh with a belt, but had dropped the belt in the hall of the cinema and was dismayed that she would have to go back and get it.

John said, "Whoa, I'll get the attendant to get it for you." He went over and talked to the usher, who happily retrieved it for John, who gave him a shilling, and cheerfully brought the belt out to Olive.

When John helped Olive put the belt through the loops on her coat, he put his arm around her waist and, in that moment that he held her, a flash moved between them. She looked at him, her bright blue eyes inquisitive and full of intrigue. He felt something instantly, just as if a welding torch had touched him, and that's how the whole thing started. They just looked at each other and then stood there talking.

"Where are you from, Miss Meadows," John asked her?

Olive replied, "I'm from Brandon, Manitoba," and he could immediately sense her longing for home.

"Canada," she added, beaming with the thought of it.

"And what brings you here?" he asked curiously.

"I'm a nurse with the Canadian military," she replied before John cut her off.

"Enough said, I've just been released from the hospital," he squeaked out. "You folks do a wonderful job; I could never thank you enough." An expression of gratitude crossed his face.

Then Olive said, "Goodnight, I really must go now; I have a bus to catch," and then she was gone. John went back to his hotel, never knowing if they would meet again.

*
**

A short time had gone by, and then one afternoon he was on the beach at Bournemouth and saw her on the sand. She was a sight for sore eyes, sitting there in her lounge chair. Little flashes of gold and copper sparkled from her chestnut brown hair as it lay on her shoulders. She was clad only in a flowered bathing suit but a great part of her was hidden behind the large book she was reading. Beside her were two small kiddies playing in the sand with their toys. They had a brief chat, and John was struck instantly by Olive's honesty and politeness. She smelled of tulips and looked so lovely that he was compelled to make a date to meet with her again.

John was working in Parkstone quite near there, and he said, "Well, I am going to play golf tomorrow afternoon. Why don't you come over to Parkstone and see me?"

"I just might do that," she said with a smile

So the next day she did come over, and they scooted balls around on the golf course. Later in the evening, as they were walking around the grounds, hundreds of glowworms hung around them, lighting up the sky. They had an enchanted evening.

They didn't even kiss then and that didn't bother him a bit; he never had been a sex merchant. They walked up to the road to where the bus was running, and her bus went one way and John's the other. When they parted, they hadn't arranged to meet again, but he had gotten her number and so in the following week he phoned her and they did get together again, quite often in fact.

On Saturday afternoons, when it was nice weather, Olive would come over to Parkstone. At the golf course was a place where people used to sit and watch the golfers. She would sit there and watch John play golf with the other golfers, and then they'd go and have a drink. Just a drink, nothing else, but they would sit and talk and talk. She would tell him about her life in Canada and the interesting times while serving her years in training.

Olive was serving as a nurse at the Canadian #5 Military Hospital at Taplow during the war. She and John became good friends, and it turned out they were both lonely souls looking for a friend. This could be it, John thought, and it was!

John never told her what he had been doing during the war; in fact, he didn't tell his story to anybody. He and Olive would walk along the seashore or on the golf links at Parkstone and watch the fireflies glowing in the evening. They were really very, very happy there. It was like they were just one person, or two peas in a pod, and they were acting like children. They didn't even realize that they had fallen in love. They just met and that was it, just like two pieces of a puzzle that fit perfectly together.

Epilogue

ADOLF HITLER

The death of Adolf Hitler on April 30, 1945 was a cause for celebration worldwide. In his life he had become one of the world's most immoral monsters in history, a truly evil man.

With time, Adolf Hitler's death has become well documented, but in the beginning and for a long time it was all very secretive, especially considering that everyone wanted the facts about his end to be out in the open. His death left many people uncomfortable about his actual demise, and the latent mystery was that no body was viewed or any real proof given. In the end it was universally decided he really was dead.

It turned out the complication was because Hitler had made strict arrangements to have his body burned after his suicide by a self-inflicted shot to the head.

EVA ANNA PAULA HITLER (NEE: BRAUN)

It is now well known that Eva Braun was Hitler's friend or mistress and, in the last few days of the war and of their lives, they were married. Fräulein Braun died with Adolf Hitler in the bunker faithfully by his side, succumbing to the same fate as him. It is said that Adolf shot his newly-wed wife Eva Braun in the head before he shot himself, and once deceased they were set ablaze together.

John had thought years before that Eva Braun was quite a woman and when he heard the news, he just couldn't help but think, "What a waste of a good human being."

PAUL JOSEPH GOEBBELS

A faithful friend to Adolf Hitler since the early 1920s, Joseph Goebbels was a ringleader in the Nazi movement and stayed with Hitler to the very end. Goebbels was the minister of propaganda, the man who seduced the German people and made it possible for the horrific events to transpire. A few hours after Adolf and Eva's suicides in the Berlin bunker, Joseph Goebbels and his wife poisoned their six children before killing themselves.

HERMANN WILHELM GOERING

Herman Goering, another long time friend of Hitler's, fell out with him near the end. He just quit fighting, going back to his old ways and enjoying life. That came to an abrupt end when he was hauled off to the Nuremburg trials where he was sentenced to death by hanging. Goering was too proud to endure such public humiliation and, on October 15, 1946 — the day before he was meant to hang — the famous WWI pilot and leader of the German Luftwaffe Hermann Goering took a potassium cyanide capsule to end his life.

HEINRICH LUITPOLD HIMMLER

The chief of all police in the Nazi regime, including the Gestapo and the dreaded SS, was to be Heinrich Himmler's legacy, and he lived up to the wicked side of his persona, causing the death of millions of people.

Himmler tried to sneak away after Hitler died, but was caught by the British Army in Bremen. He was also sent to stand trial in Nuremburg as one of the Second World War's most outrageous war criminals, but he too took his own life with cyanide on May 23, 1945 before the trial began. He was survived by a wife and daughter.

This sadistic man, Heinrich Himmler, had caused such incredible damage and loss of human life. He was 44 years old when he died.

ERWIN JOHANNES EUGEN ROMMEL

When Field Marshal Erwin Rommel died, it was reported as an accident but the truth was kept a mystery for a long time. Some said that he shot himself, and others said he had a car accident. It was not disclosed what happened at the time.

Since then, we have learned that Herr Rommel was forced to end his own life by the Nazi party in order to protect his wife and son after he was linked with a conspiracy attempt to kill Adolf Hitler.

Nevertheless, Field Marshall Erwin Rommel was laid to rest as an illustrious war hero in October of 1944 at the age of 52. He will be forever remembered as "The Desert Fox."

WILHELM FRANZ CANARIS

Admiral Wilhelm Canaris, otherwise known as K, or at one time chief of the German Secret Service – the Abwehr, was another interesting person and mysterious man. Admiral Canaris played his cards very carefully, but in the end he lost.

Wilhelm Canaris wanted what was best for Germany, never a war. However, his double-dealings with the British cost him his life when the assassination attempts on Hitler increased and he was implicated in them.

Admiral Wilhelm Canaris was taken to a Flossenburg concentration camp where he was horribly humiliated before being slowly put to death by the Nazis on April 9, 1945.

ILSE LIEBERT

John found out from a private source back in England that the good doctor Ilse Liebert was interned when war was declared. It seemed that her support for the government was no longer required. Well, some people will do anything for money, even at the risk of losing their life. John was devastated at the news and never did find out Ilse Liebert's final destiny.

FREDDIE, KARL, and LILI SOLINGER

John never did find out what happened to the Solinger family, either, but he never gave up hope that they might have survived. Their names were changed for this story, but the incidents are true.

BERLIN – THE ADLON HOTEL AND POTSDAMER PLATZ

Berlin was bombed heavily during the war, and most of the city was completely devastated in the Battle of Berlin.

Surprising, the Adlon Hotel survived the war and was even used as a hospital near the end, only to succumb to a fire in May 1945 that destroyed it. Only one wing of the grand hotel was left standing, and that ended up being on the east side of the Berlin Wall, after it was erected in 1961. A fabulous new Adlon Hotel has since been built on the same location.

Potsdammer Platz did not survive at all, and the entire district was completely annihilated. It has also been fabulously rebuilt with no semblance of the past. For many years the Berlin Wall literally divided Potsdammer Platz in two.

FRANCIS EDWARD FOLEY

Major Frank Foley, a long-standing officer of the British Secret Service, would always be remembered by John as simply Captain Foley, the man he respected more than any other in all of his many years.

Captain Foley was a man who risked his own life and all that he held precious for the sake of humanity. When he was posted to Berlin with the Secret Intelligence, it was under the simple guise of a passport officer but, when the Nazis came to power, Captain Foley was there to defend the Jewish people and became deeply involved, above and beyond his duty. He was a truly outstanding man. Captain Foley was the Berlin Enigma.

Frank Foley died in 1958. At the Trial of Adolf Eichmann, a witness for the prosecution praised Frank Foley as a man who, in his opinion, was "one of the greatest man among men of the world." He rescued thousands of Jews from the jaws of hell.

A grove of trees was planted in his memory, at Kibbutz Harel.

CAPTAIN HAYSLEY

The last time John saw Captain Haysley was in Bletchley. He remained an unrecognized hero, as did many officers and staff of the British Secret Service.

JOHN SYDNEY HARRINGTON

John fell in love with Olive, and she with him. They had a lovely time in England. Olive was so happy, so very happy. They used to stroll down Bond Street on a Sunday morning and look in all the shops, and they used to say, "We'll buy this, and we'll buy that," chuckling to each other as they knew they couldn't afford to buy anything. The shops were wonderful in London at that time. Oh, yes, in the forties. They were both so content.

They were always on the go somewhere, to a theatre or a beach or out in the country. When the weather was bad, they used to lie in bed with the radio on and listen to Stewart MacPherson. Of course, he was quite a celebrity then. He was voted the top male radio personality of 1947. There was no television in those days. No other fun was needed. They just lived their lives. They weren't interested in anything else but just their two selves, and they used to have a grand time.

The visit of Olive's parents from Canada in early 1949 put the whole picture in full view for John. They toured them all around London and really enjoyed themselves. John asked Olive's father one day, "Do you mind if I marry your daughter?"

He responded with, "Well, you've got to live with her," and that was it.

So they were married on September 7 of that year in just a quiet ceremony, with a very good friend of Olive's. John was never happier as he looked at Olive with her breathtaking smile that was at the same time so innocent, and came from deep within.

Later that evening, Olive was a jolly sight indeed, when John said to her "Well, let's go back to Canada."

He had formed the impression that here was his chance to do something that he had never experienced before – to maybe go to Canada and make a home and perhaps a family of his own. Once again, as many times in his life, he was entering a strange and different country and didn't know what to expect. With a difference — he did not mind because this time, at least, he was not alone.

In October, after Olive had said goodbye to the numerous friends she had made in England, they departed the shores of Southhampton, England on the R.M.S. Aquitania of the Cunard White Star Line. It was a seven-day trip, and they had a very rough voyage with unusually high waves.

In the evening, when it was dark, they used to go on the back of the ship and cuddle up together and talk, discussing all sorts of little intimate things. That was a great time for them, and they were cuddled up on the deck every night until they got to Canada.

After arriving at Halifax, they boarded the train for Brandon, Manitoba and arrived there on a cold November day. They were met at the North Road Station by members of Olive's family and, wow, was she welcomed, as so she should be. It made him feel great to know that there were still people in the world who knew what real love really was.

It was cold, John sure knew that. All he had on was a thin Macintosh and a cap, nothing else, and it was way below freezing. Of course, even though he was really cold, that didn't seem to matter as soon as he met Olive's family who were clamouring around her. John stood there for quite a few minutes, and finally they discovered him. Those were wonderful times for John, creating memories that stayed with him till the end.

He said to himself when he got to Canada, "I am going to have a family. I am going to work hard, and I am going to have a house and I am going to retire in comfort." Yes, and that's what he did.

John felt that they had achieved their goals. He worked hard in the early years. For 27 years, he worked as a machinist at Bristol Aerospace in Winnipeg before he retired, and his beloved wife Olive also worked for just as many years at the Old and New Grace Hospital, until she too retired. They raised a family of four children, two girls and two boys, had a nice home and felt secure — something they were both very thankful for.

In 1977 when it was time to retire from Bristol Aerospace, some forms arrived in the mail from the pension offices requesting a copy of John's birth certificate for proof of his birthday. John was not a Canadian citizen yet, and so he had to apply for that also. In order to do that, John had to send away to England for his original birth certificate and a short while later it arrived in the post. It was much to his chagrin that he had to write back to the Canada pensions and request them to please amend his application form accordingly. The birth certificate showed that his name was not officially John Sydney Harrington; it was just Sydney Harrington. He must have just picked up the John early in life somehow and it stuck with him. The really strange thing was that his birthday, which he had always celebrated on February 29, was actually March 19. This threw him for quite a loop.

The year was the real kicker. The only record that John had of his birth year was from the records they gave him when he was last injured near the end of the Second World War. They were still the records from Bletchley, and John thought that explained why the government didn't know who he was; his record had been modified. It read that John Sydney Harrington was born February 29, 1912 and for the next 30 years or so, he had used this as his identity.

Now John was finding out that he was actually born on March 19, 1896, sixteen years earlier. What an incredible shock that was – and not just for him but for his whole family.

He had already figured out that the year on his passport was wrong because he would have been far too young in the first war and at the Scottish Exhibition, but he had no idea how old he actually was and had never really bothered about it. All these years later, and he was finally retiring at what he thought was somewhere around age 65 or 70, when he was actually 81 years old.

John had seen the world go from a very rough and rugged time of walkabouts and horse and buggy to the modern age of computers and space travel. He felt privileged while working at Bristol Aerospace to help with his own hands in the building and perfecting of the Black Brant, a rocket which orbited the moon for research in the early sixties and is still in use and very popular today.

As time went by, John aged gracefully, with from time to time outbursts of sentences in different languages that no one could understand. He suffered great pain from his leg in later years and wanted it removed, but Olive wouldn't let him and he listened to her, but John woke up one morning with two black toes. He showed Olive and she whisked him off to the hospital before breakfast; they had gangrene and were gone by midday. He blamed that on his trench feet in WWI, as well as his hearing loss, but he never forget the sound of the "Destiny Waltz", a song that stayed with him for the rest of his life, and sometimes when things got bad he could still hear it playing in his head.

In March 1986, on John's ninetieth birthday, he went for a two-week trip to Germany with his daughter and her fiancé. When they visited Berlin, John discovered it was now no longer the way that he had known it. He could not even find some of the places that he had known so well many years before.

John wondered until his dying day, whether his father's father was a convict or a guard in Australia, but he never found out. "Oh, what a tangled web we weave," he used to say.

His involvement in the British Secret Service remained an absolute mystery until one day in his very old age, when he finally thought it had been long enough and his duty to the British Government to maintain their secrets was complete. Duty to the king and country still meant a lot to John, as he was from the old school and quite stubborn that way.

"Now, of course the years have gone by, it doesn't matter," he said one day out of the blue. Yet, John was adamant about and used to say quite often, "I never want any of these stories to get out until after I am gone."

John passed away on May 12, 1997, five years after his beloved Olive. Losing her was the worst loss of his life. It was very sudden, with no warning at all, and he never even got to say goodbye. He always said that Olive was the most wonderful person he ever knew in the whole world. Now the ship had lost its rudder, and he was completely lost. He just missed her so much. "Funny all the little things you take for granted," he would say.

She was always busy looking after somebody and was adored by so many people. Olive was the most loving, giving and caring person that anyone could ever even hope to know. She had a wonderfully long and interesting career as a nurse of which John was always very proud. She was a wonderful mother to their children and of course a loving wife to him and he hoped their spirits would be joined again some day.

Shortly after his 101st birthday, John said, "To think I am that old, it doesn't seem possible. Where have all those years gone?"

Shaking his head back and forth with the boyish smile that never left him and the bouncing curls that were now grey but continued to make people smile whenever they looked at him, he said, "They must have just gone by, all those years. So many memories, so many people! However, you know my motto, I say one day's today and tomorrow is another day. That's how I have lived most of my life, even in the trenches. Still, I've had a good run."

THE END

This was one of John's favourite poems in later years:

The horse and cow live for thirty years,
And nothing know of wines and beers.

The goat and sheep at twenty die,
And never tasted Scotch or Rye.

The sow drinks water by the ton,
And at eighteen is nearly done.

The dog at fifteen cashes in,
Without the aid of wines and gin.

The cat in milk and water soaks,
And in twelve short years it croaks.

The modest sober bone-dry hen,
Lays eggs for you and dies at ten.

All animals are strictly dry,
They aimless live and swiftly die.

But sinful, ginful, rum-soaked men,
Survive for three score year and ten.

And some of us the mighty few,
Stay pickled till we're ninety-two.

Author Unknown

Notes From The Author

As the youngest of John's children, I was the only one still living at home when this project began. My father was sixty-two years old when I was born, but he was still a good dad. He would take me golfing with him on the weekends and even machined a set of clubs down to my seven-year-old size. I was so proud of them—my own set of clubs.

There were a few difficulties with an old dad, but also some benefits. Many of my friends thought he was my grandfather. No one could understand a word he was saying with his funny Australian-British accent, and so his children became his interpreters.

In 1975 in Winnipeg, MB, I came home from high school one day and saw my father sitting at the dining room table, clacking away on his large black Underwood typewriter. I was curious and discovered he was starting to record his experiences from World War 1.

John kept his previous life entirely secret when he started a new family in Canada. His four children had no idea of the incredible experiences he had already encountered. Neither of our parents ever spoke about the war, even though they were both quite involved in it. Children were still sheltered from such horrors.

I was immediately enthralled by Dad's project and hoped to ease his workload with the help of my electric typewriter and the photocopier at work. Computers had not been invented, and so in those early days I used to type up the notes. I would literally cut out the paragraphs I wanted with scissors, and tape them into the manuscript before making a photocopy. At age seventeen, I moved two hours east of Winnipeg for a summer job on the lake. It was so lovely there that I stayed in the Lake of the Woods region for the next thirty years, commuting back and forth to Winnipeg